Back Where We Belong

How Tranmere returned to the Football League

By Matt Jones

Foreword by Mark Palios

Edited by Nick Hilton

Photos by Richard Ault

To Emma and mum, who have been there every step of the way, and for Dad, who would have loved to have seen Tranmere win at Wembley

Foreword
By Mark Palios

If "Back Where We Belong" means an entitlement simply borne out of an inherent expectation, then I don't buy into that. If it means entitlement based on effort, then I totally get it.

This book is a veritable tour de force of one famous old football club's fall from grace and ultimate redemption. The redemption is a consequence of so many people's efforts, faith and a stubborn refusal to accept anything less than league football on the Wirral.

The account gains its raw authenticity from the viewpoint of those who made the journey: on the terraces; on the pitch; from the dugout and in the boardroom. It details the contributions made by both managers; Gary Brabin who built the foundations and Micky Mellon who finished the job. It accurately covers the rationale for decisions made along the way as well as the depth of emotions experienced by those involved and affected by the club's struggle to regain its league status, culminating in the drama of Wembley on May 12th 2018.

Above all, it charts the coming together of the various elements that constitute a football club. The gathering strength through adversity and the realisation that the whole is great than the sum of the parts. That old fashioned team spirit still works today. That the fans can contribute in a way that is ultimately more than just through what they pay. It shows the strength that can be found in a lower league club where it benefits from the access it can afford fans and the local community, something which is difficult due to the scale inherent in the larger clubs where fans can become customers.

Chapter One
The Reality Check

The boos that echoed around Prenton Park as Tranmere's players trudged back to the dressing room said it all. This was a result that defied expectations, and not in a good way.

Everything had been rosy so far. Having picked up ten points in Gary Brabin's first four games in charge, it looked like the demons of the previous two years, when successive relegations had seen the club sink into the National League, were set to be banished.

But here, on a sunny afternoon on the Wirral, Boreham Wood had other ideas. Their performance was far from sparkling; more robust and streetwise than eye-catching and full of flair, but it got the job done. More to the point, it showed Rovers what they were truly in for.

"We are not ready," was Brabin's frank assessment of a 2-0 defeat. "It is a big transition for this club. I have taken on a team that had successive relegations and they are not used to winning football matches.

"It is a long season. I wasn't jumping over the moon when we were winning games and I'm not going to be despondent when we lose them. We have no divine right to win every game in this division.

"I'm sorry I have given the fans their first defeat of the season and it was a poor performance. But we are certainly going to be winning more games than we lose this season."

The manager, a recruit from Everton's youth set up during the summer, was certainly right with that conclusion. Tranmere did pick up more victories than they suffered defeats during the 2015/16 campaign. But it was the manner of this loss that sent seismic shivers down the spine of every supporter. They had just lost to a plucky side whose average attendance would be just 544 over the course of the season. They had come to Prenton Park for a point, yet departed with all three.

Like Rovers, this was Boreham Wood's first campaign in the National League. They, though, were a club on the way up, not down. Led by Ian Allinson, a former Arsenal midfielder who would give up the role a few months later due to other work commitments, they had reached the highest point in their history by beating Whitehawk in the National League South play-off final in May.

The team were set up to play a brand of football that Rovers supporters simply were not accustomed to seeing, but one they would quickly become used to. Whilst the previous twelve months in League Two had been a bit of a culture shock to the club, this would take things to a new level.

Time wasting was an art, sucking life and momentum out of not only performances, but the crowd as well. It became apparent from an early stage that referees were not going to crack down on a player for taking a few extra seconds over any dead ball situation, be it a throw in or goal kick. Teams would do it from the first minute, even at 0-0, and it always had the desired effect on the crowd by frequently and quickly escalating the tension and frustration on the terraces. This was not what people had paid to come and watch.

Substance over style was clear too. Boreham Wood lined up in a 4-5-1 formation, using on-loan Bristol Rovers forward Jamie Lucas as their outlet. He stands at nearly 6 foot 3 inches tall and was employed primarily as a target man, running tirelessly on to long balls that were regularly pumped up field from defence.

The visitors had little interest in putting on a show. They just wanted to get the three points. In fact, even one would have satisfied them, and in their first year in the National League, that is something Tranmere struggled to get their heads around.

"The Boreham Wood game disappointed me," says chairman Mark Palios. "We couldn't find a way to break down the block. You either go round it, under it, over it or through it. We probably didn't have the players to go through it, so you go round it, over it or under it.

"For me, if you're comparing that to what we do now, we've simply improved the squad and that enables us to do it and in any number of ways. Teams don't know how to compete with us now.

"But equally, them coming here to frustrate us was going to be the game plan for every single team. This was always going to be one of the biggest things. Gary knows the league, so that's what he expected, but it was our worst fears confirmed.

"They came here, put a block on and the fans get on your back because you're playing in Non League. I've always said it though - if you get organised, you can frustrate anybody.

"In the National League, to drop two points at home was as bad as losing. You need to win games in this league with only one going up automatically. So it was disappointing, but was it unexpected? Well it was the worst case scenario. It really wasn't great."

The fans let the players know their thoughts on the performance at full time, and for many of the squad, this was to be their first experience of how vociferous the Prenton Park crowd can be.

Seven of the starting line up that day were in their first season with the club. A further three new faces were on the bench. Importantly, though, nine of those summer arrivals had played National League football before. They should have known what was coming, whereas the fans had not got a clue.

"I didn't know what to expect, in truth," admits Ben Harrison, chairman of the Tranmere Rovers Supporters Trust, "because we'd never been there before. I thought football would win through, but it doesn't. Wrexham are realising that as well.

"There's a huge gap in terms of quality between the National League and League Two. The skilful players, the ones who are capable of winning you a game on their own, they just get kicked.

"The football is a bit more brutish. There's a lot of time wasting. You don't want to harp on about referees, but they don't seem to be on to it. They just let it flow. I think we fell into the trap a few times of getting frustrated and then the crowd get on your back. Boreham Wood knew what they were doing in that sense."

There was another reason as to why this game was to be so indicative of what Tranmere were to expect over the coming months and, ultimately, years, as well. Teams coming to Prenton Park treated the match like a day out at Wembley.

Some of these players were part time. Football was more of a weekend job than a full time occupation, with plenty of them spending the majority of their careers in Non League football. For them, this was a big deal. They had not played at such a big stadium or in front of such a large crowd before, and that gives you plenty of adrenaline.

This is something Brabin would mention time and again, as would Micky Mellon when he arrived little over a year later. "It is harder to play for Tranmere than it is against them," he said, and you can understand why.

Harrison continued: "When we played Boreham Wood, they brought about 29 fans on two mini buses and it was a big wake up call for everybody. That was the point at which a lot of people thought that this is someone's day out. Mark Palios said to me that they arrived early and took photographs on the pitch. We had a season where we were everybody's cup final."

The pressure on Rovers to deliver in every game was huge. They were expected to pick up three points in almost every fixture they went into. That simply was not the case for the opposition. Anything other than a defeat was a bonus. When kick off came, they raised their performance. The venue and occasion was all the motivation they needed, and sometimes that can be difficult to match.

Allison noted after his side's 2-0 victory that: "It is an absolute privilege to ply our trade at such a large club. Today makes last season's promotion even more special.

"We defended from the front. Every player was given a specific role which they carried out to the letter. We made it hard for Tranmere and I'm pleased with the outcome."

For Brabin, though, Boreham Wood was not the turning point. Although the defeat sparked a run of four matches without victory, and just one win in seven, there is another fixture that weighs more heavily on his mind.

"One game that sticks out is Kidderminster at home," he recalled. "We were winning 2-0 and from a possession and footballing point of view, I remember speaking to the players and they loved it. They felt like they had the ball for the whole of the game.

"However, late in the game, we just didn't know how to switch off. The lads were enjoying themselves but we were screaming at them to keep their discipline. You could see the full-backs and midfielders bombing on and we got caught with two sucker punches. It meant we ended up drawing a game that we'd dominated. That was probably highlighting some of the issues I did have with that group of players.

"I remember the Boreham Wood game too. We were trying to be a bit more attacking minded. As the season grew, we created more and more chances but we were not being clinical enough in front of goal. Then we'd lose games on the counter attack."

After losing their unbeaten run, Tranmere suffered another humiliation a week later, beaten 2-1 by Altrincham, a team who would finish the campaign in the relegation zone. The Kidderminster game came a couple of days later on the Bank Holiday Monday, and then another draw, 1-1 at Welling, a fixture in which Ritchie Sutton was sent off.

The defender was shown a straight red card after the referee judged him to have elbowed his opponent, Sahr Kabba. Brabin and the fans were fuming at the time, with the manager commenting "We looked at the footage and there was no contact made".

An appeal against the decision was successfully lodged and the three match ban was overturned, but the damage had already been done. Rovers were winning 1-0 with eleven men, but after the sending off, Welling equalised. Another two points dropped.

It was a tough time for the squad and the manager, because it meant pressure was heaped on them immediately. Although so few teams get relegated from League Two and then win the National League title twelve months later, so much was expected of Tranmere.

They were a huge club for this level. Not many have sunk as low as they have over such a short period of time. Less than 20 years earlier, they had been in the Championship and a League Cup final.

But many big clubs have come down and found getting out pretty difficult. Wrexham have spent over 10 years in the National League, whilst the likes of Luton, Cambridge and Oxford also took time to acclimatise.

You have to turn yourself into a winning machine, and when the last few seasons have been so poor, that negative momentum can be difficult to turn around. Eventually, though, things click into gear. You become more savvy and find that way to win. Like those other clubs who found themselves outside the comfort zone of the Football League, Tranmere would work out a way back. The problem was they had to suffer a few more moments like Boreham Wood along the way - but over three years, things would turn a full circle.

Chapter Two
The Context

Tranmere had been one of the least successful clubs in the country since the turn of the century, so perhaps it was no surprise that they finally ended up outside of the Football League in 2015. Their downfall had been a particularly brutal one to take, given that as recently as 2000 John Aldridge had guided his side to the Worthington Cup Final. Although that day at Wembley ended in a 2-1 defeat to Martin O'Neill's Leicester City, it is still a moment that many fans look back upon fondly.

However, within a year the downward spiral started as the club were relegated to League One. Despite hammering local rivals Everton 3-0 in the FA Cup, an occasion now crowned "St Yates Day" after the full-back netted two headers, and also performing one of the comebacks of the century in the next round by coming from 3-0 down to beat top flight side Southampton 4-3, they simply could not get things right in the bread and butter of the Championship.

This caused much frustration to Aldridge, a manager full of passion who wore his heart on his sleeve. He was desperate to keep his side up but decided to step down towards the end of the campaign as he believed Rovers might have more of a chance of beating the drop with somebody else in charge. Unfortunately, assistant boss Kevin Sheedy took his place and was unable to halt the slide into the third tier.

"The fightback starts now". That was the message coming from chairman Lorraine Rogers, but it never materialised. Dave Watson was in charge for the 2001/02 campaign and Tranmere fell haplessly short of mounting a promotion challenge, despite a squad that contained the likes of Clint Hill, Jason Koumas, John Actherberg, Gareth Roberts and an improving Iain Hume.

The latter three were still on the books when Brian Little guided the club to the League One play-offs after an impressive 2004/05 season. He had added Ian Goodison, a mainstay of the defence for over a decade, and profited from the emergence of Ryan Taylor who would go on to represent England under-21s and play in the Premier League for Newcastle and Wigan.

Unfortunately Rovers came up short. A 2-0 defeat in the first leg of the play-off semi-final to Hartlepool proved a mountain too tall to overcome. They did hit back in the return game at Prenton Park thanks to strikes from Taylor and David Beresford, but were eventually defeated on penalties as Ian Sharps missed the decisive spot kick. Their opponents would go on to lose the final at the Millennium Stadium to Sheffield Wednesday, who joined Hull and Luton in getting promoted.

That was the first time Tranmere had reached the play-offs since the days of Johnny King, who came so close to guiding the club to the Premier League in the mid-90s with three successive top six finishes. It would also be the last time they did so before dropping out of the Football League ten years later.

A lot of cash was thrown at getting promoted that year. Rovers gambled on Little completing the job and allowed him to sign high profile figures like ex-Liverpool man Jason McAteer, Jamaica international Theo Whitmore and midfielder Mark Rankine. Not going up was costly and meant the budget was slashed for the 2005/06 campaign. It also resulted in Hume and Taylor being sold to Leicester and Wigan.

That made things much harder for Little, whose new look squad was unable to scale the heights of the previous twelve months. Indeed, they only avoided relegation in the penultimate game thanks to a dramatic 2-1 win at MK Dons. The manager departed shortly after that fixture, paving the way for legendary former striker Ronnie Moore to return to Prenton Park.

He would spend three years in the hot seat, gradually building a team that got stronger and stronger during his tenure. He profited from the form of Chris Greenacre up front, and also added the likes of Chris Shuker on the wing, Antony Kay in midfield and his son Ian in attack. They were not the most talented side in the division, but they worked hard and had immense team spirit.

Unfortunately, heartbreak was not too far away once again as what turned out to be Moore's final game ended in a 1-1 draw against Scunthorpe on the last day of the 2008/09 season. It meant Rovers missed out on sixth place and a shot at the Championship by two points. It was another gutting moment for a club who by this point seemed destined only for misery. They had led for 49 minutes at Glanford Park, only for Cliff Byrne to equalise with a late header after Gareth Edds had been sent off. Worse, though, was to come.

That summer, Peter Johnson returned as chairman, replacing Lorraine Rogers who had decided to step down after becoming disillusioned with some of the goings on in football. The problem was that he had no intention of funding another promotion. He just wanted to sell up.

"There was decay throughout the club," says Ben Harrison, who as chairman of the Tranmere Rovers Supporters Trust launched an attempt to buy the club in 2014. "Peter just wanted to get control back, I think that was it. He was happy to put his hand in his pocket if there was a shortfall in wages, but any business that survives on an owner like that is just going to become lazy. It's like a child with a rich parent; if they just keep giving them money and they don't have to make any effort, they aren't going to do anything.

"It meant there was a steady decline for ten years. If you think back, we did 'Les Aid' in 2010 and raised £12,000 to sign Andy Robinson. He came in and scored that wonder goal against Millwall and you just thought 'ooh, is there a chance that we could go on?' There wasn't any chance though."

One of Johnson's first moves upon returning to Tranmere in 2009 was to sack Moore after being talked into giving John Barnes another shot at management. Unsurprisingly, it did not go well. The fans never took to the former Liverpool winger who did not help himself with a disastrous start to the campaign.

Fourteen games and ten defeats later, the axe was swung again and this time physio Les Parry took charge, initially on a caretaker basis. It was a bold move but also signalled the end of Tranmere's aspirations to go up. From now on, the sole aim was to avoid relegation. There was little appetite from the boardroom for promotion, with investment rarely forthcoming and the club having to battle on with a wage budget that would have seen them struggle to compete in the division below.

A 3-0 win at Stockport on the last day of the 2009/10 season kept Rovers up, somewhat miraculously given they won just two of the opening eleven fixtures. Parry was offered the job permanently and twelve months later relegation was avoided a little more comfortably.

The manager had earned cult status at Prenton Park before his spell in charge, but the fans soon started to drip away. Games were often lacking in entertainment value, largely down to performances that were pragmatic and within themselves. This squad of players did not play with flair or excitement. They scrapped for every point they could muster in a bid to keep treading water.

Another change of manager was required in March 2012 when a 1-0 defeat to Chesterfield extended a dreadful run of form to a sole victory in 20 games. Again, Moore was called for and he immediately found that spark that had everyone pushing in the same direction at last.

For the first half of the 2012/13 season, Tranmere were simply sensational. They had a thirst for goals, with Jake Cassidy, Andy Robinson and Jean-Louis Akpa Akpro a formidable trio who could hurt any League One defence. With Ian Goodison, Zoumana Bakayogo, James Wallace and Ben Gibson, on loan from

Middlesbrough, this squad was going places. Indeed, they were still top of the league in January. The fans could not quite believe what was happening; would this finally be their year?

If anything was to highlight the lack of ambition from the board room, it was to be the underinvestment that followed as injuries took their toll on the squad. Wallace, Gibson and Akpa Akpro all missed large chunks of the fixture list due to fitness issues, whilst Cassidy was recalled from his loan spell by Wolves.

At the time, the general consensus was that only a couple of strong reinforcements were needed to get Rovers over the line. Instead, Moore had to bring in ageing striker Mama Sidebe from Stoke, and in truth just getting him on the pitch was an achievement. Then there was Paul Corry, a young midfielder from Sheffield Wednesday who struggled to settle whatsoever, and Donevorn Daniels, a raw centre-back from West Brom who was learning to play the game and as such failed to hit any kind of form.

Ultimately, just three wins in their final seventeen games saw Tranmere slip from top spot to outside of the play-offs. They failed to even score in the last six matches. This was when the rot well and truly set in. This run of form set the tone for what was to come over the following two years. There was momentum, but only in a negative form, something that is difficult to turn around.

By now, the Trust were preparing to launch their bid to buy the club. A couple of potential owners, including Club 9, had shown their interest and alarm bells were immediately ringing. "Our concern was what was going to happen," continues Harrison. "Peter wanted to sell, but he kept hanging on. There needed to be an alternative, and that's where us as fans tried to get together.

"Michael Wilde was the most serious bidder, but I didn't know much about him. He did join the Trust, I know that, and he left his £300 in as well. When you started to speak to people behind the scenes though, there did seem to be something a bit fishy about him.

"Peter got wind of it not really being what it was meant to be and he obviously wasn't comfortable with it, so he didn't accept the bid. The strange thing is he then recruits Jeremy Butler, Wilde's right hand man, as Tranmere's chief executive. That was just another example of settling for second best because there was nothing left.

"Peter was interested in us buying the club. However, he would never back us. If he had publicly said 'I want to seriously look at them', I think we would have reached our £500,000 target. Eventually, we got to £200,000, but we were doing it outside the gates. It was very hard. I thought we'd get there, but then I'm the eternal optimist. If we'd have doubled our money, Peter might have thought differently.

"What also didn't help was that the previous decade had sapped everyone's energy. If you see some old pictures when you come to the ground, it was like a prison! It was neglected. We had a few moments of celebrating survival, but when you look back, that's not what you want to do in life. It was just tired, everything about the club was tired.

"We had things like alleged spot fixing, betting scandals and all that. It was being run by absent people and when you tried to put forward ideas, it felt like stony ground.

"When we were doing the season ticket campaign for 2018/19, I got handed a box of past campaigns, which go back over the last ten years. You can almost read the enthusiasm of the club, but year after year their motivation disappears. That box to me reflected Tranmere Rovers."

The underinvestment was a major problem. There was a press conference midway through the 2013/14 season when Ronnie Moore, having concluding his interview, predicted that if the club were not relegated this campaign, it would happen twelve months later. He reckoned they could not compete with what everybody else in the division was spending.

It proved to be a remarkably accurate estimate. Although Moore was relieved of his duties in April 2014 after admitting breaching FA betting rules, John McMahon could not save Tranmere from the drop. They went four games without a goal before a 2-1 defeat at home to Bradford on the final day sealed their fate.

And this is where Mark Palios comes into the equation. A former head of the FA who had two spells at Prenton Park as a player, he and his wife Nicola decided they needed to do something to stop the club slipping into oblivion. Finally, Johnson had a bidder he approved of.

"I'd visited the club in April, only coming up to see Dave Philpotts and a few mates because I usually pop in if I'm in the North West," he said. "The club had gone through a recent history of things like former players being arrested for spot fixing, Ronnie Moore being charged by the FA for betting and things - so the reputation around the club was just wrong, especially for a club that I knew prided itself on being a family club and doing things the right way.

"They were in freefall. I'd walked into 30 failing businesses a year and this was a failing business all over the place. With morale, people had their heads down, management didn't necessarily impress me (I'm not talking about football management, just the management of the business). The whole thing had a smell of death around it.

"I knew that Peter had been trying to sell the business for a long time and when you're trying to sell something, like a house for example, the last thing you do is put a new bathroom or kitchen in. So the business suffers as a consequence, and it's not just the fabric of the business. It's the whole atmosphere around the place. That spreads out onto the terraces. For years they had been fighting against getting relegated from League One, so there was a very negative spin around the place.

"We went to our house in France, we were on the way back on the last day of the season and we were listening to the results. Notts

County jumped over us; they scored with fifteen minutes to go and we conceded. The radio flips between the important relegation and promotion games on the last Saturday and I just turned to Nicky and said 'that's it, they're going down and they'll go down again and they'll go into administration'. I didn't think Peter Johnson would start funding things once they went into Non League.

"Nicky just turned to me and said 'Do something about it', because that was my job. When I was working, I was head of business regeneration for Price Waterhouse Coopers and I'd developed the whole turnaround product in the city. I said 'I will if you will', because I knew that I'd get involved in a big way. We were living down south at the time. I knew Nicky was enthusiastic. She's somebody who likes sport and would like a project like that.

"I came away and you always ask a mate who will give you the right answer, so on the Monday I rang Ray Stubbs [the former Tranmere youngster turned television and radio presenter]. I said 'Is this totally stupid?' and he replied 'No, it'll be great!' If credit is due, he now claims responsibility for us going in. I then rang Peter and I said 'look, I can see what's going on. Are you interested in selling out?'"

It took a few months for things to go through. Naturally, Palios did his due diligence on issues on and off the field. In the meantime, things where continuing from a playing point of view as Rovers prepared for their first season in League Two for nearly 30 years.

Rob Edwards, a former Bristol City and Preston defender, was recruited as the club's new manager by Jeremy Butler, coming in after an impressive stint as part of Exeter's coaching staff. He was tasked, for the first time in his career, with building a squad, but had a minimal playing budget with which to do so. It was an extremely difficult task, made even harder by the expectations of a fanbase who believed the club should mount a strong challenge for promotion.

Away from the playing side of things, Palios realised there was much to be done too. Tranmere had been trying for years to sell their youth training base, Ingleborough, in order to pay off some long standing bank loans, but had had no success whatsoever. Prenton Park meanwhile was of little use away from match days and was costing hundreds of thousands of pounds to operate each year.

"The business was making a structural loss," Palios admits. "I knew I couldn't turn it around straight away. They were starting to recruit a squad and going into League Two and it would probably take two years to make a difference. The suites, for example, I couldn't do them then - I had to do them the following year. So I prepared for us to have enough funds to live through those two years and then start to make a difference.

"When you start to make a difference, you look at investment coming in. The only thing that was left outstanding really in that two years was getting the Ingleborough deal through. They'd been trying to do that for years. I believed I could negotiate that and we subsequently did that around the Christmas time. That has now transpired to become The Campus and paid off some bank debt. So that was the start."

On August 11th 2014, two days after Tranmere had started their season with a 1-1 draw against York, Mark and Nicola Palios were announced as the new owners of Tranmere Rovers Football Club. After years of waiting for change, this was a perfect match.

The fear was that whoever took over would be an asset stripper; somebody looking to make a quick buck by selling the land the club owned. But here, they had a former player who was an expert in turning around failing businesses and knew football inside out. On top of that, Mark and Nicola both possess an incredible work ethic. What more could you want? At last, there was something to be positive about.

"You go on your gut reaction," said Ben Harrison. "Straight away, after dealing with Peter for a long time, I could tell it was different. Nicola and Mark upped sticks to move here and they gave The Trust the associate director role, which is something Peter would never have gone for. They wanted us involved.

"My first meeting with them was positive. They were very receptive to us. They came in and went around for the first month and looked at everything that needed doing. I think it was written on twenty sheets of paper!

"Mark said they could only do so much, so they wanted to work with us. Because we had that takeover attempt, we had some money available and we wanted to put it back into the club. Quickly we agreed to a deal where we put in £75,000 over three seasons for improving the surroundings and things. It worked well for them.

"The one thing that Mark did that made me know he was genuine was with the marquee. We had it up for the Chester game on a temporary basis. It got dismantled afterwards, but the club wanted to keep it. They ran it and they'd be the first to admit they didn't know how to. Mark said 'put it in the directors car park and the fans should run it.'

"It was a masterstroke. It sent so many messages out to the supporters. Rather than have Bentleys and what not in the car park, there's a facility for the fans. It's most probably the number one thing where I thought 'I like these two'. You look at it now and all the players, Micky Mellon, Mark himself, they've been in there dancing. It's justified itself."

The only question for Palios was why get involved? He was living a successful life away from football and, as Peter Johnson has said himself, nobody makes any money out of owning a club. Indeed, this business was haemorrhaging cash. It did not appear to be an attractive proposition at all, but the former Rovers midfielder had his reasons.

"A lot of people have asked me that," he added. "I was a senior partner at PWC, I had been Chief Executive at the FA, why did you come back? I was never hankering to come back to work at a football club. It wasn't something I aspired to do. I was offered chief executive jobs after I left the FA, and before as well, by Premier League clubs, but I wasn't really interested in doing that.

"The only reason I came back was because it was my club. In my life, they were a massive piece of the jigsaw. The two things that gave me stability as a kid, because I didn't have the richest of upbringings, were my school and the football club. It was an element of pay back that I felt was due.

"I knew it was difficult, but when I used to go into businesses, it didn't matter what the industry was. I was industry agnostic. This was the first industry that I knew a little bit about. I'd very often go into a business, like British Steel, and the guys at the top would say 'What do you know about British Steel?' They'd been in it for 30 odd years, I was an accountant. I'd say 'what do you know about my business?' Mine was about working the situation out, rather than the industry, and I'd bring in industry specialists if I didn't understand. So coming into football was probably the only industry that I knew relatively well from the shop floor, the pitch, right the way up to administration and the top level of the game."

The day after Mark and Nicola bought the club, Tranmere were beaten 1-0 in the first round of the League Cup by Nottingham Forest. A 2-1 defeat to Shrewsbury followed a few days later, but they did not have to wait too long for a first win under Rob Edwards as Cole Stockton and Max Power scored in a 2-0 victory against Wycombe.

That looked like the perfect platform to build on, but Rovers continued to struggle. Edwards registered only one more victory, against Morecambe, as error strewn performances cost them dearly. A 3-2 loss at Accrington stands out, a game that the visitors led until the 77th minute, only for their soft underbelly to allow Stanley to turn things around.

This alarmed Palios, and when a 1-0 defeat to Plymouth on October 11th left the club bottom of League Two, he decided it was time to act. Edwards was dismissed and the experienced Micky Adams came in as his replacement.

Again, this was a decision that fans largely agreed with. Although Edwards' tenure was short lived, lasting only five months, the on field results simply had not been good enough and things needed to turn around quickly.

In Adams, a manager with bags of experience was available and interested in the role. He had just left Port Vale, but could count the likes of Leicester, Brighton and Fulham amongst his former clubs. This was somebody who knew how to get the best out of a group of players. It looked like a positive move.

Palios explains: "The important thing was not to get into a situation that we couldn't salvage, and so to get somebody in to have a look at what was going on and have a chance in the window to replenish the team. That was the theory of it.

"We brought in Micky Adams, who everybody at the time said 'what a great appointment'. If you look at his record, he had some ridiculous win percentage, but not over 100 games, over 750 games, up and down the leagues. He'd never been relegated either."

Things went well under the new manager to start with. After three draws in his opening three games, Rovers registered wins over Bristol Rovers and Bury in the FA Cup and Johnstone's Paint Trophy. It gave the squad some confidence, and that elusive league victory finally followed in late November, a convincing 3-1 win over Portsmouth.

A 3-0 hammering of Accrington in January lifted Tranmere out of the relegation zone. Everybody was looking up the table at last, but soon things started to turn sour. Palios had kept back £300,000 to spend on new players, be it on loan or permanent transfers, and those signings seemed to have a negative impact.

"When a load of loanees started arriving, it just went downhill," recalls Ben Harrison. "There was a game at York and that was a real eye opener for a lot of fans, but Mark and Nicola didn't go. When they heard the feedback, they knew we were in trouble. I think Adams might have been sacked earlier if they had been there.

"Also, though, Mark doesn't want to be seen as an owner who just fires somebody when the going gets tough. The one thing we said as fans is the club needs continuity. If you chop and change all the time, it doesn't work. We're seeing it now with players signing two year deals. Before, the fans had no identity with the players. They didn't know who some were!"

The York defeat, however, was followed by a superb 2-1 victory over Micky Mellon's Shrewsbury. They were chasing promotion, but left Prenton Park empty handed thanks to goals from Rory Donnelly and Danny Holmes. Even a late strike from Connor Goldson proved to be only a consolation for the visitors.

But Palios continues: "Three days later, on the Tuesday, we went to Portsmouth. They were flying high and we played probably the best football we played. We were 2-0 up with about 20 minutes to go, had an injury, had to rejig things and we lost 3-2.

"We won one game after that, at Cambridge, and we were on a massive downward spiral. Everybody said get rid of Micky, but you have to make a decision and a call, and that call was with ten games left, would you bring somebody else in who could make a difference?

"You flip a coin at that point in time. I stuck with Micky because I'm a believer in stability and working with the managers as long as we can. It was not to be and we just couldn't stop it going down the plug hole."

Adams eventually left after a 3-0 home defeat to Oxford. Tranmere were shambolic and heads dropped as soon as Kemar Roofe handed his side the lead just after the break, with two more goals coming within the next 17 minutes. The writing was on the wall.

When wandering through the corridors underneath the Main Stand shortly after full time, the manager was spotted sitting on his own, away from the changing room, slumped in a chair. He knew the game was up. Assistant boss Alan Rogers fronted up to the media afterwards, and he was confirmed as caretaker manager alongside Shaun Garnett 24 hours later when Adams was sacked.

Unfortunately for the new leadership team, they were left with a near impossible task to keep the club up. Tranmere had Plymouth away on the penultimate day of the season, but were two points from safety with only six to play for. They lost 3-2, and that, coupled with victory for Hartlepool, confirmed their relegation. All that said, it is still a day that Palios has fond memories of.

"The Plymouth game cemented the relationship I already had with the club," he says. "Nicky and I said 'let's go and front it with the fans' who'd gone to Plymouth knowing we could be relegated out of the league. I remember the players were warming up in front of them, we went down there and the fans were fantastic. It still chokes me up now when I think of it.

"We went back to our seats and I sat down and I said to Nicky 'we'll come straight back up.' I'd planned for the day for the whole week, because I'm a great believer in alliteration, so I said 'It's devastating today, but it's not disastrous tomorrow' because we had a business plan. We started working on that from day one.

"That business plan is the same in the league as it is in the Non League system, it's just harder lower down because you've got funds dripping away from you. There has been £3m in funds that we've lost because we've been down here for three years, despite parachute payments. We knew it was coming, but it just meant harder work.

"I drove back from Plymouth, so I wasn't on my phone, but it ran out of battery because of the messages I received from people all over the game who were sorry to see Tranmere go out of the league. A lot of people have that affection for the club. When I went to the EFL meeting when we had gone back up, a lot of people came over and said 'It's great to see Tranmere back'. The club is well liked in the game. That's a testament to everybody who's come before and what the club's about."

And so there we have it. For the first time in their history, Tranmere were a Non League club. A second dreadful season in a row, a second relegation.

"It was soul destroying," adds Ben Harrison. "I remember when we went down to League Two, Mark Bartley, who's taken over from me as an associate director, said 'Tranmere are in League Two! How far have we fallen?' I don't think he realised that a year later we were going to be out of it!

"Tranmere fans are quite tenacious. They like to back the underdog. But everybody's energy had been sapped from the place. I realised, by looking at Wrexham and Chester, that there was a potential scenario to end up like them.

"Talking from a fan's perspective, I do think we could have avoided relegation. Micky Adams kind of had unlimited resources. He used a lot of players. But it is very difficult to turn around that negative momentum.

"Soon after the relegation was confirmed, we had a working day looking at the club. The first objective Mark and Nicola had set a year earlier was to retain the league status for the 3 to 5 year plan. That day, he just scribbled it out and changed it to regain."

Chapter Three
Gary Brabin

One of Tranmere's first tasks following relegation to the National League was appointing a successor to Micky Adams. As the club approached their first season in the division, it was vital they found somebody who had experience of managing at this level. There would be no point getting in a high profile figure who did not know what it took to win games outside of the Football League.

Mark and Nicola Palios were also desperate for some stability. This would be Rovers' fourth permanent manager in little over a year, and in football, constant upheaval does not do anybody any favours. Each boss wants his own players and coaching staff, something that proves pretty costly, and they all take time to settle. Whoever came in had to see the club as a long term project.

For Ben Harrison, the managerial appointment was crucial and one that could not go wrong. After successive relegations, there was a worry that Tranmere could follow in the footsteps of Stockport, who sunk through to the National League North in their second season after being relegated from League Two.

"It was the most important appointment in the club's history," he said. "We hadn't done very well up to then. Mark and Nicola had been there for a year and they aren't the type of people who like to change managers. This was going to be their third one and it was crucial.

"It sounds negative, but the manager's job was almost to stop the rot to start with, and then build the club back upwards. Someone with experience in that league was what we were after. If it had been the wrong appointment, they could have got relegated again. When you're in that downward spiral, that could happen.

"We could have lost the first four or five games and the mood within the crowd wouldn't have been good at all. Mark and Nicola would have been in the spotlight a lot more, too. Thankfully we got off to a reasonable start, so we avoided that.

"My expectations as a fan were to at least make the play-offs. That was the same as my expectations as an associate director and chairman of the Trust. We wanted promotion. I know that's ambitious, but top five is what you want. To be fair, we were near enough there. Certainly towards the end of the season, we were fairly well placed."

The emerging candidate was a former Blackpool, Doncaster and Hull midfielder by the name of Gary Brabin, who was beginning to forge out a reasonably successful management career after hanging up his boots. He had mounted promotion challenges with Cambridge and Luton, two teams with a high profile. Leading a team with huge expectations would not frighten him.

Indeed, during his time at both The Abbey Stadium and Kenilworth Road, he had come mightily close to winning promotion. Only a 2-0 defeat to Torquay in the 2008/09 play-off final prevented him from taking Cambridge back to the Football League, whilst he suffered penalty shoot out heart break at the same stage two years later as Luton were defeated by Wimbledon.

Another bonus was that he was a scouser. Palios has always been keen on getting people in who understand what Tranmere are all about. To the people of the Wirral, or even Merseyside, they are not just another club. They have values and traditions, something somebody local would get.

"Gary had done well in the National League and knew the division," explains Palios. "You want somebody who understands what it's like to go to an unfancied club with 600 men and a dog watching on a wet Tuesday night in January. I've had that experience with some of the players and sometimes you've thought do they fancy it? You've got to pick the right players.

"What Gary did very well was completely cleaning out the team. The strategy I like to have, if I can, is to shop for the division above. I tried to get half of the team on two year contracts at the end of the season, or with another year on their contract left, and the other half coming out.

"You've then got the ability to move it around. You add in four or five first team players, whatever you need. Gary built a good squad quite quickly. We had a squad of players who were capable of playing in the division above but were equally good players in the National League. He knew the league very well."

Brabin was offered the job at Prenton Park after meeting with Palios, but there was a snag. After a period in charge of Southport, he had decided to step away from management for the time being. He was still in coaching, having taken up a position working within Everton's academy. For him, this was a dream come true. He had followed the club as a boy and still supports them now. As such, it would take quite something to prize him away from Finch Farm because he had no intention of making a return to the dugout.

"I was really happy in my job at Everton," he admits. "I'd made my mind up that that was the path I wanted to take. I was proud of what I had done in my managerial career beforehand, I just I felt the opportunities were limited.

"When you start out in management, you always have your eye on certain clubs. They can be former clubs or realistic ones that you feel you can manage, and Tranmere were one of them. I remember coming close to it once, when John Barnes left and Les Parry took over. I was close to it that year.

"It was always a club that I'd had an eye on who I'd like to manage. When they were relegated, I dismissed it because I didn't want to go back into the National League. I was happy doing what I was doing."

Mark and Nicola therefore had a fight on their hands to convince Brabin that he wanted to come to Tranmere. The job, though, was a pretty easy one to sell. Although there was huge risk in taking it, given the successive relegations, there was the potential for massive rewards too.

Get this right, and you could turn yourself into a club legend. You could forever be known as the person who took on the club at their lowest ebb and returned them to the Football League. And that teasing prospect of earning Rovers their first promotion since 1991 was one that excited Brabin.

"Mark and I had mutual friend," he continued. "He knew a bit about me as a character, and my record as well. I'd just left Southport who were struggling when I took charge and I kept them in the league and got them to third round of the FA Cup. Previously I'd managed big clubs who'd been in the same position as Tranmere before - Luton and Cambridge - and I took them to play-off finals.

"I was approached by Tranmere and the first couple of times I turned down the job. I told them I was happy. I arranged to meet Mark just to give my bit of advice or help on managing in this league, and it ended up snowballing from there. Eventually, though, and not because I needed talking round, I took the job. I decided I was going to have a go and I did."

As things moved forward, the Supporters Trust were kept in the loop with what was happening. Mark and Nicola were keen to make sure they got this appointment right, and that meant Ben Harrison was asked whether or not he thought Brabin was the correct man to take the club forward.

It was a bold move. Such a question had not been posed by previous owners, although it almost certainly should have been six years earlier when John Barnes was controversially brought in to replace Ronnie Moore. However, it underlined just how much the owners valued the input of the fans. They wanted everybody to feel involved.

"It was during the very, very early stages of me becoming an associate director," Ben explains. "They said 'what do you think' and, on paper, from what he'd done, I thought it was a good appointment.

"To be honest, I was still in a daze after the second relegation! But once I'd come to terms with it, I felt we needed somebody who knew the National League and how it worked. The logic was explained by Mark and Nicola, and you couldn't disagree with it.

"Brabin had a fairly good history in the division. He'd never got promoted, but he'd come close, losing the play-off final twice, once on penalties. On paper, he was a good appointment.

"I did not know too much about him, but I remembered him managing Southport. They were very tight defensively and had a good FA Cup run. I also looked at how he got on at Luton, which must have been tough. The other thing I realised is he got sent off once for a tussle with a steward.

"Anyway, it looked like a good appointment. Of course the jury was out and everybody was in a whirlwind state after what had happened. But the Trust looked at it and could see there were only six players under contract, a few of whom had had back to back relegations. They were scarred, so it was a rebuilding job. The Trust therefore thought it would take two to three years to get out of the division. We didn't have any doubts over his appointment."

After getting that seal of approval, Brabin was appointed on May 5th 2015, just three days after Tranmere ended their League Two campaign with a 1-0 defeat at home to Bury, a result that was enough to earn The Shakers promotion. The rebuilding process had started and the man to take Tranmere back to the Football League had been chosen.

"Gary was my main target for this role for a number of reasons," announced Mark Palios. "Firstly, he is a manager with a strong win rate, over 48%, and a fantastic track record of getting his clubs into the Conference play offs. He achieved this feat in all three of his full seasons as a manager in the Conference, and left Luton when they were still in a very strong position.

"Importantly, the job requires a strong character and someone who knows what the weight of expectation of managing a larger club in the Conference feels like. Gary has done this at both Cambridge and Luton.

"But he is not someone who relies on playing ugly football to win matches; he is a young, progressive manager who has taken the time to study other successful managers both in this country and abroad, and who is very keen to use the best that sports science can offer to ensure that players are at peak fitness and continue to develop throughout their careers.

"Finally, he is a local man. Although that wasn't a pre-requisite for the job, I do think it means he has both a natural affinity for and understanding of the area and more importantly what Tranmere Rovers means."

Brabin meanwhile admitted the the lure of taking charge of the Wirral club was simply too good to turn down, adding: "I have had approaches from other clubs and declined them, but the Tranmere job is special. The chance to lead one of the three famous old Merseyside clubs back to where it belongs in the League is a fantastic challenge that is hard to resist.

"The decision was also partly down to the chairman. It is unusual to be able to work with a chairman who is a football man through and through and Mark and I have a shared vision of what was needed to get the foundations right for the future.

"I know that the club and its fans are hurting right now because of relegation, but I am confident that we can restore the club to its former glory and play some football that will put a smile back on the fans' faces."

His hardest task would prove to be managing expectations. Ensuring fans left Prenton Park happy was one thing, but could he keep them content without promising a promotion push in his first year in charge? After all, that was the demand of many supporters, some of whom thought the National League would be as easy as a stroll in the park.

"The biggest challenge for Tranmere and certainly the supporters is the expectation," said Brabin when he was unveiled as the new boss. "It's hard to accept that we've fallen out of the league and we want to get there as quickly as possible, but we've got no divine right to do that.

"It's going to be difficult. As long as we can understand that and work together, we're confident we can get out of the division. I've been inspired by what's going on behind the scenes and I want to try and put things right on the pitch."

Brabin insists finishing in the top five was never a demand, from himself or from Mark Palios. He just wanted to turn around that negative momentum after two relegations and start the club moving in the right direction at last.

History went against Tranmere, too. Bristol Rovers had been promoted at the end of the 2014/15 season, going up via the play-offs, but this was the first time a team had returned to the Football League at the first attempt in a decade. The division usually requires a settling in period, something Brabin knew very well.

Indeed, until you really study the division, something few supporters had done before ending up in it, you do not really realise just how competitive it is. It is a graveyard for former Football League clubs, all of whom are fighting to go up. However, there are only two promotion spots available. Just one team will go up automatically. As such, a bottleneck is created at the top end of the table with some extremely strong sides.

"Mark Palios was really low when I arrived," Brabin says. "He'd admit that. He had come into the club and had an affiliation with them. He'd just started taking over after they were relegated from League One and in his first season in charge, they were relegated again.

"He was desperate to get success, but looked a little bit low on confidence. It reflects on him. He's the owner. He always tries to put a positive spin on things, but it's hard to put a positive on successive relegations.

"I was always confident that I'd be challenging. However, I said on numerous occasions and kept on repeating it myself to remind people, the arrangement was that we'd be up there, in and around the play-offs. The first year was all about rebuilding and getting us winning more games than losing.

"There wasn't too much emphasis on getting promoted in that first year. That was part of the agreement from my point of view. I needed those first few months to build a squad after successive relegations. When I went into the building, they only had a handful of players, some who weren't classed as regular first team players but were eating up half of the budget."

***

Soon after Brabin arrived came Tranmere's first signing of the Non League era, a striker by the name of James Norwood. He was 24 and, apart from a handful of appearances for Exeter as a youngster, had spent his entire career outside of the Football League.

The former Brighton man arrived at Prenton Park with a terrific goal scoring pedigree. He had represented his country at England 'C' level, where he played with Andy Cook, and had scored over 50 goals during two stints with Forest Green.

However, he had grown tired of being pushed out on the wing at The New Lawn and was looking for a challenge. Fortunately, Brabin was searching for a striker who he could rely upon to find the back of the net. It did not take long to convince Norwood that he wanted to make the move.

"The first three phone calls I got were from Halifax, Torquay and Ebbsfleet, who were in the Conference South at the time," he said. "I'd run my contract down at Forest Green and I was questioning whether I had done the right thing.

"Then Gary Brabin rang me, a week after the season ended. I'd played against him when he was Luton manager and he said 'I'm at Tranmere'. I'd never heard of Tranmere! He asked why I'd left Forest Green and I told him how I'd spent five years playing left midfield. I hadn't played upfront since I was 18, even though I'd been telling them I was a striker.

"Gary wanted me to play upfront and he wanted me to play every game. I just said 'where is it?' He told me it was near Liverpool and how the city was great for a night out! Then he asked me to come up and have a look.

"I met the chairman in the centre circle, which was a clever ploy as it is a big stadium. Gary Brabin came out and we didn't talk about contracts or anything. We went for lunch and he just kept telling me about Tranmere. We went for dinner and still didn't talk about contracts.

"He asked me to stay another night and I wasn't in a rush so on Wednesday, I came in and talked contracts. They asked me something I've never been asked before - 'how long do you want?' I replied 'can you sign a five year deal in the Conference?' It took about 15 minutes to do in the end. I signed for two years."

Over the next three seasons, Norwood would turn himself in to a legend at Prenton Park. He frustrated the fans at first, with his finishing in one on one situations sometimes a let down. But what was always there was a willingness to run, an ability to always find space in the box and a clear desire to improve himself each day.

"I wouldn't say that James is what you'd call a natural finisher," says Brabin. "He's somebody who works hard to get his goals and he deserves his goals because he works so hard.

"He'd admit himself he was getting five or six chances before he was scoring. To be brave and dominate those leagues, you need somebody else who's chipping in with goals or a better ratio than one in five or six chances. I did struggle to find a partner for him in that first season."

Norwood soon became crucial to the team though. He made his debut on the opening day against Woking and quickly settled into life at Prenton Park. Indeed, after three years on Merseyside, he now feels totally at home here.

"I've always lived away," he continued. "I was five hours from home at Exeter and then three and a half hours away when I was at Forest Green. But this is the first time I'd been living away. I've got a girlfriend, bought a house, we've got dogs. It's changed my life in terms of giving me more stability.

"I'm somewhere where I'm happy to be and I'm happy to play at the same time. At my other clubs, I was either happy playing but I didn't like the place, or I didn't like the club and I didn't like the place. This is the first time it's fitted me.

"I really liked Gary Brabin as well. The first time I played against him I thought he was a nutcase! When I met him, I'd grown my hair back, because I used to have it shaved, and he told me to get it shaved again because I looked like a pansy!

"He is such a nice guy and had so much belief in me as a player. Rarely do you go into a club and have the manager tell you that 'no matter what, you're going to play every game and you'll be upfront'. That was the confidence I needed because I hadn't played up front for so long."

***

Frustratingly for Brabin, Norwood and everyone associated with the club, the striker would endure a difficult start to life at Prenton Park. He had a niggling injury that kept him out of a 4-1 win over Gateshead, the second game of the season, before picking up a three match suspension that came completely out of the blue and had nothing to do with his time at Tranmere.

"In my first game, we beat Woking 1-0 with Jay Harris scoring," he recalls. "I thought to myself 'corr this is big!' Then I got injured and when we battered Gateshead I believed we were going to absolutely piss the league. I had been around the division so I knew they were not an easy team to beat and we hammered them.

"I picked my ban up when I was at Forest Green. I wasn't playing at the time, so I was made to play in the reserves and we played a university team. In games like that, there's no team sheets or anything.

"We had an 85-year old ref and his two mates who he played bingo with. He didn't have a clue. He started asking for team sheets, telling people they couldn't wear this and that and our manager started to lose his head. He was writing fake names on the team sheet, like Lambert and Butler up top, Mike Bassett kind of stuff. The referee was ruining the game by blowing up for everything. Both teams were getting frustrated.

"I was playing right midfield wearing orange boots. Connor Jennings' brother James was playing left-back wearing orange boots. He fouled somebody on the other side of the pitch and he's a bit of a hot head, so he's swearing and all sorts. The referee walked over the to the manager and told him to take James off, but he wouldn't.

"The referee has followed him and seen me and shown me a red card. I was trying to tell him it wasn't me and he wasn't having any of it. In the end, I thought 'it's just a mess about game. Walk off.' It got to the point where the two teams walked off the pitch and refused to play until the referee and linesman left. In the end, we had one of their substitutes referee it and didn't have a problem.

"I then sign for Tranmere and the chairman pulls me to tell me I've got a three game ban. I couldn't believe it. I asked why and he told me for a sending off in a reserve game. I had signed in June. It was August by now. The game was in February.

"I had video evidence, their manager and our manager, their team and our team all saying it wasn't me. The FA wouldn't have it. It just proves how bad they are when it comes to disciplinary action. It's not innocent until proven guilty. It's guilty, even if you can prove yourself innocent. They don't want to undermine the referee or back down, even though we had 50 witnesses. I ended up serving a three match ban and therefore in the first month I played three games.

"I came back for a match at Welling and then we played Chester at home. After Liam Hogan had opened the scoring, I got my first Tranmere goal after a mazy run. We had about 9,500 there and that was the first time it hit me.

"I made my professional debut at Elland Road in front of 30,000 people and it felt like that many at Prenton Park that day. I thought 'this is massive'. The next game I scored at Southport and we took about 1,500 away. It was mad. It was the same amount of people that Forest Green had at home."

Chapter Four
The Beast From Eastleigh

There are not many occasions when a Tranmere team have been applauded off a pitch having lost a game. Of the 34 matches in which they suffered defeat in the National League, there is surely only one, and that was a 2-1 reverse at the hands of Eastleigh in October 2015.

Rovers headed into the match unbeaten in nine outings, and although over half of those fixtures had been drawn, a 1-0 victory away to Cheltenham and 4-0 thumping of Bromley had fired them back up the table.

They were beginning to look in good shape but, like the Boreham Wood game, things quickly went wrong. The finishing was abysmal, but also, not for the first time, the officials seemed to be against them.

The hosts were excellent in the first half, but they simply could not put the ball in the back of the net. James Norwood missed the best chance, a penalty that was saved, whilst they would rack up 16 shots during the 90 minutes, double the amount that Eastleigh managed.

A furious looking Brabin said at full time: "We played really well in the first half with some really good play. We dominated and should have had a penalty before the one we got. We had some one on ones, one saved on the line and then got given that penalty. You fancy our leading goalscorer in those situations, but he's missed, and it gives them a lift before half-time."

Naturally, Eastleigh made them pay after the break, something that would become a familiar theme throughout the club's tenure during the National League. Joe Partington got the first, heading home the opener, and that lead was doubled only a few minutes later by experienced striker James Constable. In between the two goals, Lois Maynard was sent off after picking up his second yellow card and that gave Tranmere a mountain to climb.

They did manage to get one back through Steven Jennings who sent a bobbling shot into the bottom corner from inside the area after Liam Ridehalgh's swinging ball into the box was poorly dealt with. It was not enough though, and Rovers actually finished the game with nine men, with Andy Mangan hobbling off injured after all three substitutes had already been made.

To be fair to Tranmere, they huffed and puffed and gave their all. It was just one of those days where nothing seemed to go right. One of those things was referee Ryan Johnson who made a number of baffling decisions and did not endear himself to the 5,133 fans present at Prenton Park. Eastleigh, renamed "Beastleigh" after this, were heavy handed and physical, but at no point did he crack down on their forceful tactics.

Brabin though refused to blame the officials for the defeat, saying: "The end product was where we were beaten. I'm gutted over that. It was a game of mixed emotions - which is probably an understatement!

"After the break, we go out looking for the same again and we start very sloppily with a wayward pass which puts us under pressure and results in us defending a set play that they've scored from. It's a big disappointment because we've looked quite strong in that department."

Looking back on the game now, Brabin is not quite so diplomatic. The officiating at that level is poor at best, with the referees regularly getting a number of game changing decisions wrong. Indeed, some seemed to come to Prenton Park with the intent of making a big call early on to show everybody who was in charge.

It damaged Tranmere. It was not their fault that they were a large club with a large fanbase for the division. Regularly, though, key decisions would go against them and it cost Brabin, and later Micky Mellon, several points.

"I remember the Eastleigh game," Brabin reflects. "Everything went against us, but there were a lot of games like that. You try not to moan too much about referees, but it's hard when decisions go against you and that game was one of them.

"We played really well. The sending off was very harsh. We weren't getting the rewards we deserved. At this point, I kept on reminding people that the expectation was to be in and around the play-offs. I had to keep reminding people of that message.

"I remember us going top of the league in our first year and I think I came out publicly and said 'we're not ready'. It sort of raised the expectations a bit more when I knew we weren't ready. I knew we wouldn't be far off and we were going in the right direction."

The game did follow a worryingly similar pattern to the Boreham Wood fixture earlier on in the campaign. Rovers had most of the ball and the best of the chances, but they were not able to find a way through. Their opponents, on the other hand, were more savvy and more clinical and therefore went home with the three points.

"Chesterfield have come down into the National League for the 2018/19 season," says Ben Harrison. "My message for them is to watch out for teams like Eastleigh and Boreham Wood! They're the ones you have to contend with, and it's not easy.

"In the National League, you have to play with wingers. We struggled a bit there. A lot of teams play very narrow. That was our problem at the start of our final season too. We couldn't score because we were just trying to play down the middle."

***

Tranmere's form hit a bit of a nosedive after the Eastleigh defeat. To be fair to Brabin, the lack of players did not help, with Adam Dawson and Andy Mangan both out injured when their form had been crucial in the nine game unbeaten run.

A 1-0 loss to Barrow at Prenton Park followed just a few days later, and although high flying Forest Green Rovers were beaten 2-0 in mid-October, further defeats to Lincoln, in the FA Cup as well as the League, and Dover were just around the corner.

Rovers by now were beginning to sink down the table and the fans were becoming frustrated. Brabin, too, was finding things difficult as he tried to manage expectations.

"We needed to be realistic and think about getting the momentum moving forward. Any club who are moving forward, that's a positive. I still feel and felt at the time that we were moving forward. We weren't quite ready to take the league by storm, but we were heading in the right direction."

James Norwood reckons the poor form was because some of his teammates simply had not adapted to life in the National League yet. A handful of the squad had spent most, if not all, of their careers higher up, so were not used to the physicality of the division - or how much the officials let go.

"I don't think we were prepared for the type of football that's played here," he explains. "We had the likes of myself, Jay Harris, Martin Riley and Ritchie Sutton who knew about the National League. But then there was Michael Ihiekwe, Liam Ridehalgh, Steven Jennings and Matt Hill who hadn't played in the Conference.

"The challenges that were going in, they were turning to the referee and asking for the foul, but it's not at this level. You can get away with much more. So it took a bit of adapting to the rules. You knew you could be dirtier off and on the ball. It took time for them to acclimatise.

"We got a 0-0 draw at Braintree and there was no hot water in the showers afterwards. Jennings lost his head. He's ranting 'how can we come to a place like this and not win' but Jay and I just turned around and said 'it's a good point'.

"We knew if we beat them at home and so took four points off them in the season it would be a good return. They ended up taking a lot of points off people at home because they were horrible. The game was horrible. Everybody who went there would find it the same. It was a horrible place for years."

What piled more pressure on Brabin and Tranmere was the form of Cheltenham. They had been the other team to come down from the Football League that summer, but had taken to the National League like a duck to water, winning seven of their first eleven fixtures.

In fact, their third league defeat of the season did not come until the start of March. Tranmere supporters looked on jealously. Why could they not do what Gary Johnson had achieved at Whaddon Road? Why did they need to be patient in the quest for success when Cheltenham were achieving it so readily?

"The way I looked at it was that Gary Johnson was part of the club who had got relegated," explains Brabin. "The club stood by him and he was able to keep the group of players he wanted and build on the previous year. He'd been part of that process coming down. They stuck with him because they believed the club were moving forward, and they got that success the next year.

"As well as that, Cheltenham were used to it. They had been in the league before and had no expectation of dominating the league. Expectation is a massive thing in football. No matter what level you're at, you've got to work hard to gain victories. Sometimes, just because of your history, it raises expectation. With Cheltenham, they had yo-yoed before, so they knew what it was about.

"We actually went top early in the season and it was possibly the worst thing that could have happened, in a perverse way. I remember coming out publicly and saying 'we aren't ready'. I remember getting a negative response from that, but I was just purely being honest about it. We'd had a fantastic start, but there was enough expectation on the club anyway to bounce straight back up. Then with the start we had, I think it raised it even more.

"On the other hand, I remember going to watch a Fleetwood game when I was at Luton. Micky Mellon was in charge, and I've spoken to him about it because it was one of the worst games of football I've ever seen in my life. They were getting beaten by relegation threatened Tamworth and it was terrible.

"They were losing 2-1 and then Jamie Vardy scores an equaliser. The mascot and the music came on and I looked at the atmosphere for getting a draw and it was so jovial. I remember coming away thinking 'they've won the league'. It was the level of expectation. Everything was a bonus and you were competing against that."

Cheltenham would eventually go on to win the National League in the 2015/16 season. They accumulated an incredible 101 points, 23 more than Tranmere, and racked up 30 wins. It was a sensational campaign and the best anybody has had points wise since Mellon's Fleetwood team in 2011/12.

They came to Prenton Park later in the season and beat Rovers 1-0 thanks to an early goal from David Wright that completely killed the game. Once ahead, they wasted time and pretty comfortably held off a team who created bags and bags of chances but, again, were unable to finish them off. This was becoming an all too familiar pattern and perhaps showed exactly where each side were in terms of their development.

Ben Harrison admits that having Johnson in charge from the previous season clearly helped Cheltenham when going into the National League, as the stability within the club was key. He does not, however, have fond memories of that 1-0 loss.

"They had this bizarre free-kick that went viral because it was so bad," he says. "Loads of them all queued up to take it, ran over it and the last lad skied it and it went down Borough Road! We were unlucky that day though to be fair.

"In a way, there was frustration because they went up and we didn't. It put pressure on us, but you look at them and think they only get 3,000 fans! There were expectations, but you've got to manage them. Look at Micky Mellon. He's done really well with that.

"It helped that Gary Johnson stayed in charge and they had some of the same players from the previous season. They were a few steps further down the line. Look at what they've done since though. I was speaking to a Cheltenham fan recently and he said 'I think we might get relegated again'. They're only ever going to be able to cope with one thing."

Chapter Five
Squad Building

Perhaps one issue behind Tranmere's patchy start to the campaign was that, even going into the second half of the season, the squad was still gelling together.

When Brabin arrived at Prenton Park in the summer, he only had a handful of players who were under contract for the following season. Other than Michael Ihiekwe and Liam Ridehalgh, none of them had played enough to be classed as first team regulars.

Firstly there was Marcus Holness, a central defender brought in twelve months earlier as club captain. He, though, was recovering from a serious knee injury picked up at Morecambe in January and would hardly play for the club again. Jake Kirby and Cole Stockton meanwhile had been around the first team for a handful of years, but they were more out of the team than in it. Aside from that, only the even younger Mitch Duggan and Evan Gumbs had professional contracts, but they were some way off establishing themselves.

It gave Brabin a difficult task, and he was quick to tie down Steven Jennings and Matt Hill, a couple of experienced professionals, to new one year contracts.

A trickle of players arrived throughout the summer, including several who would make their mark during Tranmere's three year stint in the National League and eventually help the team to promotion, such as James Norwood, Scott Davies and Jay Harris. Things were beginning to take shape.

"There wasn't much to build around," said Brabin. "It was a group of players who weren't classed as regulars apart from Steven Jennings. I had to build from that.

"Contrary to the reports, people thought we were going to be big spenders. It was far from that. Half the budget was taken up by that group of players who were already here. It was a tough rebuilding thing, but something I was confident I'd have the time to do.

"My first signing was James Norwood, who I'd liked for a while. He was always being played wide but wanted to play upfront. He was one I knew would be a real asset as a centre-forward. The bit that I did find hard was somebody to partner him in his first year, but that's always hard with strikers.

"I liked Cole Stockton, but he just hadn't played enough games of football. With him and Jake Kirby, the conversation was that I liked them as players. They had a lot of ability. But just looking at their records for the last 4 or 5 years, they'd not played many games. It was coming on as sub or having the occasional reserve game.

"I felt they both needed to go out on loan and that they'd benefit more from playing competitive football regularly. They'd come back as better players. We needed something that was a bit more ready."

As such, both Kirby and Stockton left Prenton Park on temporary deals, with the former moving to Stockport, whilst the latter spent some time at Southport before heading into the Football League with Morecambe.

It was brave of Brabin to send both players away, but as he saw neither as part of his first team plans, he needed to get some money off the wage budget, however little or small that was, in order to bring some more experienced players in.

Looking back on it now, he admits he would have liked to have had a few more players to work with when he arrived. After all, with only a few weeks pre-season training behind them, it was always going to be difficult to gel the new players together in time for the new campaign.

"There are pros and cons to not having much of a squad to work with," he continues. "I've been in situations where you go in, as a coach or an assistant as well, and there's a big squad of players who are on a lot of money but they aren't going to feature in your plans. At that point, you're wishing you had a clean slate.

"But then I've been in other positions where you come in and you're working with the group of players and you're thinking these aren't as bad as the position or results suggest. You feel you can get more out of them. So I think it depends on the personnel.

"I would have liked a bit more of a base to build on. I felt that I had to rebuild from scratch. Part of the plan was to recruit locally. I felt it was important that we got players who were good enough but local. Not only is that financially better in terms of relocating, but it's more painful for players down south than up north.

"It was also important that people understood the size and potential of the club. It's got to that stage that is rock bottom and we had to try and build from that. That was half my selling point. Some players were taking a pay cut to come to the club and not enough gets said about that."

Ultimately, though, the manager did not quite convince everybody he wanted to join the club that summer. One target he missed out on was Omar Bogle, who preferred a move to Grimsby from Solihull and has subsequently joined Wigan and then Cardiff in deals worth hundreds of thousands of pounds.

He also had to be patient in trying to convince a couple of other players to drop out of the Football League to come to Tranmere. He had his eye on Jeff Hughes, a former Northern Ireland international playing for Cambridge, and Luton captain Steve McNulty, but started the season without either of them.

Eventually, after much negotiating, both players arrived at Prenton Park midway through the campaign. McNulty, one of the top centre halves in the division above in the previous campaign, made his debut on Halloween in a home defeat to Dover, whilst Hughes came in shortly after Christmas.

"Steve McNulty signing is a big plus for us," said Brabin at the time. "He is a local lad, a leader and was in the League Two Team of the Year last season. He is the type of player and character that we want at the club and I think it strengthens our squad even more so I'm delighted to be able to bring him here."

James Norwood was also impressed with the impact Steve McNulty had on the squad when he arrived. Rovers were craving not only somebody who could lead the side from the back, but also that bit of Non League experience that was perhaps missing through some of the squad.

"Everybody knew and knows about Steve McNulty," he jokes. "People in the Premier League know him as the big footballer who's unflattering but also so flattering. He's Paulo Maldini, if he isn't Maldini. He's such a good player and you don't argue with him.

"He's been there and done it and has got loads of promotions. He very rarely makes mistakes and he knows his game and what he's good and bad at. That's the way he works.

"Also, when a lot of people might not tell you something, he'll turn around to you in training and say 'you're crap. Sort yourself out or you can just go. It's embarrassing for you and us.' You won't find that with a lot of people.

"We had a certain player who wasn't training well and it got to the point where he wasn't allowed to train with us. I've learnt from Macca that if you're not pulling your weight, we don't want you in there. All you're going to do is be bad for the squad and you won't help us reach our goal."

However, it did take the former Liverpool youngster some time to bed in. He would eventually go on to captain the team when Jennings left in 2017, but as Brabin recalls, things were not too easy early on.

"I started speaking to him in the summer," he confessed. "I've tried to sign him in the past - on one occasion when I was at Luton - but he went to Fleetwood, of course managed by Micky Mellon.

"He's a player I've known for a while and he's a friend. He admitted himself that his body shape has probably stopped him from playing even higher. He's a big lad and people are quick to judge with his appearance, but he's a talented player with a great attitude. I knew he'd be good.

"In a perfect world, I'd have got him in pre-season, but Luton didn't want to let him go easily. It took as long as it took to get him in, but he's proved to be a real good asset.

"He eventually joined on the day of arguably our best game - a 2-0 win at Forest Green. Liam Hogan put in possibly his best performance, but it was going to be his last one because he needed an operation. We signed Macca and he came in and said 'why've you signed me? You didn't need me!'

"Even he would admit it took him a few games to settle down. It was 7 or 8 games before he got going, but he was outstanding, and he's been a real big asset to the club. I knew he'd be important going forward because he's a leader and a really good player, plus he's quicker than people give him credit for.

"But I was delighted to get that over the line. They were all little things where we were adding towards the jigsaw of what we wanted to achieve. He's great around the dressing room, too. He's fair and good from a management point of view because he won't just side with the manager or the players. He'll give his opinion and you want that from your players. He's honest and it hurts him in defeat. He's not afraid to point the finger.

"Jeff Hughes was another player I'd spoken to in the summer. I wanted to sign him in pre-season and always kept an eye on his situation. He was a fantastic signing and it's a testament to him that he came, because he took a really big hit in terms of wages. Not only that, but he has dropped out of the league, and he's an ex-international.

"We kept in touch with him from the summer and always made him feel like he was going to be a part of it. I think he was fantastic when he finally signed. What a great player."

Mark Palios too saw McNulty's arrival as a vital piece in Tranmere's building process. They already had some talented and experienced defenders in Liam Hogan and Ritchie Sutton, but perhaps something was missing from the heart of the team.

"We sort of finished that team building in November," recalls the chairman. "Steve McNulty comes in then, so you've finally got that final piece of the jigsaw. And if you look at that second half of the season, apart from some of the big games, we actually had a fantastic record and broke records."

Another mid-season signing was Lee Vaughan, arriving from promotion rivals Cheltenham. He added a new dimension to the side at full-back, allowing Lois Maynard to move further forward into a more natural midfield position.

All three of Hughes, McNulty and Vaughan were successful signings. At times, they had their critics, but always found a way of proving the doubters wrong. Whilst the latter would break his leg and sadly miss out on the play-offs the next season, Hughes and McNulty formed an integral part of the side that finished second in consecutive years.

There were a couple of less successful additions to the squad, though. The search for a man to partner James Norwood stretched long into the season. Andy Mangan scored seven times in his first thirteen games, but never fully regained his fitness after hobbling off against Eastleigh.

His time at Prenton Park ended with a run of eight games without finding the back of the net before the end of 2015. When January came, he made a surprise move to League One, returning to Shrewsbury, the club he originally left to join Tranmere.

"I couldn't stand in Andy Mangan's way" insisted the manager. "By his own admittance he wasn't fit when he first came in. We had to work him up to speed and get him fit, but he did well. Then when the opportunity came for him to go to Shrewsbury and play in the Football League, it was better for him. At his age, he wanted to play as high as he could, and financially as well it was great for him. He had a longer contract and better wages."

By the time the striker left, Gary Taylor-Fletcher had already been brought in on a free-transfer, whilst former Sheffield United striker Michael Higdon was recruited in February after being released by Oldham.

Both players came with a great pedigree and both, importantly to Brabin, were local. The former had spent over a decade in the Football League with the likes of Blackpool, Huddersfield and Leicester, whilst the latter had been the top scorer in the Scottish Premier League just a handful of seasons earlier with Motherwell.

They were a promising pair of signings who really could have taken the National League by storm. Unfortunately for Tranmere, their best days were behind them.

In fairness, both showed glimpses of quality during their short stints at Prenton Park, particularly Taylor-Fletcher who scored a screamer on his debut against Forest Green. But he also lacked match fitness, and the odd tweak or strain never seemed too far away.

Higdon, meanwhile, took too long to get up to speed in a Rovers shirt, and that put Brabin in a tough position. As much as he wanted to persist with the striker, Tranmere were not only running out of games, but they were falling short in the battle for the play-offs as well. In the end, he would score only twice before being released in the summer.

"They fitted the bill because they were local players," Brabin explained. "They were good signings, but I still felt we missed that young, hungry striker to partner James Norwood. Those two certainly gave us something, but not enough in the end.

"I did feel a little bit for Michael Higdon. He hadn't played much football but his pedigree is second to none. He'd scored a lot of goals at a higher level and with him coming back home to play for Tranmere, I thought it could have been the catalyst to find that form again.

"But he found it harder than he imagined. The league doesn't get the respect it deserves and he was getting a negative response from the fans. It seemed to nosedive a bit and didn't work out as well as we expected. Yet although we were signing somebody who was coming to the end of his career, it was as near to the quality as we needed.

"Gary Taylor-Fletcher meanwhile was unplayable at times. I'm going to praise him and criticise him in the same breath now - he's good because he wanted to play every single game, but that led to us having some heated debates because I didn't think he was ready.

"He played more football for Tranmere that year than he had in his last three or four seasons at his previous clubs. He felt like he wanted to play more, and I compliment him for that, but I didn't see him as playing every minute of every game. I wanted him to be the impact I knew he could be when needed."

You could not use either signing as a yardstick for Brabin's success in the transfer market though. More often than not, the players he brought to Prenton Park went on to be a hit.

James Norwood and Andy Cook are the best examples, each scoring in excess of 50 league goals for the club, but you only have to look at the side that beat Boreham Wood at Wembley in the 2018 play-off final to see how much of a mark Brabin left on the club. Six of the starting eleven that day were his signings, whilst a further two,

Jay Harris and Connor Jennings, came off the bench.

"I think I have a good eye for a player," he says of his transfer dealings. "You look at the players they've brought in since I left and it's still basically the group of players I brought in.

"I wanted people who I thought were going to move the club forward, and that takes time, unless you've got millions of pounds to spend and you spend silly money on players as and when you need them. That wasn't the case.

"We had to be patient. We were speaking to players and analysing players and waiting for the right moment to bring them in. It was turning into a frustrating season but I felt that it was a tough job in terms of recruiting the right players and turning the club around.

"I pride myself on value for money for players. I signed Andre Gray for £25,000 from Hinckley and Luton have made millions off him over the last few years. Ultimately, it was him who scored the goals that got them promoted. The same goes for Tranmere; I worked hard to get James Norwood and Andy Cook into the club and I think they've been a fantastic partnership.

"We missed out on players who went to bigger spenders. I look at two players now and they've moving for millions of pounds - I was close to getting them at Tranmere. I had them in the door and we were close to signing them, but we couldn't quite meet the wages. It wasn't astronomical money, but they're the fine lines.

"One of those players was Omar Bogle. He went to Wigan for about £2m. There was another, but I'd rather not mention him at the moment. Bogle was well publicised at the time.

"They go to a bigger spender and move on for a lot of money. It does frustrate you at times, but you'd always rather manage a club with history and expectation as opposed to money. It is a better challenge."

Chapter Six
Barrow Bouncebackability

When Tranmere made the trip up to Barrow on January 9th 2016, Gary Brabin was under ever increasing pressure. They had failed to build on their early season form and did not look capable of mounting a challenge for the play-offs, let alone top spot.

A 2-0 win against high flying Forest Green in October had raised hopes, but it proved to be a false dawn. A run of one victory in ten followed, and even that was only a narrow one as James Norwood popped up to score in the 90th minute to earn a 2-1 win over Guiseley at Prenton Park.

Some real dross was served up in between, including a 4-1 hammering at Woking on a Tuesday night when Rovers were absolutely dreadful. This would prove to be the heaviest defeat of Brabin's tenure, but it is not the only one that sticks out.

There was also an embarrassing 4-2 hammering to local rivals Wrexham in the first round of the FA Trophy. Although the competition held little interest to the club that season, coming way behind earning promotion back to the Football League in terms of priorities, the defeat was gut-wrenching.

A decade earlier, Brian Little's Tranmere side had battered Wrexham 5-1 at the Racecourse en route to reaching the League One play-offs. It is a result that still sits fondly in the memories of all Rovers fans as Theo Whitmore and company ran the show and thoroughly humiliated their cross border rivals.

Wrexham were relegated that season, and it was not long before they found themselves in the National League. This was the first time the two clubs had been in the same division since that 2004/05 campaign, and the Welsh fans were desperate for revenge. That day they well and truly got it.

"That was a defining moment," recalls Ben Harrison. "Micky Mellon understands those derby games, but to Gary Brabin it was just an FA Trophy game. He had to be reminded that it was against our arch rivals. They rolled us over far too easily."

A 1-1 draw at Halifax, managed by Tranmere legend Jimmy Harvey, appeared to show some light at the end of the tunnel in mid-December, and eventually things started to turn for the better with a 2-1 win at Macclesfield on Boxing Day. That was followed by a 1-0 victory over Altrincham, a team who until that season had only played Rovers in pre-season friendlies. According to Brabin, they were beginning to turn the corner.

"Just before Christmas I thought we were heading in the right direction," he says. "We were starting to get better and stronger, although we didn't have that killer instinct that I would have liked. We were more suited to the counter attack and we were creating more chances.

"We were sharing the goals about a bit more. I just felt we were still another striker away from not only competing, but being good enough to win the league. We'd given other teams an advantage points wise, but I still felt confident that we'd get in the play-offs.

"That win at Macclesfield was a turning point. It was a good, solid performance. Macclesfield is always a tough place to go. Steve McNulty and Michael Ihiekwe scored and I was pleased because it was from two set plays.

"From there, I thought we could still get in the play-offs. I started feeling more confident that we had a group of players that were going to pick up points. I always felt if we got in the play-offs, we'd win them. It was just catching that pack ahead of us."

The return fixture against Macclesfield on New Year's Day did not go quite as well as Rovers were beaten 1-0. It was a clash bereft of quality, but also one in which the hosts were lacking luck as Steven Jennings had a perfectly good goal ruled out in injury time. It left Rovers outside of the top five and things were pretty desperate.

A few days later, they made the trip to a bleak looking Holker Street to take on Barrow. Heavy rain in the Lake District in the weeks leading up to the fixture had destroyed the pitch, leaving the surface lacking in grass but offering plenty of muddy patches that would make passing difficult. To be honest, it was a surprise the game even went ahead, with the coaching staff giving the pitch a good inspection before sending their players out to warm up.

One man who was missing for the visitors was James Norwood, with the striker worryingly sent to hospital before the game due to a stomach complaint. "I was warming up and I had a pain that got worse and worse," he explains. "Very rarely would I go and see the physio but when I did, I immediately got called to the doctor. He thought I had appendicitis so wanted to rush me to hospital.

"Brabin has since told me that when we were losing, people were shouting 'you've sold him haven't you, tell us', even though I'd been warming up! He couldn't believe it. He wanted to say 'you've just seen him!'

Even without their top scorer, things started pretty well as Adam Mekki netted from the penalty spot mid-way through the first half to hand his side the lead. "I was sat in hospital with our kit man when he scored," Norwood continued. "My first thought was 'shit, I'm on penalties!'"

Things soon took an alarming turn for the worse though as Tranmere's defence was repeatedly carved open by a Barrow team who had won just two of their ten league fixtures since a 1-0 victory at Prenton Park in October.

They equalised with a quarter of the game left as Jason Walker converted from the spot following a foul by Steven Jennings. An unmarked Simon Grand then headed home from 10 yards in the 82nd minute before future Rovers man Andy Cook was picked out in space near the six yard line and tapped past Scott Davies to make it 3-1.

It was a disaster and the Super White Army were fuming. Some left, disgusted at how their team had been picked apart, whilst others vented their anger at the manager. Although stuck away in a corner, several metres down the touchline from the dugout, they still made their feelings known. Some had to be held back by stewards as they attempted to get closer to Brabin and make sure he could hear their abuse.

The manager was less than impressed with their behaviour, insisting they were doing more damage than good. Indeed, he was quick to let them know that there was still a long way to go in the season - and reiterated his belief that Rovers remained on course for the play-offs.

"We sense there's one or two who have given up on us," he said in the aftermath. "We certainly won't be giving up. It's a tough league.

"We feel like we have enough hurdles to overcome in every game without the one or two who are making life a little bit harder for us who are supposed to be on our side. But a lot of the fans are brilliant and when you score that fourth, those ones that have been singing, you're right up there and you want to be in the crowd."

Looking back on it now, Brabin's thoughts have not changed too much. And he reckons that, like on several occasions through the season, Tranmere's performance was not getting the result it deserved. In his eyes, they were having the majority of the ball and looked the more likely to win - yet, not for the first time, they could not finish things off.

"The atmosphere in the away end at 3-1 was toxic," he recalled. "It was a strange game. I think Barrow only got in our half three times and they scored on each occasion. You're thinking we're moving forward and feel like we're getting over one hurdle, and then that happens. It was surreal.

"We were actually playing well and we were the better side, but it was the problem of killing teams off. As soon as teams were getting a chance against us, we were getting punished. I understand the fans' frustration - they've travelled all the way up to Barrow and watched us go 3-1 down. It's all built up from that expectation, but also when you go somewhere, you don't expect to be getting beat 3-1, especially when we'd now built a squad of players who were good enough."

It was a pretty grim few moments, but there was life left in this game yet as it took a remarkable and dramatic turn. 87 minutes were on the clock when Cook scored, but as the match entered injury time, Tranmere drew hope from Lois Maynard thumping into the top corner from just inside the box. Jeff Hughes then profited from two defenders colliding as they challenged for a long ball that fell invitingly in his path, and he duly skipped around the 'keeper before tapping home.

And then, with just seconds left, Rovers completed a sensational comeback as substitute Jake Kirby, only just back from a loan spell at Stockport, fired a deflected shot past Joel Dixon from 20-yards.

"It's unbelievable," he said after the match. "When we went 3-1 down, a lot of the fans weren't expecting us to come back, but credit to the lads. They had heart and fought back and it was great to get the winner.

"I thought we were comfortable at 1-0 up. It was a bit of a scrappy game, but when they equalised, I still thought we'd push on. What actually happened, you couldn't have written it.

"The manager's got the fans shouting at him. Obviously they're not going to be happy when we're losing 3-1 having been 1-0 up. Once the winner goes in though, it's all forgotten. Everyone went mad!"

Social media went wild. Football fans up and down the country took to Twitter to express their thoughts on one of the most sensational comebacks of the decade. It was quite incredible. This team had been dead and buried going into injury time. A section of the fanbase had turned. Yet somehow the players picked themselves up and pulled off one of the most unlikely victories in the club's history.

At this point, Norwood was still in hospital. The test results were yet to come back, so nobody really knew exactly what was up with him. One thing was for sure though - he was desperate to join in the celebrations.

"When we went 3-1 down, I told our kit man Adam not to update me again," he said. "But about 20 minutes after full-time, he looks and tells me we've won. I wanted to get on the coach. It would have been brilliant.

"They wouldn't let me go and I had to sign something to say if I died, it wasn't their fault. Eventually I got the results back and it wasn't appendicitis. I still don't know what it was. But I got on the coach and it was a brilliant atmosphere."

The manager, meanwhile, had just felt a huge release of pressure. Ten minutes before the full time whistle, he was receiving all kinds of abuse from a handful of fans. Yet when the referee eventually brought an end to proceedings, he had just witnessed one of the most incredible games of his career.

"I've never seen anything like it," Brabin admits. "It was brilliant and I think it was what we deserved. You could see the emotion on the players' faces and I loved the fact that they all ran towards me. That was a show of support and it was good.

"It was a great moment. Although we were disappointed at being 3-1 down and you can understand people's frustrations, sometimes it is nice the manner in which you win a game. That was certainly one of those occasions."

Ben Harrison has a different take on things though, explaining: "It was an interesting game because Gary was getting a lot of grief. The players didn't celebrate in front of the fans. He had his team spirit there, but it's sad to see. A football club can't work that way."

Mark Palios admits he cannot remember a game like it either. With five minutes to go, he was looking at a team who had crumbled and looked set for a twelfth defeat of the season. Instead, they picked up a famous win that would spark their best run of form of the campaign.

"I tell a story about buying the club and that game," he jokes. "You've always got to make it the wife's idea! It's called "Socratic Nature" in Greek by Socrates. You persuade people by making them think it's their idea.

"In the 89th minute, you're 3-1 down at Barrow, it's the pits and we're not looking like doing anything. It's a horrible place to be and it's a night game. Our fans are giving dog's abuse to the manager and you're sitting there thinking is this doable? Can you fix this?

"Nicky turns to me and it's all my idea again! Then when it's the 95th minute and we're winning 4-3, it's all her idea again. The flip round was incredible. I've watched it back, and I still think we're going to lose! I still don't know how we did it!

"What was quite interesting was when we scored the third, I'd have been telling them to slow it down. Our lads ran, got the ball, grabbed it out of the net and brought it back to speed up the kick off. I've never asked the lads about it, but I wouldn't have been thinking we're going to win this, but they did. It was a fantastic turn around."

Just a couple of days before the Barrow game, Mark and Nicola had been at a fan meeting, where the question of support had come up. Certain parts of the Prenton Park crowd had been known to get on the manager and the team's back for the last few seasons, and that had carried over into the National League

It was something that the Palios' were desperate to turn around. They knew that if those fans could become more supportive and work together as one with the team, Tranmere could become almost unstoppable. The sheer volume of people they got through the turnstiles compared to other teams in the division would mean they could make a huge difference.

Mark continues: "When Nicky and I came to the club, one of the pieces of potential was the fans. It was a negative to begin with, but it turned. I worked with the Trust and set up TROSC and the Disabled Supporter's Association and it's all about them helping themselves. That's what community is all about. So I will give them tasks to step it on from where it is.

"Those can be things like getting the fans onside and closer to the team and realising they can avoid stress by doing something about it on the pitch. I brought the band in. I got the drum first to try and get the atmosphere going and it didn't really work. I tried again when I got TROSC set up. I said there's your job, get the atmosphere in The Kop right. They've been working on that and it's been fantastic. There's more to go on that.

"I get so many anecdotal stories now about kids buying season tickets - even more so after Wembley. Everton supporters coming to Tranmere and stuff like that. You've got momentum in the fanbase but you've also got it closer to the team, and Micky Mellon understands that and relates to the fans. He works it quite well. The players love it, because if the fans are helping you when you're down, it just creates this bond.

"I remember having a go at the fans because I remember them booing a substitute coming on at Halifax in our first season. How does that make him better? I said to them at that fan night 'you can come to the car park at 8.30 in the morning and boo me and Nicky when we get out of the car. Do you think it's going to make us work any harder?'

"So on the Thursday before Barrow, I'd been berating the fans. I told them they had to go the 90 minutes as well. There was a big issue that they were getting on our back and making it worse. On the Monday, I was looking for everybody who left before the 90 minutes. It was great."

There was also a feeling amongst some supporters that Brabin might have been sacked if Tranmere had lost at Barrow. Their form had begun to turn slightly, but it was still not at the level you would expect for such a talented bunch of players. They were underperforming, and this would have been a really damaging defeat just when things had been looking up.

"I think he would have been under pressure with a defeat there," says Ben Harrison. "Mark and Nicola wanted at least the play-offs. They had put the money into the place and they looked at the league - Braintree made the play-offs, we didn't!"

Palios though insists that that is not the case. Although Rovers were not hitting the heights expected of them, he was not about to make another change and bring in a fifth manager in less than two years.

"He was under pressure, but not from me," he says. "My role isn't to pressurise the manager. To be honest, he must be totally thick if he thinks he isn't under pressure. I don't need to add to that. If anything, I need to take it off him.

"What I won't do is make a statement supporting the manager. I never will do. I've done it bleakly, saying 'so and so is a great manager' when I've been interviewed, but I won't make the statement, because that leads to pressure when you don't make the statement. So I won't get involved in it. It's between me and the manager, not the fans, as with any employee in the club.

"I said it when we went down - people were trying to get me to comment on whether Micky Adams was responsible for all this, but I just said 'everybody at the club works in the best way they can' and I'll give them the benefit of the doubt. They've got the right to walk away without me commenting in the press. I wouldn't comment on any other employee, like the catering manager going.

"So Gary was under pressure from the fans, but the way I do it is I will ask the manager to come in and ask him how he saw it. I will let them tell me, and if I see it radically differently, I will probably challenge that. But if it gets too often or they just don't see things, you make a decision on their position.

"You've got to go somewhere better and have somebody who's going to make an impact in a different way and move the club on. Unless you do, you're just responding to the ebb and flow of defeats and victories. That's the landscape of football.

"We didn't get promoted under Gary Brabin at the end of the day, but I never even thought about sacking him because we were making progress. We would continue to make progress, I hoped, in the summer. He wasn't under particular pressure from me."

***

In football, the manner in which you win games can have a huge effect on the team. After such a topsy turvy few months, coming from behind to snatch victory from the jaws of defeat in such a dramatic fashion gave Tranmere something to build on. They now had some momentum with which to move forward.

Perhaps unsurprisingly, they quickly found their best form not only of the season, but since October 2011, winning four games in a row and throwing themselves back into the promotion mix. Victories over Bromley, Torquay and Southport followed, all of them by a one goal margin, and Brabin reckons the Barrow success was the catalyst for such a push.

"It gave us momentum," he continued. "That belief was growing stronger every day and with every game. We felt we didn't always get what we deserved from games but we always believed. The group of players were getting stronger and stronger and I'm looking at the squad more than confident that we'll get even better next year.

"I knew it was a club heading in the right direction. They had spiralled two divisions into the National League. It's not easy just getting back up. You've got to fight and scrap for everything. But I always believed we were going in the right direction. I knew I was building a squad of players who were good enough to get out of the league. We felt that if we got into the play-offs, we'd win them, and we spoke about that as a squad at the time."

Ben Harrison agrees that the win over Barrow had a positive impact, but he also thinks there was still something missing. Even as Tranmere racked up the wins, the pressure on Brabin did not subside.

He was concerned about the relationship between the manager and the supporters, and believes it was one of the reasons behind his downfall only nine months later.

"There's usually something that triggers off a good run in football," he says, "But the relationship with the fans wasn't there. It's always hard to put your finger on why, but nobody chanted his name.

"Micky Mellon plays that side better. He's more of a seasoned professional and he played for the club. Some Tranmere fans have got this scouse and Birkenhead divide as well that they use when things aren't going well.

"If I was ever offering Gary any advice, I'd tell him that at a club like Tranmere, you've got to get close to the fans. He came to an event we did for the Leyland DAF. He's a nice guy. But maybe he just wasn't comfortable doing it. At a club like Tranmere, you can't avoid doing that."

Chapter Seven
The Death Of The King

Tranmere have had their fair share of legends, a list bursting with people who have scored important goals at Wembley, helped the club to promotion, or amassed a huge number of appearances over years of service. A select group even fall into all three categories. There is one name who stands above all others though: Johnny King.

The wing half actually started his career across the River Mersey with Everton, racking up nearly half a century of games for the Blues before signing for Bournemouth in 1960. He was on the move again a few months later, and it is at this point that he would start his love affair with Rovers.

King spent eight years on the Wirral as a player, making in excess of 250 appearances and earning promotion to Division Three in 1966-67. Twelve months later, he moved on to Port Vale and later finished his career with Wigan.

Upon hanging up his boots, a move into management always looked likely and it was in the dugout that King really enhanced his reputation. He received some help and advice from Liverpool legend Bill Shankly, who once described King as the best young manager in the country when recommending him to Sheffield Wednesday.

That, though, was long after Tranmere came calling in 1975 as they searched for a replacement to Ron Yeats, and despite being a rookie, Johnny duly delivered a promotion in his first season in charge.

Rovers would comfortably stay in Division Three for a couple of seasons before eventually being relegated in 1979-80. A few months later, King was subsequently sacked, making way for Brian Hamilton.

He went on to manage Northwich and Caernarfon, where he also left a charming footprint that still exists decades later.

When local businessman Peter Johnson bought Tranmere in 1987, one of his first moves was to bring King back to the Wirral, making him manager of the Super White Army for a second time. In his own words, he took them on "A trip to the moon". The success he brought was unparalleled as, after avoiding relegation in 1987 thanks to a crucial win over Exeter, Tranmere made five trips to Wembley and were promoted twice, in 1989 and 1991.

It was an incredible period for the club and the second of those promotions, thanks to a famous play-off final win over Bolton courtesy of Chris Malkin's winner, took them up to Division Two. They had a squad of superstars, including the likes of John Aldridge, Pat Nevin and Eric Nixon, as well as several local youngsters who would go on to much bigger and better things.

This was dream land. The club were on the brink of the Premier League, the type of dizzying heights that had never been scaled before and have certainly not been matched since. The fans were in nosebleed territory. When this club had been crumbling and at risk of extinction just years earlier, now they were trying to break into a division that included Manchester United, Arsenal, Everton and Liverpool.

Yet all good things must come to an end and despite three successive appearances in the play-offs to reach the top flight, the curtain was brought down on King's managerial career in 1996. The greatest era of Tranmere's history came to a crashing ending.

Unsurprisingly, he is revered on the Wirral to this day. He was adoringly taken into the hearts of every supporter who lived through those halcyon days, but not just for his footballing prowess. This is somebody who was as great a person as he was a manager, much loved by everybody who had the pleasure of working with and under him.

It was those famous quotes that strengthened the bond between man and club, too. Jim Steel was a "maypole" who the rest of the team danced around and John Aldridge "The Gunslinger", but perhaps best of all is his description of how Rovers compared to their rivals across the water. "Tranmere will never be able to compete with Liverpool and Everton," he said. "They're big liners like the Queen Mary, but I see Tranmere like a deadly submarine."

Quite rightly, his time at Prenton Park has been honoured by the club. The Borough Road stand is now named after King, whilst the Supporters Trust erected a statue in his honour in 2014. Everyone remembers him fondly, especially those fans lucky enough to witness those golden years. Speak to any of his former players, and they will shower him with the praise that such a glorious period deserves.

On March 30th 2016, one of King's former players Mark Palios announced: "It is with enormous sadness I have learned that Johnny King has passed away peacefully with his family at his side after a long illness. He was a great manager, a great man and a true Tranmere legend. Our thoughts are with his family." He was 77.

There was an immediate and huge outpouring of grief, not only across Merseyside, but the world of football. Thousands paid tribute to one of the greats of the game who had left his mark on so many.

One of those people was Ray Mathias, a lifelong friend who played with and under King before becoming part of his coaching staff. "He brought quality, quality players to Tranmere," he said a few days later. "The likes of John Aldridge, Pat Nevin and Neil McNabb. To control them, in the divisions that we were in, and then challenge for the Premier League was an absolutely fantastic feat.

"When we used to have team meetings, he would always come out with one or two anecdotes and they were fantastic. The players used to go out of the room afterwards and start laughing, but that was John. He was always right with what he said, too! There was one where he said 'if we all grab an oar and start rowing, we'll achieve our goal of getting to the island. If anybody drops that oar, we're not going to get there. We're going to fail.'

"That's the way he was. I can assure you though in the dressing room before games, he used to really get the players going. Then you'd go out of the dressing room and he'd give you a massive big slap on every part of the body he could touch! You used to grimace as you were passing him going out on to the pitch!

"He was the best manager I worked with. Just look at what he achieved at Tranmere. We went to a certain limit and could probably have brought a few more players in, but John was loyal to his players. We got to one March and we might feel we needed a player or two, but he'd say 'No. My players will get us through this.' It proved right, because we went to Wembley so many times."

As with so many others, though, this relationship was not purely built around King the football man. There was so much more to him that made him so endearing. The pair used to live on the same road as each other on the Wirral and that meant, even after Mathias left Tranmere, they remained close friends.

"Over the years, we used to meet more or less every day and have a chat about football," he continued. "When I was manager of Wigan and he was still at Tranmere, Granada did a little thing with us with the Neighbours theme tune! They did a thing as we both came out of our house singing it and met in the middle of the road!

"He used to love his dogs and he used to take them out at the same time every morning. He was very, very superstitious. He'd have the same coat on and the same wellies. I could put my clock to him every morning when he went out of the house, and in the evening as well.

"He was just such a likeable guy. He would come into training every morning looking immaculate in his jacket and tie. He lit the place up as soon as he arrived and he'd always sing. He was the life and soul of the place, lifting people as soon as he came into the room."

There are many great stories about King from during his time at Tranmere. One involves getting Dave Higgins to head a cushion in a hotel corridor before an Anglo-Italian Cup game to see if his neck was still injured, whilst he once sent Shaun Garnett into the sea to try and heal a strained muscle, hoping the cold water would speed up the process.

Mathias, meanwhile, fondly recalls one of the post season trips to Tenerife. "We'd been to this bar and had a few drinks," he said. "We were walking back and on one side of the road was a bit of a hill with some bramble bushes at the bottom of it.

"Next minute, John has disappeared. He'd slipped down the hill and landed in these bushes. He came back up with scratches on his face and all over his arms. We said to him 'what are you going to say to your wife, John?' He replied 'I'll say I was in the sea and the sea took me into the rocks.'"

Tranmere had a National League fixtures just a couple of days after King's passing. They were set to play Welling at Prenton Park. Attentions tentatively turned to that game, with plans put in place so that the club and fans could mark the occasion in a poignant and respectful way.

"He was Tranmere's Bill Shankly" explains Ben Harrison. "We had to do something. Everybody was emotional and the game meant a lot. The family were there and perhaps we knew it might overshadow things, but sometimes you've just got to do what's right at the time.

"In the same season, Everton's greatest manager, Howard Kendall, had died. They played Manchester United at Goodison on the same day and lost 3-0. We kind of expected the same thing. We did a mosaic but it was just so flat."

Flat does not even come close to describing the performance that day. Tranmere were beyond dreadful. They well and truly failed to live up to the occasion and give King the send off that he deserved.

Many fans would point to this as being the club's worst ever performance. On a day when they had to deliver, let alone were expected to, they were beaten 2-1.

Lee Vaughan had actually given his side the lead, acrobatically volleying into the far top corner as he received Gary Taylor-Fletcher's lobbed pass. That was as good as it got for the hosts though. Ian Gayle equalised two minutes later with a deflected strike from near the penalty spot after Tranmere poorly defended a free-kick, and then disaster struck in the second half when Kadell Daniel slotted home from close range after Welling opened the defence up with uncomfortable ease.

Gary Brabin was furious at full time. "I thought one to eleven were very poor," he fumed. "We were in a good position, I still feel we are, but that was a good opportunity for us. We were sloppy and we were way off the standards we've set ourselves.

"The first 20 to 25 minutes, they looked almost frightened of us and I don't think we took advantage of that. We've taken the lead and then they've got back in the game with a ludicrous equaliser. We huffed and puffed and still had a couple of chances but we were nowhere near it.

"It would have been nice to get three points for such a fitting day. Johnny King is part of the club's history and it's been a sad week. It would have been a small consolation to have a good performance and a good win."

The manager's assessment of the performance is just as honest when he reflects on it a few years later. It is a game that sticks out in the mind for all the wrong reasons; a performance so desperate that it ruined what should have been an occasion when Tranmere celebrated one of the true greats of Merseyside football.

"I can't even gloss over it" he admits. "I came off and I remember there were a lot of heated words after the game from the players. I think everybody knew they'd let themselves down. We never turned up. I remember that second goal - the lad danced around three or four of our players to score. It was not a good day. It was so poor."

Harrison adds: "You look at the mistakes in the game; it was almost as if the team had not been prepared. I'm sure that's not the case, of course, but they almost walked the ball through our team for their goals. It just needed somebody like Jay Harris to plough through the lot of them!

"I don't know if the occasion got to them. I just remember looking at a few of the players and thinking their heart wasn't in it. They probably didn't know who Johnny King was - the manager who put Tranmere on the map.

"I think that was the lowest I've been as a Tranmere fan. I was completely deflated afterwards. We had the fan park up and running and by being in there, you're getting a lot of honest feedback from the fans. People start tell you 'it's shite that, you need to sort that out'. They wanted to blame somebody and I've now learnt to not get into any PR! You just agree. Everybody was deflated. The statue was covered in all kind of things, scarves and flowers, and it was a hard night."

James Norwood meanwhile remembers the scenes in the dressing room after the game, because things were threatening to boil over. Tranmere were desperate to make the play-offs and this result did their chances of finishing in the top five no good whatsoever.

"There were groans and boos at full time and that was the first time I started to see people turn on us," he admits. "They had been patient. That was the first time I realised making the play-offs was going to be difficult.

"But there was a lot of testosterone flying around in the changing rooms. I guess that's the mentality of winners when you lose a game. Even this season we've had problems in the tunnel with other teams, more recently than you'd think. Then Big Mac has come to the rescue!

"People have come here with a big game, match and club mentality and you don't accept losing. Teams have come here thinking 'they're one of the best teams in the league, we go again and play somebody else of our calibre of team'. We wouldn't go anywhere and accept a draw or loss.

"That Welling game was where it all spilled over into everyone saying exactly what they felt and doing exactly what they wanted to do. I like that, as long as it doesn't carry on after. As long as it's sorted in the changing room.

"I've had it with Macca. We've had a couple of slaps or something like that, then we've got in the shower and shook hands. It's what happens in the moment, it's what you need to say to move forward."

Mark Palios had a special relationship with Johnny. He had two spells as a midfielder at Prenton Park, from 1973 to 1980 and 1983 to 1985. King was in charge for the majority of that first period, and Palios holds that time in high regard. He also fondly remembers when the statue that now stands proudly outside the gates of Prenton Park was erected in 2014.

He recalls: "When I first came to the club, the Trust stood up and said 'this is a statue that's done by the fans, not the club'. I heard it and thought I'm not letting it rest, because the fans are the club. That's my phrase. They are the club. Just look at Milton Keynes. They took the franchise out of Wimbledon, but Wimbledon are still alive. It's just a different guise.

"Anyway, the fans rightly hold Johnny in great esteem. I played a lot of games for him. He came back when we got the statue put up. When he came back in his wheelchair and he was suffering from the illness that he had, it was quite upsetting.

"I leant down in front of him and I could just see the light of recognition come into his eyes. That was great. It gave me the opportunity to see him before he died."

Johnny King lives on at Tranmere. His legacy will be there for years to come. And if anything tells you how much he did for the club, it is that when Rovers were eventually promoted in 2018, it is the first time they had gone up without his assistance since 1938. King was involved in all four promotions in between.

Chapter Eight
The Play-Off Chase

When Tranmere played Grimsby on the final day of the 2015/16 season, they still had a slim chance of reaching the play-offs. They had followed up the Welling defeat with a 1-0 win on Grand National Saturday at Torquay thanks to a rare strike from Michael Higdon. A fortnight later they beat Eastleigh on the road by the same scoreline with James Norwood getting the only goal.

Unfortunately, in between came another damaging home loss and once again it was to their bitter rivals Wrexham. "This is a crucial time now," said Gary Brabin beforehand as he called on the supporters to get behind the team through the 90 minutes.

"We all want the same thing. I speak to opposition managers when they come here and their message is 'let's frustrate the crowd. Let's get them turning against their own players'. That's their game plan. It has been proved though when our fans really support us, through thick and thin, we do get that extra bit of energy, enthusiasm and will to win. When you've got the support we've got backing you, it does push you that little bit further."

Unfortunately, it did not take long for those fans to have something to be frustrated about as after just 15 minutes their team went 1-0 down. Steve McNulty massively under-hit a back pass from the touchline, and that allowed Kayden Jackson the chance to run towards the box and slot past Scott Davies.

Tranmere equalised deep into the second half with a penalty that was well dispatched by James Norwood after a foul on Adam Mekki, but they could not cling on. With just five minutes left, Sean Newton rose highest to connect with a corner and head past Jay Harris who was guarding the far post. It was a bitter but deserved blow for Gary

Brabin and his side.

"It was another opportunity for us to get some points," he said afterwards, "but it was two bad goals conceded. I don't think they created enough to create us any problems and it's two of our most experienced players who are at fault for their two goals.

"It's disappointing because we had a lot of possession. We dominated their half and when we got back into the game, you felt like we were going to go on and get that second. We're hugely disappointed that he's got a free header from a corner. There's still a lot to play for though, we're certainly not giving up."

The victory at Eastleigh a week later gave Tranmere hope. It meant they could still make the top five going into the last day, and if you had offered Brabin that on the opening weekend of the season, he would probably have taken it. All they needed to do was pick up three points, and hope that Braintree slipped to an unlikely defeat to Altrincham, who themselves needed to win to avoid relegation.

"We're all going into the game optimistic," said the manager. "We're looking forward to it. It's another game in front of our fans and one that we go into full of confidence, wanting to put in a good performance. Hopefully we get the right results elsewhere.

"I just want to focus on ourselves. I'm sure, as has happened in the past, if anything positive elsewhere is happening, you normally hear from the reaction of the crowd. It's important that we get it right here. Let's see what happens elsewhere."

Opponents Grimsby meanwhile had already secured their place in the top five. The only thing they had left to play for was third place and therefore having the second leg of their play-off semi-final on home soil. When they arrived at Prenton Park, it quickly became apparent they were not too bothered about that as Paul Hurst rested a number of his first team regulars.

That left the door open for Tranmere to strike, but with matters out of their hands, things were always going to be difficult. They were also hindered by missing a handful of key players due to injury, such as Ritchie Sutton in defence, meaning a rare start for Martin Riley.

Things started brightly though, and the hosts had captain Steven Jennings to thank for taking the lead midway through the first half as he tapped home from close range after Lee Vaughan's cross was poorly defended.

Unfortunately, the news from elsewhere was not so good. By this point, Braintree were already beating Altrincham 1-0 courtesy of Michael Cheek's 17th minute strike, and he would double their lead before half-time. As if Rovers were not already out of the frame by the break, The Iron cemented their play-off spot by adding a third through Mitch Brundle just after the hour mark, therefore relegating their opponents.

It was a tough day for the club, but Nick Hilton's match report in the Liverpool Echo sums things up pretty well when he concluded: "They were kept out of the top five by teams, a couple of them part-time, who turn out to be a little bit more savvy about playing the division than Rovers were."

That was the thing, in the end. Tranmere had not quite learnt from that initial culture shock provided earlier in the season by the likes of Boreham Wood and Eastleigh. They were not industrious enough. They refused to lower themselves to a level of time wasting and play acting that had so often been a cause of much frustration for themselves. Indeed, even if they had employed such tactics, the Super White Army would have been quick to turn their backs.

"We're all disappointed," concluded Brabin afterwards. "We thought lady luck was going to be looking down on us and we'd get in the play-offs. All we could do today was concentrate on ourselves and win this game, which we did, but unfortunately other results haven't gone for us and we just miss out.

"We've lost the last couple at home which probably dented our chances. It was important we got back to winning ways. I thought it was a good, solid performance from the lads.

"I do feel the squad has got stronger. The way we finished the season means we are excited for next season. I think we will be better prepared for it. It was always going to be a big ask and tough to completely rebuild the squad. I'm delighted with the players we've brought in. We've looked better and better since the turn of the year and we felt we were going to sneak into the play-offs.

"We've got to deal with the disappointment at the moment, but I think there are a lot of pluses. We've just missed out by two points, so we dust ourselves down and look to go again."

As it was, Tranmere ended the season in sixth place, two points off a play-off chase. They actually accumulated 78 points over the course of the campaign, just two fewer than the club record set by Ray Mathias in 2002/03, when, ironically, they also narrowly missed out on extending the season.

There is no doubt the campaign ended in disappointment with a strong feeling of what might have been. Things could have been so different; if only they had clung on to that 2-0 lead against Kidderminster in the opening weeks? What if the Welling performance had not been so abysmal? How about the Wrexham game a couple of weeks later? Win either of those latter two fixtures and they would have made it.

There was muted applause as Rovers left the field, with the fans well aware things had not gone their way at Braintree. Ben Harrison recalls: "Lots of people didn't bother coming out for the second half because they had heard how they were doing. It was like a pre-season friendly.

"I was so disappointed to finish sixth. Friends and family have banter, and that was when they said Tranmere really are shit. My belief was always that Tranmere would get out of the league. I just didn't know when."

Brabin was equally as hurt by where they ended the campaign. For him, like losing in the play-offs with Cambridge in 2009 and then again with Luton in 2011, it was a near miss with a club who had huge expectations in the division.

"It was so disappointing," he admits. "I remember sitting in the office after the game, I was so disappointed but I was trying to keep a brave face when I was speaking to Grimsby as they had got in the play-offs. They were the eventual winners, but we felt we grew into a better side than anyone.

"Sitting in that office after the game was hard to take. The goal, though, was to be challenging, which I felt we did. 90 minutes to go before the season ends, we're around the play-offs. We're then looking forward to the next season and hopefully building on the squad we had and hopefully achieving that goal next season."

James Norwood meanwhile had got over the disappointment of not reaching the play-offs before the game against Grimsby even kicked off.

"We weren't expecting to make them because of who Braintree were playing," he says. "The form they were in and the team they were playing made it unlikely. We knew Grimsby were resting everybody so we knew we could win, but we couldn't see Braintree slipping up. They were playing a team set to be relegated.

"If we got in, great, but realistically we hadn't put ourselves in a position to put it in our hands. It was a hard learning curve for our lads. We had played 4-3-3 and all sorts and I'd scored 21 goals, but the next highest had seven, so we didn't have goals coming from elsewhere.

"Once that season finished, I wasn't unhappy with the way I'd played, but I wasn't happy with what we'd achieved as a team. At the start of the season I thought we'd piss the league and batter teams by 4 or 5. It just didn't turn out that way. I was disappointed that that never happened."

Another frustrating aspect for Brabin is how the rules for the play-offs were changed less than a year after he left Prenton Park. For the 2017-18 season, qualification was extended down to the teams who finished in sixth and seventh as well. If that had been in place for his campaign in charge, Rovers would have got their chance to reach Wembley.

"The way it's changed around, I wish we'd had that," he says. "But you know what you've got before the season starts. I do think it's good as it gives people more opportunities and more to play for."

***

The inquest into the season started immediately. Fans were quick to point to moments in the season that they felt cost Tranmere a place in the top five. Ultimately, it was the home form that was the biggest problem, with Rovers beaten nine times at Prenton Park.

On the road, things were much better. After the 4-1 hammering at Woking in November, they went on a club record run of away fixtures without defeat until losing at Aldershot the next season - there were 15 matches in between.

"I don't think there is any one defining moment," says Brabin. "But if there was for us not doing it that year, it was that Welling game. It wasn't a good day at all. It is harsh to just blame the one game, but that was the biggest disappointment. In the building process, we gave away too many cheap points. Sitting in that office after the game was hard to take."

Ben Harrison agrees with the manager's assessment, adding: "It was the defining moment in not reaching the play-offs for me. You look at not being in the top five of the National League, it's crazy. That feeling at the end of the season when you've not got there is awful.

"Sixth wasn't that bad a finish. But being a little bit critical, we flopped in some games where you thought there wasn't something quite right about the mentality. They didn't look motivated in some games. There were a couple of players who'd come in where you thought it just isn't working."

Mark Palios meanwhile picks another home defeat as the let down moment of the campaign. As bad as Welling was, it is the Wrexham fixture two weeks later that sticks out in his mind.

"There are a lot of what ifs in football," he said. "In the 2017/18 season, if we'd have scored any number of goals that we could and should have scored, we'd have won the league by a mile.

"For me the defining moment was the 2-1 defeat at home to Wrexham. It gave me a lot of concern. I wasn't happy after that, but you stand back and look at it and keep perspective. Somebody doesn't become the wrong manager after one game."

Chapter Nine
The Summer

That debrief from missing out on the play-offs continued long into the summer. Everybody was disappointed; the fans, the manager, the players and the owners. That was hardly surprising, given Rovers had finished below Braintree, a club who only a handful of years earlier had made half and half scarves for Tranmere's visit to Cressing Road in the FA Cup.

Speculation mounted that Gary Brabin's position at the club was under threat. He had narrowly missed out on the top five but plenty of fans would have been glad to have seen the back of him. They were unhappy at the club's failure to extend their season given the budget available compared to those some of those 'smaller' clubs above them.

There was also speculation over the future of the Braintree management team, brothers Danny and Nicky. They had done a stunning job in Essex, guiding a part time club to the play-offs in their first season in charge. Lincoln were sniffing around, and that move to Sincil Bank was subsequently made in mid-May, but only after rumours that they were being considered to replace Brabin at Prenton Park.

All the talk frustrated Brabin, who felt as if Rovers had pretty much achieved their minimum target of at least mounting some sort of challenge at the right end of the table, even if they did fall just short. He was now trying to build towards the 2016/17 campaign, but admits it was a difficult period for him.

"I didn't think my position was under threat straight after the Grimsby game, but as the summer went on, I did," he concedes. "You try and stay professional, but I don't think Mark and I were singing from the same hymn sheet. There was certainly a breakdown of communication somewhere along the line. It wasn't as positive as when I first took the job."

Palios though was content with the job Brabin had done. Once again, a lot of it comes down to consistency and not wanting to be seen as somebody who sacks managers as soon as the going gets tough. Often, these situations can be worked through. The chairman also admits that the strength of the squad made it an easier decision for him. Rovers were clearly getting stronger and stronger, the Welling and Wrexham results aside, as the 2015/16 season went on, and that showed they should be capable of mounting a more serious promotion challenge in the following campaign.

"I stand back and look at it and look at the bigger picture and the momentum we had," he reveals. "We had had a record number of wins and win percentages. We'd improved from the start to the end of the season and had a great platform.

"I was disappointed, of course, but I'd reconciled the fact that we weren't going to get into the play-offs. I did think we should have made them though. Gary had assembled a good squad.

"You're always going to leak a few points, but we just hadn't gathered enough in the early part of the season. That was that really. I was resigned to going into the close season, having a debrief with Gary and sorting out what we were going to."

There were some people who would have liked to have seen a change made though. Brabin never had the best relationship with the fans. A few did not like his style of football, others were unhappy at how he had, on one or two occasions, called out some supporters for not getting behind the team.

Ben Harrison admits some members of the Tranmere Rovers Supporters Trust board would have welcomed a new face in the dugout. "On the whole, a lot of them didn't think Gary should carry on," he reveals. "They felt if a decision was going to be made, they should do it there and then.

"Personally, I was for the continuity. I thought surely you can let him have a full pre-season. That's the way we actually went in the end and some good signings came in. Connor Jennings arrived from Wrexham and Andy Cook came from Barrow. At that point, you thought 'hang on, we can do something here'.

"Nicola actually asked me what my opinion was - and I told her what the Trust board thought. But Mark and Nicola make their own decisions and you have to give them some credit for that. They stuck with him."

Mark Palios believed, like Harrison, that Brabin had done enough to earn a second season at Prenton Park. Their job was to now build a squad more capable of finishing in the top five. How could the team be strengthened? Who should and should not get a new contract?

The signings of Cook and Jennings were the only two major arrivals that summer, both on two year contracts after impressive seasons in the National League. It showed that the club felt the squad only needed tweaking slightly in order to mount a serious assault on top spot.

One person who was delighted to see the new arrivals was James Norwood. The striker had spent a lot of his first season at Prenton Park playing as a lone striker, particularly after Andy Mangan's departure in January.

To be fair, Norwood appeared to thrive in the role. His work rate was always unquestionable and playing on his own up top appeared to give him more licence to find space in behind the defence. However, he was always desperate to have someone up there with him.

"I played with Andy Cook when I made my England C debut in Bermuda," he says. "He looked exactly the same then! He'd just won Young Player of the Year for the Conference. I'd played against him and have been friends with him since, so I was delighted. I knew we were going to be playing 4-4-2.

"As for Connor Jennings; well, there was one year when he was on loan at Macclesfield and I'd hit the ground running. I had nine goals by the end of November. I looked at the goal scoring charts and he was already on 16! That was when he played upfront. Now he's on the wing.

"To give the fans an idea of how good a player he is, he got 16 in three months up front, then ran Wrexham from centre-midfield as their captain before making left midfield his own and scoring vital goals for Tranmere. You can't pin him to one position.

"He thinks he'll end up at wing back soon! He works so hard for us. He sets goals up. Play him anywhere and he'll be an 8 or 9 out of ten every week. That's a testament to how good he is."

With the arrival of Jennings and Cook, Tranmere's squad immediately looked stronger. Brabin, though, felt it was not enough. He only brought in one more player that summer, a youngster called Darren Stephenson from Chorley who would barely feature in his twelve months at Prenton Park.

The manager wanted more and felt he was not getting the backing he deserved. This worried him as the season drew ever closer. He feared the sack might be about to come.

"I didn't think I was going to start the season as Tranmere manager," he reveals. "I don't feel I was backed. I brought in three signings, so we only had a squad of 17 players when we started the season.

"The budget was not as healthy as the year before, though. We had one player, Johnny Margetts, who I wanted to keep. He was a good player and had signed the previous summer after a fantastic pre season.

"I really liked him, but he wasn't always fit. He always wanted to play but he had a couple of little injuries. You could see he was a real talented lad. I wanted to keep him the next year, but we couldn't stretch the budget."

Palios though felt the squad only needed tweaking slightly, hence the arrivals of Cook and Jennings. With them, he believed Tranmere had what was required to kick on the following season.

"My view was that we had a stable base and we just needed to add the firepower," he adds. "That was when we brought in Andy Cook and Connor Jennings. I remember saying to people 'he's ungainly, but you'll like Cooky'. The fans like Connor too because he works hard and he's a great pro.

"The key thing for me was to have that debrief. We had most of the squad in place, so I wasn't looking at having to make a decision on the manager quickly in order to get new players. We had most of the squad sitting there, so I had the time to go through and talk to Gary as to how we went forwards.

"My view at the time was that he deserved a chance because he'd built a good squad, we had some great stats in terms of momentum and therefore you just build on that. To build on that, we just needed the firepower that we were a bit short of. We sat down, talked through what players he would and wouldn't sign and went and got Connor and Cooky.

"We had a team who had been built by the manager and had had a great second half of the season, albeit they were not that good at home and that was a difficulty. I thought one of the advantages of coming down was Prenton Park, where you could build the fanbase and the atmosphere. We didn't really have that, but we had a fantastic away record.

"I keep coming back to it, but do you think if you make a change, you're going to put the club in a better position or not? My job at the start of every job was analysis. That's what I'm trained to do.

"People will disagree on a different information base or experience base to me, they'll just disagree, but I'd prefer people to have an opinion than not have one. I just don't have to agree with it or debate it. That might sound arrogant, but it's difficult to do the job if you're debating the opinion."

Ben Harrison reckons that Mark and Nicola were also keen not to bow down to fan pressure. It is important for any chairman to show strength and courage if they believe that they are doing the right thing and others do not. The Palios' have displayed that in abundance.

"I think they wanted continuity," he says. "Mark's a turnaround expert and Nicola is smart. If you chop and change, you'll be doing it forever. Then once the fans know they can get you into a chop and change situation, you're on a bit of a hiding to nothing.

"You can't be blindly loyal, but we've all had jobs and worked in places, we all have bad moments and days. You don't want somebody to tell you to get lost - but football and society have become very like that. I admired them for sticking with him."

Season 2
2016/17

Chapter Ten
The Beginning Of The End

Tranmere started their second season in the National League on fire. A 2-0 win over Bromley on the opening day got the ball rolling, with James Norwood netting a brace - and a supporter dressed as a hot dog invading the pitch for good measure.

"Just look at the first goal," says Norwood. "Jay Harris hooks it up to me, I chest it down to Connor and he plays in Cooky. He runs with it for a little bit and plays in Connor, who passes to me and I put it top corner. As a manager, you're thinking I've signed those three, they've linked up and I've put it in the back of the net after only a few minutes.

"For the second goal, Cooky heads it up and a I run in to tap home. We had a good understanding. We were all the same age and had played in the division for a long time. We knew each other's quality and respected each other. Now we're all good friends. It's the recipe for success."

It was a really positive way to get the campaign underway. Rovers were comfortable and both strikes were well taken. They shook off the disappointment of missing out on the play-offs just a few months earlier straight away and looked ready to take the division by storm.

"I was delighted with that," said Gary Brabin afterwards. "We've worked really hard in pre-season and it's always nice to get a good start. It would have been an injustice after the pre-season we've had not to get the right result!

"In the first 20 minutes, we looked really good. The opposition made it difficult for us at times, but we looked strong and hard to break down. We were always a threat and had some good chances at the end. We acquitted ourselves really well and I thought it was a really good performance."

Further victories followed against Barrow, Eastleigh, Boreham Wood and Maidstone. Nine goals scored, just two conceded and, for the first time in the club's history, five wins in a row to kick off a campaign. It left them top of the National League, three points better off than Dagenham and, like twelve months earlier, everything was looking rosy.

"We deserved it," said Brabin after the Maidstone game, a match that turned into a tough contest for Tranmere, but they eventually came out on top courtesy of a late strike from Steve McNulty after Andy Cook's first half goal had been cancelled out by Alex Fisher.

"I felt we'd limited them all afternoon until that moment where they got back into the game. We kept on playing some good stuff, creating some good chances and thankfully we got the winner. We could have had a third at the end too.

"I sensed that little bit of frustration coming in because we hadn't scored in the first half an hour. We just kept on plugging away and we've gone a goal up and looked comfortable. They've got back into the game against the run of play but we've dug in there and got our noses back in front. It was another good three points and I'm delighted to have got a well deserved win."

Ben Harrison always had a few concerns about how Tranmere had started the campaign though. Yes, they were winning, but only by slender margins. Despite having the likes of Andy Cook, James Norwood and Connor Jennings in the side, Rovers were struggling to put games to bed. One of those occasions was when the run finally came to an end at Southport. ←

"It should have been seven wins out of seven," he said. "We won the seventh game by beating Guiseley 1-0, but Southport got lucky in the sixth, which ended in a draw. Louis Almond, who we signed

Bol went AWOL & ruined the 'Southport - Leeds fest', weekender!

about a month later, crossed the ball and it just happened to go in. After that, we were thinking we could win the league.

"Now I'm not being hard on Brabin here, but there was no rapport with the fans. Absolutely none. He could have won ten games in a row and the fans wouldn't have chanted his name. I don't think I heard them do that once."

The Southport game had certainly opened up a few cracks that some supporters thought were being papered over. Andy Cook had given Rovers the lead just after half time, netting in front of the huge army of travelling fans, but they were not able to put the game to bed. Wayward finishing, both before and after the equaliser, meant they failed to claim the three points.

"It was one of those games where we could easily have stolen the three points with the chances we've had," admitted the manager at full time. "It was a tough game. We can't be too despondent though. I think it's a good point as I think the opposition showed what they can be capable of this season."

Brabin though was not shocked whatsoever with how his side had started the season. In his eyes, they were stronger than the previous year, and this result was a club record 15th away game without defeat - a run that extended back to that 4-1 hammering at the hands of Woking in November 2015.

"I wasn't surprised we were top of the league," he insists. "But despite starting really well, I knew it was never going to last. Contrary to the results, I believed we needed to bring players in. In fact, I had some who were waiting to come into the club, but I wasn't allowed to do it.

"We still only had seventeen players. Jeff Hughes got suspended against York a couple of games later, we had injuries and we had players playing injured. I knew it was only a matter of time before we'd struggle to put a team out.

"I think the week I got sacked, they then signed three or four players. Ben Tollitt was one of them, and I had him on my list. Louis Almond came in too and Elliot Osborne arrived on loan.

"Straight away, they strengthened the squad and continued to bring in players from then, such as Andy Mangan and Adam Dawson. They were two players who were fans favourites but I didn't think they were good enough. They brought them back, and Dawson barely played."

The Guiseley game would prove to be Brabin's final win as Tranmere manager as they never really recovered from the draw against Southport. Things took a turn for the worse with a 3-1 defeat at Aldershot on September 3rd when they conceded two late goals.

"The manner in which we got beat is disappointing," was the manager's assessment afterwards. "It's never nice to lose but I thought we deserved something out of the game. They were sharp in the first 25 minutes and caused us a few problems.

"I'm certainly disappointed with the first goal we've conceded but for the 15 or 20 minutes before half time, I thought we were excellent. We got back into the game with an equaliser and started the second half brightly. I thought we were the better side to be honest.

"The two goals we've then conceded - we're better than that. I've said that to the lads. Rather than feel sorry for ourselves, we need to learn from that and hopefully go on another run."

Their next match was against Lincoln at Prenton Park, and Rovers were wretched. Macauley Bonne scored the only goal with a quarter of the game left, knocking the hosts off the top of the table - with their opponents replacing them in first place.

Of course, at this stage it was far too early to tell who would finish the season in what position, but this defeat would prove telling. Fast forward to April, and Lincoln were lifting the title, finishing four points above Tranmere. True, the Imps did ease up in their final couple of fixtures, but who knows what could have happened if the tables had been turned on the Wirral that day.

Next up came a 0-0 draw at York, a bad tempered game in which the usually mild mannered Jeff Hughes was shown a straight red card following a foul on Richard Brodie. In fairness, it was not the best of tackles from the former Northern Ireland midfielder, but the reaction from the striker did not help things either as he rolled around in a manner not befitting of the contact made.

Brabin was understandably fuming, and made his thoughts known post match. "You could see the anger on our fans faces," he said. "From where we were standing, he hasn't gone anywhere near him. If you'd watched the game clearly, you could see what was going on. It was like a pantomime.But that's out of our control. All we can do is try and control what we're in control of, and that was our performance."

Worse was to come for Hughes too. The red card produced by referee Andrew Miller resulted in an automatic three match ban, but that suspension was doubled by the Football Association because of his reaction to the dismissal.

Chapter Eleven
The Sacking

After the draw at York came the straw that broke the camel's back - and it was live on BT Sport. Rovers were beaten 1-0 at Sutton, and in truth, they were hopeless. The hosts had lost three in a row, but Danny Flitchett's header just after half time sealed a win against a Tranmere team who worryingly created very little.

This was another cornerstone in the club's history, and it was stick or twist time for Mark Palios, who was faced with quite a dilemma. Gary Brabin had the best win percentage in the club's history, nearly 47%, but statistics do not always tell the full story.

Two days later, a decision had been made and it was game over for the manager. A statement on the club's website from the chairman read: "I would like to thank Gary for his hard work and contribution over the past 16 months in building a strong squad of players, getting us back fighting for the promotion places and setting some club records in the process.

"However, we have agreed that it is best now to allow someone else to take the club to the next stage. The club will make a statement regarding interim arrangements shortly."

The Sutton defeat was another one of those games where everything seemed to go against Brabin. His side would have gone top of the table with a win, but they did not complete the 90 minutes with a full compliment of players, despite the fact that nobody picked up a red card.

"We finished the game with ten men," he said. "That wasn't because we had anybody sent off but because people picked up injuries. There were people playing injured. Steve Jennings played injured for the last two or three games. Jay Harris started the game injured and came off early. Jake Kirby got a freak injury in the game. There were those silly moments. I knew, I wasn't soft, that it was going to be the end."

The little tweaks and niggles were picked up because Sutton play on an artificial pitch. Micky Mellon would air his thoughts on 4G surfaces when he took charge because muscles can react differently to them than they do to grass and the recovery period can be much longer too.

However, the Tranmere fans did not care about the injuries. They had made their minds up, and they were helped by the fact that Gander Green Lane is an unsegregated ground, and therefore they could move wherever they wanted in the stadium.

Several congregated behind the away dugout and made their thoughts known to Brabin. The BT Sport cameras picked it all up and the manager cast an extremely lonely figure. It looked like there was no coming back.

"It all started going pear shaped after a defeat at Aldershot," said Ben Harrison. "Lois Maynard played right back and gave a penalty away and you could start seeing a few odd decisions. We drew 0-0 at York too; Jeff Hughes got sent off and got a six match ban, whilst the Lincoln defeat came in between. Gary said he might have got sacked after that.

"I was actually away for the Sutton game - and my wife always reminds me of this, as we were in Ibiza. We went into a bar in the town and the guy had seven televisions showing the football. Barcelona were on one and loads of others had the Premier League. I asked him to find Sutton v Tranmere and we watched it without the sound on.

"That was the moment for me. They were shocking. It was worse than Welling the previous season. We picked up three bizarre injuries and sadly a lot of the fans rounded on him that day. That was when I thought something had to be done, and so did the Trust board. We all exchanged texts and we were thinking that something had to change.

"To be honest, some of the fans behind the dugout didn't exactly crown themselves in glory that day. They shall remain nameless, but from the club's point of view, when you see the real die hard fans turning, it's not good.

"Unfortunately, that's football, isn't it? There was no coming back from it. I think if we'd have carried on, things would have got worse. Confidence had gone out of that team. Somebody said to me that in the Football League, you can afford to draw at home. In the National League, you can't. You've got to at least draw on the road. We weren't. Lincoln and Forest Green had clicked into gear and we were slipping away."

The players trudged back down the tunnel and they started getting it in the neck from the screaming fans too. It was a walk that seemed to take an age and James Norwood has revealed there was a different atmosphere to normal once they finally reached the dressing room.

"Brabs got it a lot from some fans, especially at home," he said. "He'd be in the right hand dugout and people would be trying to get to him. They'd be shouting this and that.

"In the Sutton game, he was quiet and he shouldn't have been, but Paul Carden, the assistant manager, lost his shit. He started calling people out. He was pointing at the players and saying 'shitbag, shitbag, shitbag'. He gave it big time to Lee Vaughan, shouting 'you can't play in big games'.

"It all went back and forth and then Gary just said 'stop it. You can only blame yourself for what's going to happen'. I'm sitting there thinking 'that's a bit weird'.

"What he meant was somebody was going to come in and they

97

might not pick us. He'd stuck by us, but the new manager might not think we were good enough. He knew after that game that he was done for."

The call from Mark Palios came the next morning. The chairman had not actually been at the game as he was away on a business trip. But before he jetted off, his decision had pretty much been made. The Sutton defeat was the final straw.

"It wasn't actually that match that caused me problems," he admits. "I didn't think we'd been playing compelling football. We'd won five out of five at the start. We were strong and solid but we hadn't been convincing.

"Then against Lincoln, we were tactically poor. They were fairly simple. You knew what they were going to do before they came. We didn't combat it. We had a debrief after the game because I was going out to China. I wasn't happy with that debrief.

"When I was out in China, we played York and had Jeff Hughes sent off. To be honest, I think it wasn't a bad performance with ten men because he got sent off just after half time. People were complaining about it, but it wasn't bad.

"The fans were very anti-Brabin. We weren't playing attractive football. If you play winning football, then the fans eventually like it. I just think we were losing pace. I didn't want to do it from China, but I had to act.

"I decided to part company with Gary at the time and again I'm looking at it with the bigger picture. We had a good squad and I think we were underperforming, relative to what we should have been doing. I was thinking that I needed to give somebody a chance to come in and have a good go at it."

Brabin admits he knew it was the end of the road as well. Once you lose the fans like that, there is often no coming back, and he was expecting the phone conversation with Palios.

"It wasn't frustrating because I felt it was going to happen," he admits. "Mark phoned me up and I knew what was going to happen. Like I said, I didn't think I was going to start the season. It probably had to come to an end."

One big problem for Brabin was that he had lost some of the fans the previous season after failing to make the play-offs. To a degree, the damage had already been done with some of those home defeats. Ben Harrison reckons, for some supporters, there was no coming back.

"I think the Welling game had a huge lasting effect on Gary's relationship with the fans," he says. "Yes, he won 5 or 6 games on the run in the next season, but he could have got another four and there was still something missing. Nobody was chanting his name.

"I realised at that point that the fans were starting to galvanise behind what the club were trying to do. We took 2,000 to Southport - we didn't take that anywhere in the Championship. We were seeing the green shoots of the relationship where the fans were believing in the ownership, but if you drew a line, there was Mark and Nicola Palios and the Trust all in a line, but Gary off on a branch."

Brabin though does not believe that is the case. He felt plenty of supporters remained behind him until the end, and holds no bitterness over his departure.

"I had some of the fans on board," he continues. "The ones I took the time out to go and meet. But look at Micky Mellon; when you're an ex-player who has an affiliation with the club, you always get longer in a job. Other than that, I think the managerial merry-go-round is getting quicker and quicker and quicker. There's people getting sacked left, right and centre and social media doesn't help.

"Some of the fans were brilliant, and even now I still get messages from some of them thanking me for signing players like Andy Cook and James Norwood. That's nice to hear. Genuinely, I'm delighted that they're now back in the Football League.

"Whenever you get big clubs, even the one's who've struggled, eventually they will get back to where they belong. Whether it takes one, two, three, five or seven years, I think you eventually get back to where you belong.

"To be part of that process with Tranmere, I do feel proud, especially when I see James Norwood and Andy Cook scoring in the play-off final. You still feel like you've added something to it. It's part of my history.

"I'm not one of those people who lives in the past and you do move on, but watching the Boreham Wood game reminded me that I felt like I was doing the right thing."

Gary Brabin was sacked by Tranmere on September 19th 2016. He was the National League's reigning Manager of the Month and had been in charge at Prenton Park for 60 games. 28 of those matches had ended in victory.

Chapter Twelve
Mellon Returns

Tranmere were yet again at a pivotal point in their history. They were already in their second season in the National League and were desperate for that stay to be as short as possible. As such, Mark Palios was in no rush to appoint a replacement to Gary Brabin. He was prepared to take his time in order to get things right and give his side the best possible chance of going up.

Rovers only had to look at local rivals Wrexham to see what can happen if decision making is poor. They had been in the division for over a decade and with each passing year, their promotion challenges were wilting earlier and earlier. Granted, they made a strong fist of things in 2017/18, but the inevitable crumble eventually came and they did not even make the top seven.

Palios promoted from within as Paul Carden was given the reigns on a temporary basis. A former Cambridge, Chester and Rochdale midfielder, he had managerial experience from a short stint at Southport, where he took over from Brabin.

He had then moved to Tranmere as part of the backroom staff in the summer, so he was somebody the players knew extremely well. Crucially, it also gave the owners a chance to assess their options.

"Paul Carden was around and he's well respected," says Palios. "I think he did some good coaching under Gary Brabin. He came in as the interim manager and that gave me the time to look around for managers.

"One of the things you've got to be aware of, and it's not the determining feature, is how well does the manager get on with the fans? Unfortunately for Paul, he'd have probably been seen as a creature of Gary's. As a consequence, it would have been more of the Gary regime.

"The fans at the time would probably not have given him a realistic chance. He did well and got a couple of results, but then we lost 1-0 to Gateshead on a Tuesday night and it was horrible."

That game appeared to speed up the recruitment process, because Rovers really were terrible. Team selection did not help, with Lois Maynard on international duty and Jeff Hughes, Steve Jennings and James Norwood all unavailable. A makeshift side, including on loan pair Elliot Osbourne and Ethan Jones, was not up to scratch.

It was a shame for Carden, whose reign had actually started pretty well. They beat Woking 3-1 at Prenton Park in his first game in charge as Andy Cook netted and brace and James Norwood got the other.

A week later, Michael Ihiekwe was sent off but Rovers managed to hang on for a 0-0 draw away at Dagenham before, on a cold, wet, dreary Birkenhead night, Sam Jones netted the only goal of the game as Gateshead picked up a 1-0 win. Suddenly, the hopes of mounting a promotion push seemed to be shrinking away.

It looked like Carden's time was up as the gap up to top spot grew larger and larger. Palios knew he had to act. "I'd already been speaking to managers who I was allowed to speak to," he admits.

Two days later, the local radio and newspaper journalists had congregated at Prenton Park for a pre match press conference ahead of a huge local derby against Wrexham. They were due to speak to Carden and Mitch Duggan, who was enjoying a run in the team for the first time in his career.

However, reports were beginning to circulate that Tranmere were closing in on a new manager. Moments after the latter had finished speaking to the media, Carden's interview was cancelled, protecting him from the inevitable barrage of questions that would have come his way.

The name being linked with the post was one that the fans were extremely familiar with: Micky Mellon. The Scotsman, currently in charge of League One side Shrewsbury, had enjoyed two stints at Prenton Park as a player.

His affinity with Rovers stretched back to 1997 when he was bought from Blackpool for £300,000 by John Aldridge. He made his debut in a 2-1 defeat to Sheffield United and went on to make 65 appearances before joining Burnley in 1999.

Two years later, with Rovers struggling at the wrong end of the Championship and staring relegation in the face, Aldridge signed him again in the hope that he could help keep the club up.

Unfortunately, it was not to be, but Mellon stayed for another three years and played in a further 139 matches. He even went on to wear the captain's armband under Brian Little. He was, however, not everybody's cup of tea.

"Micky Mellon wasn't liked by a lot of people when he was a player," jokes Ben Harrison. "He got a lot of grief from the Johnny King stand! A lot of fans don't understand football and what his role was in the team. They saw him as being a negative holding midfield player.

"When he came back as Shrewsbury manager in League Two, we beat them and thought we might stay up. He was applauding the Tranmere fans then. When Brabin went, he was the main man because he does have some affinity with us."

That was the first time Mellon had been back to Prenton Park since being released in 2004, but he held the club in high regard. One moment from his playing days that stands out came during a run to the FA Cup quarter finals in the 2003/04 campaign.

With a fourth round tie at Luton looking destined to head to a replay, the midfielder scored a late screamer, crashing home from outside the box with just nine minutes left to secure a 1-0 win. Swansea were then beaten in the last 16 before Rovers eventually lost 2-1 in a replay to Championship side Millwall.

After a short stint with Kidderminster in 2004, Mellon hung up his boots. He would soon start to forge out a thoroughly impressive managerial career though, beginning with Fleetwood, a Non League team on the way up, four years later.

He guided them to the Conference Premier via the Conference North play-offs in 2009/10 and within two seasons they were on the move again, reaching the Football League for the first time in their history.

After being sacked by Fleetwood in December 2012, despite being more than handily placed in fourth in League Two, he had a spell as David Flitcroft's assistant manager at Barnsley, and even had a brief stint as caretaker boss of the Championship club.

He left Oakwell in March 2014, but did not have to wait long for another managerial position as Shrewsbury came calling just a couple of months later. In his first season at the New Meadow, they were promoted to League One as runners up in League Two.
It was a formidable record for somebody who was still at the start of his managerial career. In just six years, he had amassed three promotions.

It was therefore no surprise that when news filtered through that Tranmere were interested, the fans were extremely excited. But they questioned one thing. Why would he drop two divisions to take charge of Tranmere? After building up his profile and leaving the National League behind, why slip back down?

"I never thought about dropping two leagues to come back," he admits. "I didn't quite know until I got here how far they had dropped though, to be honest.

"You get a feel for all of your old clubs, but when I thought the opportunity would be there for me to come back, I was excited. I knew what a big club Tranmere were and I knew going back was going to be a strange situation, because it had suddenly become a club with massive potential again.

"When I was playing here in the Championship, we were at our glass ceiling. We couldn't really get any bigger. We were playing top Championship clubs every week. When John Aldridge was here, we were getting to a cup final and quarter finals and people weren't blinking. It was just what we did. We had full houses regularly against the likes of Sunderland, Newcastle and Manchester City. To see where it had gone and where it had been excited me.

"I put all my chips on one colour, if you like. A lot people asked me why I dropped all those leagues and went into Non League again, because it is so hard to get out of Non League, but from speaking to the chairman and knowing the size of the club, it would be an exciting challenge to take on.

"It was also an emotional challenge. I'd spoken to a lot of ex-players and everybody was disappointed about where the club had gone to. I just thought it was an opportunity that excited me and I wanted to be a part of."

What was key, then, was how far a club like Tranmere could go. They had been in the Championship within the last two decades. They had a solid fan base and a large ground. Everything was in place for them to kick on once they got things right on the pitch. According to Ben Harrison, that meant that despite being in the National League, they arguably had a higher glass ceiling than Shrewsbury, who were two divisions higher at the time.

"They were only getting 4 or 5 thousand fans," he said. "He probably looked at Tranmere and saw the potential. They can get 10,000. There's still massive potential here."

Mark Palios was made aware that Mellon was interested in the role and a meeting between the pair was quickly arranged. "I told Shrewsbury that I wanted to speak to Tranmere," continues Mellon. "I met Mark at the Riverhill and we had a conversation about why I was there really.

"It must have looked, if you didn't know me, strange that a League One manager would want to drop all the way down to the Conference. After the conversation we had, I told him why it excited me. Professionally that was down to the challenge and emotionally it was because of those reasons I've just mentioned."

Palios was impressed when he met Mellon. This was somebody who had huge pedigree within the game, yet at 44, he still had the majority of his managerial career ahead of him. There were, however, other people interested in the job.

"I had another candidate," he reveals. "I'd prefer not to say who, but it was between the two of them and both have been successful.

"Micky Mellon gets the club. I think you've got to respect the club. That's massively important to me, but you've got to respect the club more than going 'yeah, it's a big club'. You've got to understand the personality of the club and what you see now is fully extracting that personality. You won't always get that.

"He also had the knowledge of the league and knowledge of promotion; he knew what it would take. Also, when you talk to him, he was tactically astute and flexible in a way that it wasn't my way or the highway.

"That was massively important, because he understood that I wanted to build an infrastructure that stayed when the manager goes. It doesn't all just disappear with him. You couldn't really ask for more."

As with when Gary Brabin arrived at Prenton Park, Mark Palios was keen to get the thoughts of the Supporters Trust before the appointment was ratified. Ben Harrison was asked whether or not he was excited by the prospect of Mellon taking the reigns and the answer was an emphatic and easy one: yes.

"I looked at what he'd done at Shrewsbury and Fleetwood, getting teams promoted, and I was delighted," he said. "Unanimously, the Trust board said it was a good appointment.

"Everybody had identified that we needed the owners, fans and manager to be aligned and you thought if anybody had a chance, it was him. It was welcomed. Mark and Nicola say they are guardians of the club. Not many owners say that, but it's true. The club have been around for over 125 years. It's very important.

"It also turns out the timing of the Gary Brabin sacking was perfect as it meant Micky could come in at that time. A lot of people jumped for joy. When you get a manager who's dropping a few divisions, it makes a statement to other people. It's not making do with the best in the National League."

On the evening of October 6th 2016, less than 48 hours before that huge local derby against Wrexham, Micky Mellon was confirmed as the new Tranmere manager.

"I am delighted to bring Micky back to Tranmere Rovers for a third time," said a statement from Palios. "His track record speaks for itself. He already has a number of promotions to his name and we are confident he will add to that record once more at Prenton Park.

"We are especially pleased to bring in a manager currently managing in League One and who sees the potential in the club. Micky knows the club and what the fans want to see. He will take over a strong squad, albeit that it is depleted at this time."

Interestingly, Shrewsbury did not seem too concerned to see the back of him. Despite Mellon taking the club up that summer, life in League One had proved to be quite tough. They were struggling at the wrong end of the table and had won just three of fifteen games in the league and cup competitions.

"Let's be honest, the team hasn't performed to how we would have expected this season," said chief executive Brian Caldwell as Shrewsbury confirmed Mellon had left by mutual consent to take on the Tranmere role.

"We've tried to be as patient as possible with how it's going and I think it's in the best interests of everybody that we make this decision."

Such things did not bother Mellon whatsoever though, as upon his appointment he said: "I'm delighted to be at Tranmere Rovers and really pleased to be taking part in such an exciting project. I'm looking forward to meeting the players tomorrow and the fans on Saturday for what should be a good game against Wrexham.

"It's easy for me to say 'it's great to be back', because that's what people will expect me to say, but it truly is. I never looked at it as dropping down, although technically and physically it is league table-wise. I'm coming to a club that I've got so much regard for and I am so excited about trying to win games.

"To come back to a club that you have such affection for in a different capacity as manager is a bit surreal for me to be honest, because I still walk around the place and see how it was when I played here. I see a lot of familiar faces and familiar things. Of course, a lot of things change but it's still a fantastic football club."

Mellon would soon be followed to Tranmere by his assistant manager at Shrewsbury, Mike Jackson, another former Rovers player who had also had two spells at Prenton Park.

The first, initially on loan from Preston when Ray Mathias was in charge, coincided with Mellon's second spell, whilst Brian Little brought him back to the club on a permanent basis in May 2004.

Everywhere you looked, there were people who knew Tranmere inside out, be it the owner, manager, assistant or players. The revolution had started. The only way was up.

Chapter Thirteen
A Record Breaking Start

Having hung up his boots in 2004, Micky Mellon had only returned to Prenton Park once - for that 2-1 defeat when Shrewsbury manager in February 2015. He had not been to the old training ground, spent much time wandering the corridors in the Main Stand or visiting the offices used in the Kop. After signing his contract as Tranmere manager, he was shocked with what he found.

"I was surprised at how far we'd fallen," he admits. "I hadn't actually been inside to have a look around the ground or to the training ground at Raby before I came back.

"When I went through that journey, the dressing rooms and stuff, I could see how it had decayed. It used to be immaculate. The offices and changing facilities were immaculate. Everybody made sure that it was top drawer. But you could tell it had had no money spent on it. The first team dressing rooms were still the same as what they'd been years ago. A lot had decayed.

"Then when I went to Raby, that was the saddest part. Raby used to be immaculate and it used to be great to train there. The pitches were amazing and the goals were immaculate. Everything about it was pure professional.

"When I got up there, it was the exact opposite. The pitches had been left to go to ruin and it was a real mess. It was almost untrainable. The equipment that we had was inadequate for a club of this size. Everything just smacked of deterioration really and it was sad.

"That's when it dawned on me size of the task that I knew that I had on. It was much, much bigger than what I first thought. All around the place, you could tell it had been neglected. We very, very quickly worked hard to change that."

Perhaps Raby had been ignored because the club had been trying to sell their youth training base at Ingleborough for nearly a decade until Mark Palios took over from Peter Johnson. The plan had always been to buy a new facility for the youth and first team to use once that deal went through.

By this time, thankfully, the wheels were in motion. It would not be too long before Tranmere shifted everything up to Solar Campus in Leasowe. They had purchased the facility from Wirral Borough Council in 2014, but it took some time renovate the building and grass pitches before they were ready for use.

Midway through the 2016/17 season, Tranmere eventually moved to their new state of the art training base. It houses their first and youth team and has space for several grass pitches, whilst also containing a gym, offices and a cafeteria. It is this kind of change that Mellon was yearning for.

From a playing point of view though, Rovers could not have made a better start to life under Mellon. He had the chance to make an immediate impression on the fans in his first game in charge against bitter rivals Wrexham. His players duly delivered as Andy Cook scored in second half injury time to complete a 2-0 victory after an own goal had given the hosts the lead.

"We're delighted," said the manager as he beamed throughout his post match press conference. "It's been a tough time for the players, I've got to say that. They've lost their manager and it does affect people because a lot of them were brought here by Gary.

"They've worked hard all week with Paul Carden and to go out today and turn out a performance like that, I've got to be really pleased.

"A lot of the time at this level, you'll get asked certain questions within the game. Today, that game asked us if we could deal with some direct play from Wrexham? Could we win the first headers and then get control from the knock downs before punishing them? Could we shift quickly across the pitch from side to side and keep the two units of four and still be a threat with the front two?

"I believe that we did that brilliantly well today. Of course, people will say that we want to play like Barcelona or whatever, but that might be for another day. Today, the questions that we got asked in this game, I thought the players were fantastic and answered them brilliantly well."

It was the perfect start. Suddenly Tranmere had some positive momentum. Their fans, after a run of one win in seven, were looking up the table once again. Their team were back.

"Micky Mellon did three things straight away in that Wrexham game that Gary Brabin had never done," says Ben Harrison. "It was a huge positive. He applauded the fans and little things like that. Yes, it's PR, but it's important work."

Next up for Rovers was a trip to Barrow in the fourth qualifying round for the FA Cup. The manager rotated his squad a touch as he took the opportunity to look at a few of his other first team players, but not many made a lasting impression in a 2-1 defeat.

When the league action returned, however, Tranmere continued to build momentum. First came a win over Solihull, with Jake Kirby netting a brace and Andy Cook getting the other in a 3-0 win.

A few days later there was a nervy 1-0 win over North Ferriby, one of those frustrating teams who would have quite happily settled for a point at Prenton Park. Thankfully, there was some late drama in store as Cook scored an injury time winner, whilst James Norwood was shown a straight red card for an incident involving visiting goalkeeper Rory Watson.

It capped off an irritating month for the striker, who now faced a three match ban having only just returned from injury. This was the first time he had started a match under Mellon and if he wanted to secure his place in the team, he could not afford to be out of the side for too long. There was no chance the new boss was leaving him out for an extended period though.

"I didn't know much about the gaffer, but I have known Andy Mangan for years from our time at Forest Green," he reveals. "He only every spoke about two things: all the goals that he scored and Micky Mellon. I knew about him and had played against his teams when he was Fleetwood manager. I knew a bit about his management style.

"When I was suspended, we had a training session and I played in the number ten role. It was the best training session of my life. I don't know why! I got called into the gaffer's office and we had a chat about where he thinks I can go and where he wants to take the club.

"Then, out of the blue, he offered me a new deal. I had eight months left on my contract - that's not something that happens in this division. They wait until the end of the season to do deals.

"I rang my mum and said 'we've got this new manager, he believes in me and wants to sell me on' or whatever. He likes doing that because it makes him look like a good manager. He had Jamie Vardy at Fleetwood, for example. A lot of managers want to keep players for themselves to be selfish and do well, but he thinks it's a sign of how good a manager you are. John Still at Dagenham is the same. He gets a player, makes them good and sells them. He wants everyone to improve every single day.

"I had an upturn in my training and then Scott Davies pulls me at the Christmas do. He says 'you don't feel safe do you?' I said 'no', because before Micky, I was the only striker scoring and I was playing every game. He says 'he'll keep you on your toes. He will be on you and if you don't perform, he'll drop you. He doesn't care'.

"That was exactly what I needed because I was in a bit of a stale patch. The gaffer hammered me about my training and was on me constantly. He wanted me to be better if I wanted to be at Tranmere.

"You eventually get into that routine of having to do it. You had Steve McNulty telling you that every day and you just think 'oh piss off will you', but you can't tell the manager to do that. He wants every single player that plays for him to have a good career and as a minimum, improve every day. He's the best manager I've worked for."

With Norwood missing, Tranmere went to Dover for their next game, and thumped Chris Kinnear's side 4-1. It was a terrific performance and one in which Ben Tollitt, at that point still only on loan from Portsmouth, really came to the fore.

The winger had shown glimpses of what he could do in a Rovers shirt so far, but put in a scintillating performance at The Crabble, using his pace to good effect as he found the back of the net for the first time for the club.

It helped Tranmere secure their fourth successive league victory and it made Mellon the first manager in the club's history to win his first four league games in charge. The turnaround since that Gateshead game had been quite incredible and despite the earlier dip in form, they had now recovered to trail leaders Forest Green by just four points. The manager though is quick to praise his predecessor for the upturn in results.

"Gary Brabin has got to take a lot of credit for that," he says honestly. "The recruitment before I came in was very good. There were a lot of good players here. I knew a lot of them.

"I could see that we would score goals and keep clean sheets. That is the recipe you look for as a manager. Can I score goals and keep clean sheets? I had to put my own spin on things and try and create the football club in the way that I wanted it to look like, but certainly

Gary gave me a lot of ingredients that allowed me to move forward with that.

"I would say that Gary started the turnaround at Tranmere. I don't think there's any doubt about that. I have got to be a part of that journey until now. How far that journey will go, I don't think anybody knows, but certainly so far I would say that between me and Gary, we've stopped the rot and started the turnaround."

Despite the results, though, Mellon was still not completely satisfied with the way Tranmere were playing. He believed he could still get more out of them in order to close that gap on Forest Green.

"I knew that there were good players here," he continues. "I could tell that right away. But even though you've got good players, you still don't know if they have the appetite or ambition needed to want to keep driving something forward. You learn that as you go along and that's up to the players really.

"I just had to go with what we had. I brought a few new faces in, like Andy Mangan, as I wanted it to be the team I wanted it to be. I'd be lying if I said I was entirely happy with how we were playing, even in the early stages. I think we were just winning games.

"We weren't functioning in the way I wanted us to function, but it was winning games and gathering a bit of momentum, which was important. Then with all the other things that we changed around about the club, it seemed to help gather that momentum."

Rovers were well and truly on the crest of a wave. They were beginning to churn out the results that had not come under Brabin or Carden. Lincoln and Dagenham were also above them in the table, but only on goal difference, so did the manager think his side could challenge for the title?

"I don't really ever think that far ahead," he adds. "I've heard people say 'what is it you want to do at the start of the season?' I think we all want to win the league, but I don't really set targets to do that. I just deal with training from day to day and with life from day to day. Then when the games come, I try and win them.

"If there's something to work on after the game, I'll find out what that is and work on it. Some of the things to work on are just consistency and what you're already doing. I couldn't be honest and say to you that I thought we were or weren't going to win the league. I just thought we were capable of improving and obviously scoring goals and keeping clean sheets and winning games of football.

"You start to get a gauge of where that is going to take you towards the end of the season. Then when you get to the end of the season, you start to think 'we could do this here'. But not at the start. I didn't have any expectations or set any plans to do anything other than just improve the whole thing."

Mark Palios meanwhile refused to set any targets for Mellon either. He felt, quite rightly, that it was unnecessary. Everybody knew what the end goal was.

"People ask if I'd set him targets," he said. "It's so naive. Why do you think we go on the pitch as Tranmere Rovers in this league? Do you think we wanted to stay in the National League?

"Promotion was obviously the target. Why would I say your target is promotion? If I said that to him, he'd say 'so what, I know that!' You've got to get promoted."

Something else that improved hugely during Mellon's first few weeks in charge was the atmosphere around Prenton Park on a match day. There had been some pretty hostile moments for Gary Brabin towards the end of his tenure, but it would be unfair to single him out as the only person to get grief from the terraces.

Micky Adams, Rob Edwards, Ronnie Moore and Les Parry had all felt the wrath of some supporters over the previous five or six years. Indeed, as Ben Harrison noted, even Mellon got it in the neck when he was a player. There would be boos and jeers and at times it could prove unhelpful.

The manager though noticed how the fans began to pull together as one behind the team and although he would not take the credit for that, he admits it has been hugely beneficial.

"I think the most important thing is I'm told, and I did feel it myself, that there was a change in the fans," he says. "There was a flick of a switch. Even though I wasn't here for many years, I could feel it. It was almost like the fans got it.

"I think that they knew that enough was enough of us eating each other from within. The club was eating itself from within. Everyone was angry and unhappy with where Tranmere had got to, quite rightly. It wasn't helping when they were trying to recover. It just kept fighting with itself, but something strange happened.

"A switch was flicked and everybody suddenly clicked and went the same way. I never heard anybody shouting anything negative from the crowd. Usually you hear somebody shouting something or somebody getting on to somebody, but I heard nothing. Nothing at all.

"Even when we didn't win games or weren't quite as good as we all wanted us to be, we just all knew that this was it. We all had to get on with it. We just have to keep improving. We know that we've got people here who've got Tranmere's interest at heart, all of us, and the fans helped us drive that."

***

After the win down at Dover, Tranmere continued to go from strength to strength. Mellon got to grips with his team as the likes of Jeff Hughes and James Norwood were back from suspension and new signing Andy Mangan, who had returned from Shrewsbury, helped Rovers kick on.

The winning run eventually came to an end with a 2-2 draw at home to Chester when a late strike from Ryan Astles earned the visitors a point. But it would be another month before the manager tasted his first league defeat with the club.

A further win was registered against Braintree, courtesy of a stunning goal from Andy Cook, whilst Torquay, Gateshead and York were also beaten by slender margins.

There was also a terrific 2-2 draw with high flying Forest Green in what was one of the highest quality games you will see in the National League. Christian Doidge had pounced to put his side ahead after two minutes, but Lois Maynard equalised moments later, heading home Liam Ridehalgh's terrific swinging cross from a clever short corner routine.

Scott Davies was then forced into a number of saves before being beaten from 22-yards as captain Liam Noble brilliantly curled home. However, the hosts could not hold on as Mangan and Norwood linked up to allow the latter to score and level the game in the second half.

"After 23 minutes I'd have liked to have stopped the game like Sky Plus and rejigged us," joked Mellon at full time. "In the first half, we completely went off what we do every day. We were reacting rather than anticipating. I just couldn't get to the players. When you get like that, sometimes they get a bit of a fuzzy head.

"We got a valuable point. It was a good game of football, and a tactical one at times, which we enjoyed as a management team. But I want to back my players, and some of the chances we got, I think they're good players and I'd expect them to score them.

"They had some decent blocks and a bit of fortune, and Mangan's had three one-on-ones which on another day I'd expect him to score. So we're pleased with a point, but disappointed we haven't

Great Xmas awayday. Bal too hungove so I drive the Hilti mobile. Carl stays at home for Marks 30th . . . .

taken our chances."

Unfortunately for Mellon, his ten game unbeaten run as Tranmere boss came to an end just before Christmas as Rovers lost a crucial fixture in the National League title race. They went into the match with the chance of being top of a table on December 25th for the first time since 1965, but defeat would mean opponents Lincoln would leapfrog them.

The visitors went into the game without Andy Cook, who had seriously injured his hand in a freak accident after dropping a dumbbell on it. He would miss the entire festive period, a big loss for the club's striking options.

If that was not enough of a blow before proceedings even began, they were soon chasing the game at Sincil Bank as Nathan Arnold headed his side into the lead after just three minutes. Tranmere had struggled to deal with a long throw routine and the midfielder pounced to nod past Scott Davies.

Jeff Hughes equalised with a penalty on the half hour mark, but with the game petering out for a draw, Adam Marriott stole the points as he smashed home the winner late on.

"I thought we started poor," admitted Mellon afterwards. "In the first ten or fifteen minutes, we were a bit disjointed. To lose a goal from a flick on from a set play, we're really disappointed because we spoke about it and we know what their threats are.

"But we settled back in quickly. We get the penalty and we're bang back in it. I lost count of the amount of times we got good opportunities and didn't go and punish them. We popped it around them like we knew we would be able to do and played some good football.

"To be caught out on the counter attack, we're disappointed with little bits of detail in that. But apart from that, I couldn't really criticise us. We just needed a bit more composure and quality.

"Football's about how you bounce back and how you improve. We have to take this on the chin, get back to work next week and keep moving forwards. That's what we'll continue to do. There's things that are very, very good, but we also know what we have to get better at. We'll keep working hard.

"I've got to be honest and think there isn't a massive amount that I have got to speak to the players about though. Where we know that we have to be better is that final pass or taking one of those chances, because away from home, if you'd got told you'd have that many opportunities to score, you'd have been delighted."

It was one of those results that, even then, you could tell was going to be crucial come the end of the season. Tranmere had now been beaten twice by the league leaders. If you turn those results around, it is a twelve point swing in the title race.

"We got on a roll very, very quickly under Micky Mellon," says Ben Harrison. "Then came Lincoln away over Christmas. They scored and went top, we equalised and went top. It was one of those games.

"I suppose losing to them twice was the big thing, although I actually didn't think about it at the time. They were going so well in the FA Trophy and the FA Cup and I was convinced they weren't going to last. Danny Cowley was convinced they were running on empty too.

"It was definitely a moment and a turning point. History repeated itself in the 2017/18 season. We didn't take points off the team who won the league. Macclesfield beat us at Prenton Park and we should have won away from home."

Chapter Fourteen
Injuries

Tranmere seem to have been plagued by injuries for years. On several occasions, just as they were beginning to look like they could mount some sort of promotion challenge, the number of casualties would increase and the squad would not be big enough or have the quality required to cope.

The best example of that is the 2012/13 season under Ronnie Moore. In the first half of the campaign, Rovers were scintillating. Nobody in League One could handle a team that would attack you all day and had enough composure in the final third to finish off the chances that came their way.

Things started to fall apart when Jean-Louis Akpa Akpro broke his metatarsal, whilst defender Ben Gibson, on loan from Middlesbrough, required a hernia operation. Abdulai Baggie also never really seemed to recover from being physically battered by Bournemouth.

The biggest hammer blow of all though came when James Wallace, the leader of the team and the driving force in central midfield, damaged his cruciate knee ligaments. He dived into a tackle in an FA Cup clash with Chesterfield in December and would not play another game for nearly a year.

With so many key players missing, and more to come as the free scoring Jake Cassidy was recalled from his loan spell by Wolves, Tranmere's promotion push spluttered to an alarming halt. Despite being top of the league in January, they finished outside of the play-off positions.

Moore had a similar experience in the 2007/08 campaign, although the fall was not quite as dramatic. He had built a team capable of battling for the top six spots thanks to the likes of Danny Coyne in goal, Antony Kay and Ian Goodison in defence and striker Chris Greenacre, a brilliant marksman at that level.

Two other key players would barely play however due to injury. One of them was Steve Davies, a hugely exciting young winger who was bursting with pace and desperate to run with the ball. He picked up a knee problem during a 2-2 draw against Northampton in late September and did not return until the back end of the campaign.

The man on the other flank was Chris Shuker. He had speed to burn and simply loved beating his man over and over again. On Boxing Day, Carlisle's full back hit him with a horrific tackle that also resulted in a knee injury and three months on the sidelines - and even when he returned, he did not look like the same player.

They were a formidable pair and would have racked up the assists between them, but Moore could not get them on the pitch and Tranmere, despite challenging at the top end of the table at the start of the campaign, once again failed to finish in the top six.

There have been other instances too, including Greenacre failing to feature after Christmas during the 2008/09 season due to fitness issues. He even picked up a problem in his comeback game, John Achterberg's testimonial in March. He, surely, would have made a huge difference as Rovers missed out on the play-offs by two points thanks to a gutting draw with Scunthorpe on the final day of the campaign.

In the 2016/17 season, for the first time since 2012/13, Tranmere looked like they could finish top of a division. The squad was that good. They held no fear and were capable of winning even if they conceded a couple, because the strikers were so prolific. And then the curse struck again.

It was back with a vengeance. From February onwards, Rovers seemed to pick up an injury in nearly every game they played. Some were season ending, others just cause minor disruptions, but they came week after week after week. Micky Mellon was exasperated as he had to find a new way to combat each problem that came his way.

It even got to a point where, in the final game of the regular season, Mellon rested his entire first team squad for a dead rubber game at Maidstone. The youth team played instead as the manager wrapped his most important players in cotton wool ahead of the play-offs.

The first blow was to Ben Tollitt, at that point in the form of his life. He picked up a cruciate knee ligament problem against Boreham Wood (yes, them again). He actually tried to play on, taking a corner that barely reached the first man, let alone beat him, and soon limped off.

The early diagnosis was not good. A few days later, the news was confirmed. "Ben is out for the remainder of the season," said Mellon at his next press conference. The news went down like a lead balloon. Heads dropped all around the room. You could sense the feeling of disappointment.

This was another Wallace from 2012/13 or Davies from 2007/08. Tollitt had been a talisman since arriving from Portsmouth, originally on loan before making the move a permanent one. Full backs hated playing against him because his acceleration was sensational and he thrived off scoring or creating goals.

In 18 appearances, he had already found the back of the net six times, including a quite sensational solo goal away at Woking where he brought the ball down on the touchline and carried it from inside his own half before slotting past the goalkeeper.

The lad was on fire, and he was attracting interest from elsewhere. Championship and Premier League clubs were having their heads turned by a 22-year old in whose potential might not have been fully appreciated by Portsmouth. He would not play again until October.

There was worse to come though. Jake Kirby broke his leg in a freak accident against Barrow in the FA Trophy just four days later, with a foul actually given against the winger for the manner in which he challenged for the ball.

A couple of months later, in the penultimate game of the regular league season, Lee Vaughan also broke his leg. The defender had been in the best form of his Tranmere career but was hit by a horror tackle by Southport defender Spencer Myers.

This was another tough blow for Mellon, because it meant, on the eve of the play-offs, he had to find a new style of play. Vaughan had been thriving at right-wing-back in a 3-5-2 formation that was getting the best out of Connor Jennings in the number ten role and Liam Ridehalgh on the opposite flank.

Unfortunately, there was nobody else in the squad who could play that role quite as effectively. Adam Buxton had been tried there but was enjoying a stint as the right central defender in the back three, whilst youngster Mitch Duggan was out on loan at Warrington.

The latter might actually have played in the play-offs. He would have been the most able replacement to Vaughan at right-wing-back. Except he got sent off in Warrington's final game of the season, a 1-1 draw with Matlock. As it was his second dismissal of the campaign, it resulted in a four match ban. The play-off final was the fourth game.

In between Kirby and Vaughan breaking their legs, Tranmere lost a number of other key players. Jay Harris also did his knee in a 1-0 defeat to Forest Green, a game in which Rovers enjoyed total domination but failed to put their chances away. The visitors then made them pay when Kaiyne Woolery scored an 85th minute winner.

On top of that, Ritchie Sutton damaged his Achilles in training in March and missed the rest of the season, whilst Steven Jennings and Adam Mekki picked up knee injuries that proved too difficult to overcome before the campaign came to an end.

"I've never known a squad to pick up as many injuries," admits Micky Mellon. "Or as many serious ones. By the time we got to Wembley, we were limping bad. It would be easy for me to say we were one injury away from whatever, but I think we were beyond that."

Perhaps the most damaging blow came just a week before the play-off final at Wembley. James Wallace was just beginning to find his form after a catalogue of injury issues since that first knee problem back in December 2012.

He had returned to Prenton Park in November 2016, determined to give something back to the club after leaving for Sheffield United in 2013 under circumstances that disappointed some fans. When he eventually got a run in the team, he was unstoppable, and he tore Aldershot to shreds in the first leg of the semi-final.

The second leg did not go quite as well though. He limped off after the break in tears. He had injured his knee again and he knew that it would be some time before he was able to take to the field. That dream of playing at Wembley had been pulled from under his feet.

"James is a very, very talented lad," Mellon continued. "If it wasn't for bad luck, he wouldn't have any in terms of injuries. It's so frustrating. It almost makes me angry at times, the luck that he doesn't get.

"The big blow was the type of players and characters that we lost. These players were characters. I don't mean in making you laugh, but they have the right mentality to win games of football and keep everybody else right.

"James Wallace was great at keeping standards around him high. He'd be digging people out if they came off the plan. Steve McNulty is the same, but James would take his share in doing that. So you've lost a strong player out of your spine.

"You also lose Ben Tollitt who makes a big difference when sometimes the game is very even. He can dribble by somebody and create something. You lose that as well. You're losing vital players. Lee Vaughan is another, he got a bad broken leg and he was doing great for me."

Mark Palios points out there was another important player who got injured, although he did return in time to play at Wembley. Jack Dunn had arrived on loan from Liverpool and with him on one flank and Tollitt on the other, Tranmere were on fire.

Unfortunately, the winger, who had impressed whilst at Morecambe in the first half of the season, only managed seven appearances for Rovers. He injured his ankle against Boreham Wood, the same fixture in which Tollitt picked up his knee problem, and would not feature again until mid-April.

"It was just week in, week out and they were important players," says Palios. "Ben and Jack were ripping up the league. At Eastleigh, the two full backs had their shorts on the wrong way round at the end of the game.

"When they were both going at it, it was just incredible. You can imagine playing against that constant pressure down each flank. Tollitt was a devastating blow, but we still had enough firepower and strength in the team to get through.

"Then Wallace comes back in and he's playing well, only to lose him. He was an immense player when he was fit. Little Jay Harris has come back in and provided massive energy and then there's Lee Vaughan, who's probably playing his best football for the club as a wing back. He gets that stupid tackle from that lad - I'd have chinned him if I was on the pitch. He breaks his leg and you just couldn't write it."

Tranmere would eventually limp into that play-off final at Wembley with eight absentees. Six of them would probably have played, and although you cannot say for certain, they would surely have made a telling difference. Ben Harrison reckons the Tollitt was the biggest loss.

"When he tried to take that corner against Boreham Wood, he only got the ball about half an inch off the ground," he laughs. "It was very damaging because he was in such good form. When he got the ball, there was a buzz. He knew it, the fans knew it and the other team knew it.

"He could win you a game on his own. Just look at the 4-1 win at Dover. That was when we started to see how good a player he was. He ripped them to shreds.

"The injuries were the other side of things to be honest. We were running out of players by the time we got to Wembley. We did have a squad - but none of them were fit!

"Jay Harris was the one that killed it for me, plus James Wallace in the play-offs. He was starting to get into his stride. He was great in the away game, played in the home leg but was out for Wembley. Imagine having those three at Wembley!"

James Norwood meanwhile has revealed that he played through the pain barrier at the end of the season. The striker, alongside Andy Cook, was rested for a couple of games due to the run in the FA Trophy, but still amassed 43 appearances over the course of the campaign, 16 of them between March and May.

"I had an inflamed bursa," he says. "As soon as I put something hard heeled on the back of my foot, it would be like somebody was sticking a hot needle in it. I used to have to pad my heel up with three or four things, strap it and wear a pair of size tens for training.

"On Saturdays, the doctor would travel away or come to Prenton Park and inject aesthetic underneath the bone and into the bursa for every game. It was the most excruciating pain I've felt.

"I had steroid injections but they don't work. You can rupture your achilles as well if you run on it within six weeks. So when I came back for pre-season, having not done a thing, we did a 1,500 metre run and I beat Steve McNulty by four seconds. The gaffer hammered me! But then when I told him, he said 'it's okay, get fit in your own time!'"

It is just as well that Norwood was available towards the back end of the season. He was crucial to how Tranmere played, and they could not afford to be without another key player. He reckons they could have coped with all the injuries - if they had come earlier on in the campaign.

"When Lee Vaughan broke his leg, we had to change our shape," he continues. "James Wallace comes in and tears Aldershot apart in the first game. With twenty minutes to go in the second, he does his knee ligaments. It wasn't just the amount of injuries though, it was the timing.

"If we'd have lost those two with ten games to go, we would have still made the play-offs. We would have also had a settled team. But we lost our right-wing-back and had to shuffle formation, then in the semi-finals, when we're 4-2 up on aggregate, we lose our centre mid.

"Injuries are a part of football. We visited Lee in hospital and things like that, but it's work. You're a professional footballer, you get on with it. You don't worry about it happening to you in training. Things happen in personal lives, like losing your parents, but people come in and play the game and they train.

"They might miss a couple of days for funeral, but it doesn't stop. Especially at this level, appearance bonuses make up a lot of people's money. If you miss a game or two, it might take you four months to get back in. That's however much money you might make in appearance, goal and win bonuses.

"People on the lower end of the scale rely on them. If you're not getting them, you can't pay the mortgage. You might have kids as well. Football doesn't stop for anything, and that's why nobody cares about injuries. Everybody gets them. You feel sorry for the people who get them all the time, but the show must go on. That's our mentality."

Chapter Fifteen
Big Wins

In football, there are two types of win that could be classified as "big". One is achieved by beating the opposition by a huge margin, whilst the second is an important victory against a rival. In the second half of the 2016/17 season, Tranmere did both.

Their form after losing to Lincoln was initially patchy. They traded wins with Macclesfield over the festive period, losing at Moss Rose before winning the return fixture a few days later. Dagenham then came to Prenton Park and won before Rovers went to Woking on a Tuesday night and smashed them 3-0 thanks to a sublime performance by Ben Tollitt.

It was a frustrating start to 2017. They only played three league games in January due to postponements and the FA Trophy, a competition in which Tranmere would reach the semi-final before losing to Macclesfield.

Micky Mellon insisted the run to the last four was not a distraction at the time. Indeed, it gave him a chance to rest the weary legs of some of his key players whilst also getting some minutes for those on the fringe who could be crucial in the promotion run in.

One of those was Cole Stockton, back from his loan spell at Morecambe. It would be fair to say that he was never a fans' favourite despite graduating from the club's academy, but the manager was a big admirer of the striker who had reached double figures in terms of goals for the first time in his career whilst with the League Two club.

He hit the ground running when back at Prenton Park, netting on his return as Rovers hammered Isthmian League South side South Park

4-1 in the second round of the FA Trophy.

The victory over Woking was when Tranmere really started to hit form though. It started an eight game unbeaten run, that also included wins over Eastleigh and Boreham Wood in the National League, as well as a 5-1 hammering of Barrow in the FA Trophy.

Stockton bagged a hat-trick in that game, his first for the club, and that caused a bit of a selection headache for Mellon. Andy Cook was, alongside James Norwood, his first choice striker. But he could not drop somebody who had just scored three goals in one match. The next fixture was due to be against Forest Green on a Tuesday night, but heavy rain caused the clash to be postponed.

Next up was, in terms of rivalry, one of the biggest games of the season: Chester away - live on BT Sport. Bragging rights were at stake as well as the three points. Rovers were still four points behind Lincoln, having played a game more, but they had a chance to put some pressure on the league leaders.

They sold out their allocation of tickets for the trip to the Deva Stadium, with well over a thousand fans making the short journey down the M53. They were expectant, and rightly so, Chester were mid-table and had not beaten Tranmere in a competitive fixture since October 1990.

However, some were left a little concerned when the team news came out. Stockton kept his place after his heroics against Barrow, as did Andy Mangan who had also scored. James Norwood and Andy Cook were on the bench, despite scoring six goals between them in the last four league games.

"We were supposed to have a league game on the Tuesday after playing Barrow in the FA Trophy on the Saturday," explains Norwood. "Cooky and I had been scoring and Micky pulls us on the Thursday to tell us we were rested for the FA Trophy game, but we'd be in for the Forest Green match a few days later.

"It was a big week. He wanted us to rest and that was fine. We trusted him. It was nice to have a rest. He told us we'd definitely be in on the Tuesday, but we then beat Barrow 5-1 with Cole Stockton getting a hat trick and Andy Mangan scoring.

"Then the game gets postponed because of the weather and we get to the Chester game and we're not in the team after being told we'd be playing, no matter what happens. We knock on the manager's door and asked to speak to him. He told me and Cooky that he couldn't drop them.

"We were travelling in and had some choice words because we wanted to play every game. Yes, we wanted what was best for the team, but we were playing well at that point. We'd hit form, we were in a purple patch. One or two games away can halt that."

Without Cook and Norwood, Tranmere made a horrendous start as their defence stopped when they thought Steve McNulty had given away a foul on James Alabi. Lois Maynard would have had possession, but he pulled up with a thigh injury and that allowed Evan Horwood to nip in and drive towards the box, where he was brought down by Michael Ihiekwe.

The defender, a former Rovers player who at that time coached in Tranmere's academy, was still outside the area when he took his tumble, but the referee awarded a penalty that Alabi converted after just five minutes.

The drama truly started after the break when Jay Harris, on as a substitute for Maynard because of that injury, netted a stunning goal from 20-yards. Chester failed to properly deal with a cross and when the ball landed to the midfielder, he only had one thing on his mind, smashing home with the outside of his right boot as he beautifully bent his shot around the defender and into the far post.

The hosts were ahead again, undeservedly so, with 22-minutes left when Ryan Astles, who had scored their late equaliser at Prenton Park earlier in the season, nodded past Scott Davies from a corner.

By this stage, Cook had already come on for Stockton who had been pretty anonymous, whilst Mellon signalled to Norwood immediately and he duly replaced Mangan. It did not take long for either to make their mark.

With 83-minutes on the clock Norwood equalised, heading home Liam Ridehalgh's delightful cross at the back post, before Cook caused pandemonium in the away end as he netted the winner in injury time by finding the bottom corner with a right footed drive from 20-yards.

"We showed the quality that is needed for a derby," concluded Mellon at full-time. "We showed some great composure and came out in the second half and really pinned them in.

"The support we had was wonderful. I said to the boys 'that's what Friday nights and being on TV is all about, so make sure you keep that in the memory bank.'

"We were finding ways of getting a lot of good quality into the box and when you've got Cook and Norwood, they're going to do that for us. To score in the last minute with that kind of following was really special. We really enjoyed it."

It was a brilliant goal to win it. The Tranmere fans went wild. Some invaded the pitch, others lost themselves in the moment. Cook and Norwood meanwhile ran straight to the Chester fans who had been shouting a few choice words whilst the pair were doing some stretches on the touchline earlier on in the game.

"We were sat on the bench saying 'we could tear these apart'", says Norwood. "At 2-1 down, I'm told to get ready and I come on and score. Cooky then wins a header, Adam Mekki blatantly dives again, which he's so good at, the ball falls back to Cooky, one touch, bang.

"When we got warmed up, we were getting loads of abuse from the fans, so we celebrated in front of them. I love the picture of us celebrating. We're knee sliding and we have our arms in the air and our faces just say 'what are you going to do?'

"It was perfect, because Jay Harris got the other and he had come off the bench too. We all scored and it was just scenes. It kept the title hunt alive. Lincoln were probably watching it and thinking 'this is it' when we were losing, but we pulled it back. It gave us a lot more belief."

From a supporters' point of view, it is a game that will live long in the memory. Matches against Chester had been few and far between since 1990, because they had sunk out of the Football League and had to reform as a club. Even if it was because Tranmere were in the National League, the teams were at last reunited, and it gave some younger fans a chance to experience the rivalry for the first time.

"I watched the Chester game back on YouTube the other night," admits Ben Harrison. "It was some game. We had two sides of the ground and it was a Friday night. The buzz afterwards of people leaving the ground was something else.

"We set off at 5 o'clock. We were drinking in Chester early and got a taxi to the ground. Somebody said we were getting beat 1-0 because we always arrive late and I didn't believe him. Then we get in and find out about it - it wasn't a penalty; it was outside the box and the lad dived!

"Neil Turner is on Radio Merseyside and it's the most biased bit of commentary I've ever heard. He said it was a penalty but it definitely wasn't! Then Jay Harris scored, they scored again and then the end was unbelievable.

"When Norwood scored, it lifted everybody. Chester weren't that confident but he ran back and I knew we were going to get another chance. Adam Mekki did his usual in trying to win a free kick by going down like a sack of spuds, but the ball fell to Cook.

"I was on the side and when it went in, it did cross my mind to get on the pitch. I didn't do it but the celebrations were bedlam. We walked back with the police escort to the pub and there was such a buzz. There weren't many moments as good as that over the decade before. Coming back from behind and in a derby, it was brilliant."

Mark Palios was a player at Tranmere when the rivalry between the two clubs was at its peak during the 1970s and 1980s, so he knew only too well what this result meant to the supporters. It also left him with a huge smile on his face when rushing off to the airport at full-time.

"I was off to China after the Chester game," he says. "What a different flight it was after Cooky smashed that one in! He scored so late and it was a typical Cooky goal. We had to race away from the game, so we couldn't enjoy it. But then you started to believe it was our year. It was a great feeling."

For Mellon, on the other hand, the win came as a great relief, but also a tactical triumph. He had not started Cook or Norwood, but both had come off the bench to score. And he loved it.

"If you could pick a game of football and ask how can you make it the most exciting game it can be, it would be that Chester one," he admits. "They thought they'd beaten us. It was a full house and we were brilliant. I've watched that game back and we were brilliant.

"The way we knocked the ball about and didn't lose it under pressure was brilliant. It was as good a performance as we had. And then to score the types of goals that we did and to have the game that we did was mega.

"All three subs scored, and that made me happy, but when you're going into the game you know you're probably going to use 14 players. So you're just grateful to win the game. I don't sit there and think 'how clever am I'. I just looked at the game and thought the changes might have to be made.

"You look behind you and it's a bit like golf. You look at the situation and think 'that might just get us out of that' or 'that might keep us in the lead'. Fortunately we had the players, the golf clubs if you like, who we knew could possibly get us over the line."

***

After beating Chester, Tranmere's form was not so good. Perhaps it was this period that would eventually cost them the title as they lost 2-1 at Barrow and drew 0-0 down at Torquay.

Micky Mellon rotated his squad for the latter of those two matches, resting Cook and Norwood as Stockton and Mangan were once again brought into the starting line up.

The problem for the manager was that Rovers were playing Saturday - Tuesday - Saturday football every week. The scheduled was relentless. Between the start of March and end of April, they played 16 games - eight in each month.

They were still involved in the FA Trophy, with the doubled legged semi-final against Macclesfield coming either side of the long trip to Plainmoor. The squad were playing a serious amount of football and Mellon was desperate to make sure they did not burn out.

He did benefit however from the return of Connor Jennings. The midfielder had picked up a knee injury before Mellon arrived at the club and had struggled to break back into the side when back to full fitness.

He was sent out on loan to Macclesfield to get some minutes into his legs and that proved invaluable as he was not only a mainstay of the team when he got back, but also one of the reasons why they started winning again. He knitted things together between midfield and attack and weighed in with some vital goals.

"Hopefully I can kick on now and try and get my place for the rest of the season," he said after featuring in the first leg of the FA Trophy tie at Macclesfield. "It was mentally very hard and tough, but I've had a serious injury before. I knew what to do.

"You just need to keep your head up high, work hard and when you get a chance you've got to try and take it. I think Micky's main thing for me was to get game time. Now I'm back, hopefully I can get some game time here."

Rovers drew the game at Moss Rose 1-1, Jeff Hughes scoring from the penalty spot, but unfortunately they lost the second leg 1-0 courtesy of a strike from Ollie Norburn. They were out of the competition. Their Wembley dream was shattered. But perhaps it was the kick up the backside they needed.

A few days after the disappointment against Macclesfield they hammered North Ferriby 4-1 with Jay Harris scoring a hat-trick and Cook becoming the first Tranmere player since Simon Haworth during the 2002/03 season to net 20 league goals in a campaign.

They were now five points off top spot, which had been taken over by Forest Green, with Lincoln sitting in second. "There'll be twists and turns along the way," predicted Mellon afterwards. "I know that. I'll never get carried away, with any of the ups or downs.

"I know that it's difficult to play under the conditions that a lot of these clubs are going to play under now, with 10 games to go. They'll learn an awful lot about themselves, but me and Mike Jackson have gone this track before and we've got a lot of players who have too.

"We're just trying to keep everybody calm and focused on the job and keep picking up points for Tranmere. We know that we've come through a difficult spell."

Braintree, Wrexham and Dover were then all defeated 1-0 before Michael Ihiekwe scored a 90th minute winner as Rovers came from behind to beat Sutton 3-2 on a Tuesday night. Five wins in a row.

The pressure was being cranked up on Lincoln and Forest Green.

And then came one of the most amazing and memorable games in the club's history. Solihull Moors visited Prenton Park for the first time on Grand National Saturday and they were absolutely destroyed. Connor Jennings and Cole Stockton both netted hat-tricks, whilst the latter also missed a penalty. That was not the end of it though. Cook, Liam Ridehalgh and loanee Aaron Collins also scored. 9-0. A record breaking margin for a Rovers win.

"We didn't start well," said Mellon afterwards. "We were slow coming out of the blocks and gave away too many free-kicks. But we're delighted. I don't know when the last time was that two Tranmere players scored hat-tricks in the same game. It's fantastic, but we're not getting too carried away.

"We're pleased with an awful lot of things but we'll quickly get back to business again. We have to, because we're in the middle of a fantastic race. We'll dust ourselves down and get the boys ready for the next few days and move onto the game against Forest Green on Tuesday night now."

Chairman Mark Palios watched on from the stands and admits he has never seen a game like it. If only Cole Stockton had not missed his spot kick - Rovers would have had double figures. It was incredible, but joy was not the only emotion he felt.

"Solihull was the one and only time I've felt sorry for an opposing team," he admits. "You've always got to respect the opposing team, but I actually felt sorry for them. When the fifth one went in, I looked at their team and there was nobody shouting at anybody, they were all just trudging back to the halfway line with their heads down.

"The slaughter just kept on coming. It was just one of those games, it was incredible. It was a fantastic result and just one of those days. We'd threatened for quite some time over months to do it with the number of chances we were creating. Everything we hit, it went in.

It didn't matter who came on, they would score. It was incredible."

Mellon agrees with Palios' synopsis, adding: "You do feel sorry for a team in a situation like that, but what can you do? We were clinical and we could have had more! We missed a penalty, we hit the post twice and we had one v ones with the goalkeeper.

"It was just a time when we were flying. We were too quick with too much pace, power and desire. The players were flying. The goals came from everywhere and we were dangerous every time we got the ball within shooting range. They were either going to hit the target and score or they were going to play it right through you. They were at the top of their game."

Chapter Sixteen
Lincoln

Tranmere spent the majority of the second half of the season chasing Lincoln in what turned out to be a thrilling title race. It was nip and tuck, right to the wire, but unfortunately Micky Mellon's side had left themselves just a little too much to do.

There were times when Rovers managed to sneak above The Imps in the table, but their rivals always had games in hand. Ultimately, however, the two defeats to them, 1-0 at Prenton Park in September and 2-1 at Sincil Bank three months later, proved pivotal.

Mellon though refused to give up on top spot until there were only a handful of games in the season left. What gave him and Tranmere hope was the sheer number of fixtures that Lincoln had left to play in such a short space of time.

Danny Cowley's side had also reached the semi-finals of the FA Trophy, where they were beaten by eventual winners York after extra time. On top of that, they became the first Non League club in over 100 years to get to the FA Cup quarter-finals.

It was an incredible run for the club, who defeated Championship side Ipswich and Premier League opposition Burnley en route to the last eight, where they were finally knocked out by Arsenal who, like York, would lift the trophy at the end of the campaign.

The result of doing so well in two cup competitions was a fixture pile up. Between the start of March and end of April, Lincoln had to complete 17 fixtures. In fact, after finally being knocked out of the FA Trophy on March 18th, they still had twelve games left to play in the National League.

The glass half full Tranmere fans therefore were hoping that The Imps would run out of steam. Surely this run of matches would take its toll eventually? Or would the run in the cups mean winning the league was put on the back burner?

"I've since spoken to the Cowleys and they will admit that they were poor at the end of the season," reveals Micky Mellon. "They said that they were limping and that they were really, really poor. We were brilliant. We were really, really good. We were scoring goals from everywhere and battering everybody, but playing some really good football."

As badly as Lincoln were playing, their results did not drop off. Somehow, they kept churning out wins and were even getting over the line in games where they looked dead and buried.

There are three results in particular that stand out, starting with a 1-0 win at Eastleigh on April 8th. That was the same day that Rovers hammered Solihull 9-0, a victory that meant Lincoln's superior goal difference, almost an extra point in the title race, was wiped out.

"They were drawing 0-0 after 77th minutes" says Mark Palios. "I've spoken to the Cowleys about it. They said that our score came through and we were about 6-0 up at the time and they could see their goal difference evaporating. He said they thought that was it. But then Lincoln nicked one at the end."

And that was the thing. Just when it looked Lincoln were going to slip up and give Rovers a glimmer of hope, they pulled it out of the bag. They did the same on Good Friday against Torquay, coming from 1-0 down to win 2-1 thanks to goals from Harry Anderson and Sam Habergham.

That trick was repeated on Easter Monday, except on this occasion the escape was even greater. Gateshead had been in the lead since scoring a 29th minute penalty, only for Matt Rhead and Nathan Arnold to net in injury time to steal the points.

he Charisma of a used wet wipe
↓

Gary Brabin [top] watches on during a friendly against Blackpool
and [below] Jay Harris celebrates scoring Tranmere's first goal in
the National League as they beat Woking 1-0

First NL game. Harris with a
rocket after someone taps it to him
sloma FK

Micky Mellon applauds the fans ahead of his first game in charge
against Wrexham in October 2016

Missed this! Derms 30th
& Grand National day April 2017

[L-R] Jay Harris, Connor, Jennings and Josh Ginnelly celebrate with Ritchie Sutton after his goal at Wrexham

Hero Status: James Norwood rises high to head Tranmere back into the Football League

Mark Palios (above) celebrates Tranmere's win over Boreham Wood in the 2018 play-off final and (below) the team assemble on the balcony at Wembley

"They were scoring a lot of 94th minute goals and all the rest of it," Mellon continues. "Penalties in the last minute, coming down from 1-0 down with four minutes to go, crazy things. The Lincoln guys would say to you they were really, really poor at the end and they were limping."

It was demoralising for Tranmere. They were winning games, but were unable to close the gap up to first place. Of course, there were a few slip ups along the way, including a costly 1-0 defeat to Forest Green when Rovers battered their opponents but just could not put the ball in the back of the net.

That was followed by a 2-2 draw at home to Aldershot, but on the whole, Rovers were picking up the maximum points allocation. In fact, their form after getting knocked out the FA Trophy was sublime, winning nine of the last 11 National League fixtures. Because of that run, the squad believed they still had a chance of lifting the title.

"You never think it's up, especially that year, until it's mathematically impossible," says James Norwood. "We were only three or four points behind. The 9-0 win at Solihull was key too because of the goal difference. If we didn't believe then, then we shouldn't have been there.

"Then Lincoln got a 90th minute winner against Gateshead. They were 1-0 down on TV and they got two 90th minute winners. Champions do that. Macclesfield did it this year. They played Woking and the ball stopped on the line. The Woking player had turned his back, but Macclesfield followed it in and scored.

"It ended up getting Woking relegated pretty much. We were celebrating on the bus coming back from Dover after our game was postponed. We were watching it and when they scored the second, we thought we were back in it. Then Macclesfield got the winner and the coach just went silent. Those two games are very similar. That's when you think maybe it's not going to be our year.

"It didn't affect the dressing room though. It's only if you win and they lose that there's a change, because you're expecting them to win. There is that expectation. It's only if you lose and they win when it goes out of sight. If you win, they can't get any further away from you.

"They're top of the league and you expect them to win. You look at who they've got to play with 10 games to go and you might think they can drop points in two of them.

"If they don't drop it in the first one, they're going to win all nine, so are we. If they do slip up, we're not, we're going to win all nine. If you win, they can't get further away from you. That was our mentality. It was different when they lost. That's when you gained points."

Mellon however admits it was demoralising to see Lincoln keep pulling results out of the bag. Tranmere would head into the dressing room thinking the Imps had slipped up, only for a couple of late goals to completely change the complexion of the title race.

"It does take its toll," he continued. "You think they can't keep doing it, but they do. But you've just got to keep professional. That's why I go day to day and Saturday to Saturday. I just get on with the next day and be the best that I can the next day.

"That's what I said to the players and that's what we did. We got to the next day. We were disappointed but that's football. You've just got to take care of your own business and that's what they did."

On the day that Lincoln beat Gateshead, Tranmere were at Guiseley. They came from behind themselves, also winning 2-1 courtesy of strikes from James Norwood and Andy Cook. Despite the victory, they remained five points behind Lincoln, who still had a game in hand. And with Rovers only having a couple of matches left to overturn the deficit, Mellon finally conceded defeat in the title race.

"I don't believe that it will happen now," he admitted at full time, as attention instead turned to the play-offs. "I've got to be honest. We've left ourselves an awful lot to do. But we just keep on trying to win games of football until the very end, and you never know do you?

"Fair play to Lincoln, that's what you've got to say to them. There's nothing more that we can do than what we've been doing. We had two tough games where we didn't collect maximum points and Lincoln did. I'm a football man and I'll be the first to say 'fair play to them'."

Lincoln eventually put the title race to bed by beating Macclesfield 2-1 on April 22nd. Rovers won 4-1 against Southport on the same day, but that five point gap was now insurmountable.

There was still one game to go in the regular season, a long trip down to Maidstone just a couple of days before the first leg of the play-off semi finals. With second place already secured, Mellon rested his entire first team squad, and that led to an extremely proud day for the Tranmere fans, coaching staff and academy set up.

With the key players left at home, Rovers turned to their youth team to make up the numbers. A couple of fringe members of the squad were given minutes too, including Adam Mekki, who captained the side but picked up a knee injury that ruled him out of the play-offs.

Seven of the starting line up were players who had graduated from the club's academy, whilst a further three came on as substitutes. Many of them were still part of Andy Parkinson's under-18 side. One of those was the man who scored the only goal of the game, debutant Sam Ilesamni. He earned Rovers a 1-0 win by battering into the back of the net from close range after some persistent work by Adam Dawson.

"It's wonderful," said Mellon afterwards. "It's good for the soul, they were absolutely brilliant. With so much young talent, it's great to see their ability and determination to do well. I'm so, so proud. They deserve all the credit that's going to come their way.

"I'm pretty speechless to be honest, because it's just such a nice feeling to see them get their rewards for working so hard. When people saw the team, who thought we were going to beat a full strength Maidstone?

"To get a clean sheet and a win here is always very difficult, so it's fantastic. When I saw them score and the way they celebrated, it was priceless. Sam has finished it brilliantly.

"I'm really pleased for them, the club and the fans who have travelled all the way down. The Tranmere supporters will be as proud of that and enjoyed that result as much as many this season. It is that big. It's so good to see."

It was a wonderful and relaxing way for Rovers to round off the season. As well as the youth team getting a chance to shine, Mellon had importantly managed to rest his key players ahead of the more important game that was to come a few days later - therefore avoiding any damaging injuries.

Tranmere eventually finished the 2016/17 campaign with a club record tally of 95 points. They had lost just nine league games all season, with only five of those defeats coming after Mellon arrived at Prenton Park in October. Their second place finish was also their highest in any division since earning promotion to Division Three in 1988/89.

Chapter Seventeen
The Play-Off Semi-Finals

For the first time in twelve years, Tranmere had qualified for the play-offs. For some of the younger fans, this was the first time they had known their club to have any kind of success. After years of battling relegation, finally their team had extended their season.

Finishing second in the National League meant they were paired with Aldershot in the semi-finals. It was a tough draw. Gary Waddock's side were an ex-Football League team and had several dangerous players in their line up, including Bernard Mensah, Scott Rendell and Idris Kanu.

They had taken four points off Rovers during the season, handing Gary Brabin his first defeat of the campaign in September when the game down south finished 3-1, whilst the return fixture at Prenton Park ended 2-2. Despite that, they had finished sixth in the table, thirteen points behind Micky Mellon's side.

"It was great to be back in the play-offs," smiles Ben Harrison. "If you're going to go up, it's the best way to do it. We had the Lincoln game on before they beat Macclesfield to seal the title, but nobody wanted to watch them lift the trophy afterwards!

"I feared Aldershot going into that semi final. They were a very good team with some very good players. They've got a nice pitch, paid for by Chelsea, and it was enjoyable watching them."

Tranmere's first choice players returned, with Cole Stockton, controversially in the eyes of some fans, keeping his place ahead of Andy Cook. The striker had netted five goals in his last eight league outings, including one against Aldershot in that 2-2 stalemate at Prenton Park a month earlier.

He immediately repaid Micky Mellon's faith in him when handing Rovers the lead after just three minutes. Jeff Hughes battled for the ball down the left and his persistent work led to a pass towards Stockton near the corner of the six yard box. He spun and lashed home to make it 1-0.

It was the perfect start, so good, in fact, that you could hardly believe it. Aldershot were stunned, and they were nearly 2-0 down when only a terrific last ditch block denied Lois Maynard a few moments later. At the other end, Scott Davies pulled off a solid save to keep out Matt McClure's powerful header.

Mensah then hit the bar as the hosts desperately searched for a way back into the game, but they could not breach the Rovers defence, even when bringing on an extra striker, former Tranmere loanee Shamir Fenelon, at half-time.

Indeed, three minutes after the break, the visitors were in dreamland as they doubled their lead. Liam Ridehalgh swung a ball into the box that 'keeper Jake Cole came to claim. Most people had turned their backs thinking he had caught the ball easily, but it was a wet night and it slipped out of his hands, allowing Norwood to tap home unchallenged.

"At half time the gaffer hammered me," laughs Norwood. "I got punched in the face by the right back but the gaffer hammered me for not doing anything in the game.

"Then the 'keeper dropped a clanger. I'd never been more scared to have a ball in loads of space and with loads of time on the goal line. I dribbled it right up and poked it over."

From then on, Aldershot threw men forward but it always left them open to the counter attack. Tranmere duly obliged by scoring a third when breaking rapidly after a cross into the box was cleared by McNulty.

Hughes won the loose ball in midfield, with his interception falling to Wallace who in turn played an inch perfect first time pass to Norwood, who had burst into the opposition half and was in acres of space. The striker slid across to Stockton, a perfectly timed assist, who slotted under Cole. 3-0.

Micky Mellon was quick to insist that Tranmere could not count their chickens and think they were at Wembley already, though. "We're obviously delighted to get to the half way stage and be in front," he said afterwards. "But I really do mean this, we won't get carried away. There's an awful lot of work still to be done.

"We know that we go back to an electric Prenton Park now where the atmosphere will be fantastic. Every credit to the fans this evening, too, as it was the same this evening. But we're only half way. We've got our noses in front. We need to fight to make sure we keep it that way or add to that.

"We know what a good team Aldershot are and they showed that tonight. We had to get an awful lot right in certain areas of the pitch. The lads were massively motivated to make sure that they did that. To a man, when it was their turn to go and represent us in those areas, they've worked really, really hard to try and make that happen.

"We've got a terrific pressing goal to start with and a countering attack goal as well. We're pleased with the performance. But I absolutely will be drumming it into the boys that it's only half-time against a very talented Aldershot side. We know that we've still got work to do."

The 3-0 scoreline meanwhile was dreamland for the Tranmere fans. They had near enough sold out their allocation of tickets for the game and had been in party mode ever since the first goal went in. It was a sensational performance.

"I remember going down to the Aldershot game and the whole car was so nervous," says Ben Harrison. "It was raining and we weren't behind the goal so we were getting wet. We took shelter underneath a tree with TV and radio presenter Ray Stubbs but still got soaked. Someone was passing a ticket around the back of the steward but he wasn't letting anyone in!

"Then we put in one of the most complete performances I've seen from a Tranmere side. They were brilliant that night. James Wallace played very well; he broke things up and set them off."

Rovers were simply sensational. They had carried their form from the back end of the season into the play-offs and had delivered in what was their most important game of the campaign. The fans could barely believe it, and neither could Mark Palios.

"It is the old adage of get them early," he says. "It was a complete shock, because in my opinion, Aldershot were the best team in the play-offs, other than us. It's a pity, because I like Aldershot's directors. If we hadn't gone up, I'd have wanted it to be them.

"It was beyond my wildest dreams, getting a 3-0 lead in the first leg. If you'd have asked me if I would you take a draw, I would have to get it back to our place!"

Mellon meanwhile still stresses that the tie was far from over. He had been in football long enough to know that anything can happen. Indeed, if Rovers could come from 3-1 down at Barrow in injury time, then Aldershot had a sniff at turning this tie around with 90 minutes to play.

"I couldn't have asked for more than a 3-0 win from the first leg," he admits, "Well, other than 4-0! But I knew it wasn't over. There is an advantage given to the team who are behind.

"People don't psychologically think about it, but there is a time where they can throw everything at you and you're fighting to keep a hold of everything. It's called the kitchen sink and it becomes 'they can do that'. You know it's going to come and we knew it was going to come for 90 minutes."

James Norwood has a different take on things though. After the way Tranmere had demolished Aldershot away from home, he was confident there would be no comeback. It was job done. There was no way they were letting this lead slip, not given the quality of players in the squad and the manner in which they had been churning out results in recent weeks.

"We knew it was two legs and we knew they were coming to our place," he adds. "In that situation, in England, they say 'job's not done, anything could happen, you've got to be scared of them'. In America, it would be 'we've just battered them. They're not coming to our place and getting any more than this. We will just do them again'.

"I just wanted to say that. The tie was over. They weren't going to claw back a three goal deficit against a team who've won that many games at home and picked up so many points. Not a chance. Of course, a goal can change anything and football is weird. But that's all I wanted to say in interviews. 'Tie over. Don't bother turning up Aldershot'. It was such a good performance. We just came out of the traps and took them by surprise."

***

The return leg on the Wirral came three days later, on May 6th 2017. Micky Mellon named an unchanged starting line up and over 10,000 packed into Prenton Park, most of them supporting Tranmere as so few Aldershot fans bothered to make the trip given the result in the first game. All of those present expected to see Rovers book their first trip to Wembley since the League Cup final in 2000.

The atmosphere was absolutely electric. This was by far and away the biggest attendance of the season. Indeed, it would prove to be their largest attendance of the National League era and was only the second time they had reached five figures since a 1-0 defeat to

Notts County in 2011 - a rearranged game that was free to enter.

There were a few pre-match butterflies, naturally. Some supporters have a thing about Tranmere not doing it the easy way, so they were thoroughly expecting another emotional roller coaster over the next 90 minutes.

"Even with 3-0 coming back to Tranmere there were nerves," laughs Ben Harrison. "We were in the fan park and we couldn't serve alcohol until 11am. It was rammed. People were queueing up and everybody's face told you 'I haven't slept, I need a drink!'"

Rovers however had history on their side. Since the play-offs were introduced into the Football League and National League, no team had blown a 3-0 lead from the first leg.

That advantage became 4-0 after half an hour when Stockton scored again, curling home from close range after being picked out by Maynard, who had done well to get Davies' long clearance under control.

Prenton Park erupted and that should have been game over, but the crowd had their spirits dampened moments before half time when Mensah beautifully found the top corner with a shot from 25-yards. It was a terrific finish, but he could have been closed down more quickly, whilst Rovers had failed to react to a hastily taken free kick.

"I knew before the match started that we had to score," says Mellon. "We did, but then we gave away a goal just before half time to make it 4-1 on aggregate. There was no need to give it away.

"The game was over. We were cruising. At 4-0 it was done and gone. I'd have got them in at half time, we'd have spoken about the first 20 minutes and it would have been done. But we gave them a glimmer."

With that shred of hope, Aldershot came out for the second half all guns blazing and they got a second when Matt McClure wriggled clear of his man to divert a corner into the roof of the net from close range. There were still 40 minutes left to play. 4-2. There was still a chance.

McClure soon had another opportunity, aiming for the bottom corner from 20-yards only for Davies to block, whilst the 'keeper then made a stunning save to deny Callum Reynolds, arching his back to claw a back post header away from the goal line.

The visitors were piling men forward desperately and that meant they were always open to the counter attack. Norwood duly finished them off once and for all in injury time when he slid home from close range to make it 2-2 on the day and 5-2 on aggregate. Game. Over.

"It's fantastic that we'll get the opportunity to fight for the last place out of the division," beamed Mellon at full-time. "It's incredible for us. We're going to enjoy the fact that we've got to Wembley, but very quickly get back down to earth and prepare for an unbelievable final.

"We had a game plan and knew that we had ourselves in front. There was no need to panic. We did the job we needed to. To get the first goal was great for us and to lose to one a minute before half time was disappointing. But if somebody had offered me the same lead at half-time, I'd have taken it.

"Every credit to Aldershot. They had a right good go at it and threw everything at us. It made for an exciting game but it's certainly not the way you want to live the rest of your life! We're just delighted that we've seen it through. It's a day that'll live in the memory for a long time."

The goal was Norwood's sixteenth of the season and his fifth in four matches. His form towards the end of the campaign was sensational, and it was important, if only for confidence, that he managed to eventually put things to bed. He insists he was never concerned about a comeback though.

"I wasn't worried, even when they were 2-1 up," he says. "They had to score two more. If they got one more, we had three players up front who would score. If you push, we'll score. It never once worried me.

"With a two goal cushion and 20 minutes to go, there wasn't a chance. Not against the team we had. That's no disrespect to Aldershot. That's my interpretation of how good a team we were. You could have put us against anyone with a 3-0 lead, playing the way we were, nobody was coming back. We were that good a team."

Mellon, however, adds: "When they got the second, the crowd got nervous and it gets to the players. I knew we were going to have to score. I always thought we would catch them at some stage because we were too quick on the break.

"We were compact, working hard in every area, and I knew we would catch them. I was sure that we were going to catch them. Thankfully we did and when we scored, we knew we were through.

"You could tell with the way the atmosphere changed and the body language of the Aldershot players. They were gone. That was too much for them to take. It finished 2-2 and was a good game and we're off to Wembley."

The scenes in the fan park behind the Main Stand after the game were jubilant. It was absolutely rammed. Supporters, former players and current club employees alike flocked there to join in the celebrations as Tranmere prepared to visit the national stadium for the first time in seventeen years.

Everybody wanted a piece of the action. After so long with nothing to cheer about, people were determined to enjoy the moment. And why not? These supporters had been starved of success.

Shaun Garnett, first team coach but also a stalwart of Johnny King's side in the early 90s and member of the Tranmere team who won the Leyland DAF at Wembley in 1990, was one of those in there.

"We had lost the togetherness with the fans," he explained, "But Micky Mellon, and Gary Brabin before him, have started to knit that back together. I thought the best way to implement this was to go and have a few drinks, hence an hour later I'm in the middle of it singing 'Oh Birkenhead is wonderful!'

"I don't do social networks, but I got up on Sunday morning and I must have had about 30 texts and whatever showing me this video of me singing, then another of me banging the drums. I was cringing! But if we get a result on Sunday, I can see similar behaviour from me!"

Some supporters have since criticised the celebrations, saying they were too much. They argued Tranmere had not achieved anything yet and as such they were over the top. They still had to win another game before achieving their goal. Ben Harrison strongly disagrees.

"I've got a good friend who's a Liverpool fan," he says. "He says you don't not celebrate a semi-final win, because if you got to the final and lose, you can't go back and celebrate it.

"Mark and Nicola have always been wary of celebrating getting to Wembley, but it had been 17 years! We are just about to do a T-Shirt with the nine Wembley tickets on. Two have been in the last 12 months. Before that it was the Worthington Cup. It makes you realise how fantastic the last two years have been.

"Eddie Bishop came into the tent, Chris Malkin too and it wasn't forced. It wasn't 'you come in at this time'. It was just somewhere everyone went and we sold every available beer we had.

"Two hours after the game it was still getting busier. People were ringing their mates and saying 'come here now, such and such is in here'. Did we celebrate it too much? I think it was just the feeling that Tranmere were back achieving something."

Despite all the euphoria, there was one man in tears because he knew he was set to miss out on it all. James Wallace had been imperious in the first leg, putting in his best performance since returning to Prenton Park earlier on in the season.

He was just beginning to find his feet again in what was just his tenth appearance of the campaign. He had been blighted by a couple of niggling injuries, but this was his fifth game since mid-April, and he was getting better with each match.

However, with 21 minutes to go and after another dominant display, the midfielder limped off. The distress he was under was clear to see as tears dribbled down his cheeks. Wallace had just torn his cruciate knee ligaments again. Even then he knew it. He had felt this pain before.

Mellon remained coy at full-time. He didn't want to give anything away to whoever Tranmere would play in the final, simply saying "It doesn't look good. It's probably another one on the knee injury list. We'll see how it is over the next 24 hours."

Even then, though, he knew the extent of the damage. Wallace was done for the season. Another gaping hole left in the team that was almost impossible to fill. It would, in fact, be ten months before the midfielder next took to the field.

Chapter Eighteen
Wembley Heartbreak

There was so much joy at getting back to Wembley. Tranmere fans finally had something to be proud about again. They had had years of sympathetic family members telling them it would get better soon, or suffered as friends and colleagues mocked them for the embarrassing tumble down the divisions.

Now, they had a chance to get back. A one off game at the national stadium. 90 minutes away from a return to the Football League. This was an opportunity too good to miss and for Shaun Garnett, caretaker manager alongside Alan Rogers on that fateful day at Plymouth a couple of years earlier, it was a shot at redemption.

"What has happened over the last few years really hurts," he said in the days leading up to the game. "It's probably a bit corny and easier said than done, but I was part of this club when it got relegated. I want to be part of it when it gets promoted. No matter what people say, we were all involved in that. As little or big a part as I might have had, I was at the club. We had been on a steady decline. Why that happened is for another day, but it did happen.

"Since Mark and Nicola have got hold of the club, they've turned things around. We've got a bit of stability as I see it. Now, coming out of this league, it doesn't matter if I'm the cleaner or first team coach, it's a massive game and a sense of achievement.

"It would mean the world to everyone to go up, from the people in the background like the groundsman to the young lad who works behind the bar; I could go on and on. We need to get back. I'm a supporter and also an employee. We need Football League football back at Tranmere. This is one of the biggest games in the club's history."

A day after beating Aldershot, Tranmere found out who they would be playing. Forest Green, last year's beaten finalists and the team who finished third in the division, beat Dagenham 2-0 in the second leg of their semi-final to secure their return to Wembley. The stage was set.

For the next week, the Wirral was in party mode. The rejuvenated fans were so excited about what was about to take place. Near enough 15,000 tickets were sold, roughly three times the club's average home attendance, despite a ludicrous pricing strategy that required families to remortgage their house if they fancied going.

On May 14th 2017, Tranmere returned to Wembley for the first time in 6,317 days. It had been a long wait. Since the Worthington Cup final in 2000, they had been relegated three times and qualified for the play-offs just once. The national stadium had even been rebuilt.

It was a lean spell, and plenty of fans fell by the wayside in the intervening years. Some had had their love for the club rekindled since the arrival of Mark and Nicola Palios though, and plenty of success-starved fans went through a huge effort to be at Wembley, flying in from far off lands like Australia, Thailand and Mexico.

It was a big deal. Everybody was full of anticipation. Given the way Rovers had finished the season and the manner in which they had destroyed Aldershot in the play-offs, there was almost an expectation that they were going to win this game as well.

"It was great to be going back there," recalls Ben Harrison, one of the many who found himself on Wembley Way before the game. "Obviously it's been redone since we were last there. We went down on the Saturday night and made a weekend of it. It was a great weekend."

The team made a weekend of it too. Some had not played at Wembley before, so after completing their media duties on Friday, two days before the fixture, Tranmere travelled down to London. They trained at Barnet on Saturday and even went to watch the

Women's FA Cup Final in the afternoon.

Subconsciously, perhaps this turned the occasion into more than just a game for them as well. They got new embroidered shirts and tracksuits and the whole experience felt like a day out. They did not take their eye off the ball, far from it, but several members of the squad would admit now that qualifying for the final felt like a huge deal in itself.

***

The injury that James Wallace picked up against Aldershot provided a real dilemma for Micky Mellon. The manager was already missing several key players, with Jay Harris and Steven Jennings also absent in midfield because of knee problems. On top of that, Ritchie Sutton was out due to his Achilles, Lee Vaughan and Jake Kirby had broken legs, Adam Mekki had a knee injury, Ben Tollitt was still out and Mitch Duggan was suspended after being sent off whilst on loan at Warrington.

There were nine absentees in total. It was a ridiculous list. Mellon was well and truly running out of players by the time he got to Wembley and some of them were irreplaceable. No club in the National League would have been able to cope with such problems.

It meant that the manager was forced to change his starting line up, shifting some players out of position. With Wallace missing, striker Andy Mangan, who had not started a game in exactly two months due to the form of James Norwood, Cole Stockton and Andy Cook, was one of those, shifted from his natural role upfront to the right wing.

Other injuries had taken their toll too. Rovers' form had been exceptional towards the back end of the campaign when they had been employing a 3-5-2 formation with Lee Vaughan at wing-back. With him and Sutton out, there were not enough defenders, so

Mellon had to switch to 4-4-2.

With Harris and Steven Jennings injured, Connor Jennings had to play in central-midfield, as opposed to in the hole just behind the striker where he had had so much success and scored bags of goals. It was a makeshift team.

"We limped into that final," says Mark Palios. "I'm not sure Andy Mangan had ever played right wing before that match. I did say to Nicky several times 'I've never really been lucky in football' and she says 'I wish you'd told me that before we bought the club!' That was how it was panning out.

"I think we had eight injuries, of which six would have played. It was of that ilk. We'd lost almost half our team. We were running on empty in the final and I felt a bit sorry for them."

Forest Green on the other hand were at near enough full strength and with the experience of losing at Wembley to Grimsby twelve months earlier behind them, they looked a formidable - but beatable - opponent.

They started brightly, with Keanu Marsh-Brown and Liam Noble coming close before Kaiyne Woolery handed his side a 12th minute lead. The Tranmere defence backed off as he ran at them, and the invitation of shooting from distance was too good to turn down. He beat Scott Davies from 20-yards.

Rovers responded perfectly though as they equalised with their first real chance of the game through a stunning strike from Connor Jennings. The midfielder picked up possession 25-yards out and unleashed an unstoppable shot that rifled into the top corner right in front of the Super White Army. 1-1 and game on.

That was as good as it got. Norwood missed a one on one that he should have scored whilst Mangan was just a couple of inches too short as he stretched to try and tap home a cross towards the back post. Tranmere were on top but they did not make it count, and before half time they were behind.

Christian Doidge made it 2-1 when the Rovers defence again backed off and he found the far corner from 20-yards before Woolery doubled the lead, capitalising on a mistake from Liam Ridehalgh who trod on the ball near the edge of the box. The winger nipped in to steal possession and slotted under Davies.

"We just made crazy errors at crazy times," reflects Mellon. "And then we lost our way, because you're playing at Wembley and you're 3-1 down. You've lost those types of goals and you're thinking 'shit, what's happened here?'

"That's where your mentality is and it's hard to turn it around. Your family are in the stand and that play-off final, it's the most do or die football match. It's life changing.

"When you get to the next season and you're going back to the league that you've just fought so hard to get out of and you've lost it in a game, and we lost it in moments, it makes it even more difficult."

The manager got his players in at half time and they were gutted. The atmosphere in the Tranmere end had changed completely. Party mode had been well and truly turned off. Some had turned into an angry mob. But there was still a chance of turning things around.

"At half time, Micky was just telling us to believe in ourselves," says James Norwood. "We weren't getting battered. They had four shots and scored three goals. We were creating chances but we were missing them.

"So why not believe? We could have been 3-3 at half time. They only time when you go in thinking it's over is when you've been battered and you can't get out of your half. So why shouldn't we believe? We've only got to score a goal with ten or five minutes to go and then they're on the back foot. It only takes one chance."

Rovers had those opportunities after the break. The best fell to Stockton, but he missed an open goal as he spun and fired over the bar, whilst substitute Jack Dunn blasted high and wide from outside the box. Jeff Hughes also dragged a low effort past the post, but they were running out of time.

Forest Green eventually saw the game out. They did not endear themselves to the Tranmere fans with some time wasting and play acting, particularly from captain Noble who did himself no favours whatsoever, but they did not care about that. They were going to the Football League for the first time in their history.

"We didn't defend the moments well enough and got punished for it," said a glum looking Micky Mellon afterwards. "At half time, being 2-1 down was bad enough. To lose another goal and go in 3-1 down gave us an uphill battle.

"We weren't good enough today. We're really disappointed and gutted for the fans who've travelled so far and paid so much money. On the day, the better side won. Every credit to Forest Green now. We'll take our medicine, dust ourselves down and get on with things.

"I have to digest things. Emotions are very, very raw and I'm disappointed that we didn't give ourselves a chance with the poor goals we gave away."

Mellon is the kind of person who would never blame injuries for the defeat. Not in the immediate aftermath anyway. He is an honest and thought provoking character who gives credit where credit is due. Looking back on it now, he admits the selection issues did take their toll, but he still had every confidence in his side picking up the win.

"It was great to get there," he reflects. "I think it helped the club's recovery, taking us back to Wembley. I think it was important to get there because it galvanised a lot of people. Getting to Wembley, you should really appreciate it and we hadn't had anything to cheer about for a long time.

"So it was 'get your old Tranmere kit out, get your scarves on, we're going to Wembley'. It stirred up the emotions and it was an important part of the start to the recovery. I'm careful to say start, because I think we've only just started. We're still only very early with where we wanted to be, but it certainly helped.

"Because of the injuries, people were playing in positions all over the place that didn't suit us. I still thought we could win, but I probably think that all the time. That wasn't anything different. I 100% thought we could get a result. There was nothing in my mind thinking anything other than that and the preparations went well.

"When you're looking back now and you aren't emotionally involved, you know that it would not have been the team that you would have picked if you had everybody available.

"I've looked back on the game, because I comb over every match. We weren't poor. We just made individual errors at crucial times that would change any game. There were huge parts of the game before the individual errors that we were in control of.

"We had chances. We had one on ones v goalkeepers to go 2-1 up, crosses flashing across the goal for people to get on the end of and stuff. So I don't get too carried away with writing it off and saying we were poor, because that wouldn't give the players credit.

"They just lost goals and if you could pick times to lose goals, every one of them would be at the time we lost them. It would have made it difficult for any kind of character to play to his max. It was soul destroying. But they weren't as bad as what a lot of people have you believe."

Tranmere were left devastated at the result, and their fans filtered out of the stadium pretty quickly after the final whistle. Many did not want to stick around and watch Forest Green lift the trophy and bask in the glory of being promoted.

"I've tried to etch the day from my memory now," admits Ben

Harrison. "To be fair, it was a brilliant day. The whole experience was good. I was just gutted that we lost.

"I kind of thought it was going to happen. Forest Green were play acting and they were playing the ball well. At 3-1 down at half time, you thought it just wasn't our time.

"We just ran out of players. We had players playing in different positions. Cook came on but we were just going long to him. We weren't going down the wings.

"To see a club like Forest Green, who are an odd club, take our place was gutting. Coming back on the Sunday is bad too. You wake up on a Monday morning and have no time to get over it. It's horrible. I'm glad the game was on a Saturday second time around!"

For James Norwood, it was a bitter pill to swallow. There is no love lost between him and his former club. The players did not have the option of heading for the exits like the fans did. He just had to stand there and take it all in.

"Watching them walk up the Wembley steps was like watching the girl you've been talking to all night in the club walk out with somebody else," he admits. "That's probably the best way to describe it! It was heartbreaking. It was easily the worst moment of my career.

"But it also made this year so much sweeter. Without hard times, you don't appreciate the good times. If all you have is good times then you don't appreciate how good they really are. So I'm thankful we lost.

"The injuries didn't make things any tougher for us, because I know Connor Jennings and Andy Mangan have played there. It's just a case of match sharpness and who has and hasn't played at Wembley before.

"We started too slow with too many mistakes. Mistakes cost you and we didn't have much luck. There's a poor header back from Charlie Cooper and then if I hit my shot from that two inches to the right it goes it. If Kaiyne Woolery has five more shots in the game, none of them go in like that one.

"In the second half, Cole misses an open goal and has a header saved on the line. Mangy slides across and the ball goes an inch in front of his toe. We could have won that game 6-4. But tiny details didn't happen for us.

"We had the luck twelve months later. There was a handball from Eddie Clarke and Jeff Hughes could have given a penalty away as well. All games of football are decided by luck. Not how good you play. Just how's your luck."

Mark Palios was equally as gutted. He had made the bold call of replacing Gary Brabin in September and it had worked. Micky Mellon had galvanised the team and the supporters, and with largely the same group of players he had picked up a club record haul of 95 points and guided them back to Wembley.

That Forest Green game just proved a step too far though. The injuries were so costly. Nine absentees. Even adding one of them back in makes a huge difference. As it was, though, Tranmere were facing a third season in the National League.

"I was flat after the Forest Green game," admits the chairman. "We had the chances to turn it around. If James Norwood had scored... 'if Nors had scored', that's what we used to say... unfortunately for Liam Ridehalgh, he treads on the ball five minutes before half time and that gives us a huge difficultly.

"I still thought we'd get a chance. They lost their ambition once they went 3-1 up. If we got a chance, it would make it 3-2 and then all kind of things could happen. We did get one, Cole Stockton got one and put it over the bar. That was the chance gone then.

"After the game, you just get on with the job. It's easier for me, because I knew what I was going to do on Sunday and by Monday morning I was doing it. I was working on the plans to get us up this season."

Chapter Nineteen
Handling Disappointment

Tranmere fans are used to a disappointing climax to the season. They knew how to handle such situations because they had been through it all before. All things told, this was the fifth campaign in a row where they had ultimately failed to achieve their goal.

Firstly, there was the promotion push under Ronnie Moore in 2012/13 that collapsed so badly and resulted in a six game run without a goal at the end. Then came the consecutive relegations from League One to League Two and League Two to the National League.

The hope was that such disappointments would be left behind by the time Rovers ended up in the fifth tier, but of course they narrowly missed out on making the play-offs in their first season down there, and then suffered this heartbreaking defeat to Forest Green.

It was gutting, especially for Micky Mellon. He had put all his eggs in one basket by coming back to Tranmere, a club he held so closely to his heart. He had dropped two leagues in order to try and help them back to where he felt they belonged.

As a manager, the Scotsman has enjoyed huge success. The three promotions he achieved before coming to Tranmere show that. He was not used to this feeling. He had never suffered something like this, and he admits now that it took him to a dark, dark place.

"It's the most disappointing moment of my managerial career without a doubt," he reveals. "It was a hammer blow. It did damage to me emotionally and mentally. There's no doubt about that. I can be open and honest about it.

"It still, even to this day, scares me of where it took me. I'm usually quite a happy-go-lucky Glaswegian from Paisley type of fellow who just gets on with things. I go again. But that took me to a place where I didn't know you could go for a long, long time.

"The disappointment of that was massive. To know that you can go to those places is not nice and a lot of people got taken there. Coming back on the bus was the worst journey I've ever had. John the bus driver just turned the lights down. There was no music. For four and a half hours, nobody spoke. Some people just had their head in their hands on the table.

"We got to the other end, got off the bus and the fans were all starting to arrive. I don't think anybody spoke. I didn't say anything to anybody. I got in my car and just went home and had a really tough summer."

It is refreshing to hear the manager talk so candidly about what he went through after that game. People often forget what the individuals involved in success or failure are going through mentally. Perhaps this highlights why what happened twelve months later felt so good to him.

For Mark Palios, the rebuilding job started immediately. Budgets had to be put in place for the forthcoming season, but the club would now miss out on significant funding due to being outside of the Football League. Parachute payments disappeared, and they would also now lose their academy status and the money that came with it.

"You've got to write the pieces to keep the people focused and not too down, plus you've got to be fair," he said. "I think I said in a statement that we were second best on the day, but hey, you carry on.

"We came back with massive disappointment, and by 11 o'clock on the Monday, I was literally working on the restructuring plan in the office. I knew roughly what we were going to do if we stayed down, but I was doing it in detail.

"Most of the fans have to have faith. They can't have an influence on anything most of the time. They don't know what's going on, whereas I can get away from the stress because I'm working on something. Over the summer, those fans were great. They stayed with the club."

The morning after the Forest Green defeat, Palios released a heartfelt statement about working towards the 2017/18 season and how the club could turn this gut wrenching feeling around as quickly as possible.

"After a bitterly disappointing day yesterday it is time to take stock and reflect on the season that has just ended," he said. "There is no glossing over the fact that the season has not ended how we wanted it to. A single 90 minute game will always have an element of lottery to it, but on the day Forest Green were better than us. They clinically took their chances and were deserved victors.

"It was always going to be a tough ask to lift the trophy with so many of our regular first team players out injured and to some extent those injuries caught up with us yesterday. But that is the nature of football and it can be cruel sometimes.

"But we should also balance the disappointment with pride in many other aspects of what we have done on the pitch this year. We ended the season with a club record 95 points - more than 2 points a game. In any other division that would have won automatic promotion. We reached the semi-finals of the FA Trophy and the play-off final, earning the club's first trip to Wembley in 17 years.

"There have been some memorable games along the way - the 9-0 thrashing of Solihull Moors, the excellent performance in the first leg of our tough play off semi-final against Aldershot and the outstanding performance of our youngsters to take the victory at Maidstone.

"But it isn't just what we have achieved, but the way we have done it, which has been striking. The atmosphere at games - particularly in the last 3 months - has also been incredible. The sense of togetherness with the fans away at Wrexham, Chester, Aldershot and Maidstone was something quite special, and we have shown we can make Prenton Park a fortress again.

"Micky, Nicky and I had last night to lick our wounds but this morning we have dusted ourselves off and started the important business of building on this year, to do everything we can to make sure we go one step better next year and secure our return to the Football League.

"One year ago today, Forest Green were licking their wounds having lost the play-off final, and today they are celebrating promotion. Everyone working at the club will be focused on making sure that next year it is us celebrating."

Little did he know at the time how accurate that statement would prove to be.

***

The 2017 summer was completely different to the one twelve months earlier. For starters, there was no pressure on the manager's position whatsoever. Whereas the year before, speculation had spread that Gary Brabin might be replaced after missing out on the play-offs, there was no chance, quite rightly, that Micky Mellon was going anywhere.

He had come in and done a terrific job with this group of players. He had found a way to get them consistently scoring much more goals than under Brabin. They were playing at a higher tempo with a much better intensity and had also displayed a willingness to get in the opposition box as much as possible.

In Andy Cook and James Norwood, the manager also had arguably the best strike force in the division at his disposal. The former finished the campaign with 23 strikes in the league, whilst the latter added another 16. A phenomenal return.

Another thing different to the previous summer was the turnover in players. Mark Palios had highlighted how at the end of Gary Brabin's only full season in charge, he felt they just needed to add a couple of new signings to the squad to give them the firepower they needed for a promotion challenge. That was when Cook and Connor Jennings arrived.

He was proved correct over the following nine months, but Micky Mellon decided he wanted to make a few changes to the squad. The likes of Lee Vaughan, Steven Jennings, Adam Mekki and Darren Stephenson all moved on, whilst Jack Dunn was tied down to a permanent deal after his loan spell from Liverpool.

A further three players left the club who the manager wanted to keep. Centre back Michael Ihiekwe signed for Rotherham on a free transfer, three years after coming to Prenton Park from Wolves. He had clearly improved during his time with the club, especially playing alongside Steve McNulty, and had earned his move to League One.

Cole Stockton also decided it was time to cut his ties with Tranmere and he left for Scotland where Hearts had offered him a two-year deal. The striker had come through the youth set up at Prenton Park but had endured a fractious relationship with the club's fans. Indeed, most thought he would not play for them again after he was sent out on loan to Morecambe, but Mellon convinced him to return - and he proved a success.

Lastly, there was Lois Maynard, arguably making the strangest of the trio of transfers as he stepped down a division to sign for Salford City. Perhaps being a Manchester United fan helped make up his mind, as the National League North club are owned by the 'Class of 92' - Gary and Phillip Neville, Paul Scholes, Ryan Giggs and Nicky Butt.

The midfielder had been a key player for Rovers over the previous two seasons. His height made him a valuable person to have in both boxes, and although he was not always the most elegant of players, he had the ability to grab the game by the scruff of the neck and drag his teammates forward thirty yards. It was that kind of thrusting burst that they would miss at the start of the following season.

In terms of incoming transfers, Chester's top scorer James Alabi was snapped up after Mellon missed out on Paul Mullin, who joined Swindon from Morecambe, whilst Ollie Norburn, fresh from knocking Tranmere out of the FA Trophy, arrived from Macclesfield.

The other new faces were Jay McEveley, an experienced former Scotland defender from Ross County and striker George Waring, who had been released by Stoke but had worked under Mellon during his time at Shrewsbury. Elliot Rokka also joined the club on a one-year deal from Radcliffe Borough, but he was always seen as a youngster who needed developing as opposed to a first choice winger.

Despite such an upheaval that summer, Tranmere only ended up playing three pre-season friendlies. These were against Cammell Laird, a fixture in which Alabi netted five times, League One side Fleetwood, who Rovers beat 3-1, and the traditional summer curtain raiser versus Liverpool. A fourth match, against Bury, was scheduled, but got cancelled due to heavy rain on the Wirral.

Season 3
2017/18

175

Chapter Twenty
A Slow Start

After their impressive 2016/17 campaign, it was no surprise that Tranmere went into the following season as one of the most fancied teams to win promotion. Indeed, they were the favourites to land the title with most betting firms, and as short as 2/1 to go up.

The disappointment of the defeat to Forest Green appeared to have been shaken off. With the new signings on board, the fans were confident. In their eyes, it was not a case of this 'could' be Rovers' year, but it 'should' be. They were eager for the action to start, and so were the squad and coaching staff.

"You've really got to question yourself if you don't get excited about an upcoming season," said Micky Mellon on the eve of the opening game down at Torquay. "I love it. I'm looking forward to getting going.

"We've worked hard all through pre-season and we've got a full squad to pick from for the game on Saturday, which I always look at as being a success for pre-season, because you want to have them all available. You don't want to over do it in the six weeks. So by looking at them, I'd say we're good to go.

"It's always been a tough league, but we know that we can be very competitive in it. We have high expectations of ourselves and are looking forward to getting going now. We've worked hard. There's no excuses.

"We believe we've brought in good quality players who will help replace the ones who have left and continue to move the club forward. The evidence so far is very, very good.

"We know what it felt like and how tough the summer was following the Forest Green game. We were able to recover together and work together and if we need to refer back to that at anytime to try and get results for the club, we'll psychologically turn that around.

"We're determined that we're going to go one further this time. Since I came in, it was all about trying to add to the great work that Gary Brabin had done, first of all in stopping it's demise and then moving it forward. I was able to pick up from there and add my little bit of spin to it. There's been a lot of change. Tranmere's a very different place all the time. We're building on that."

Unfortunately, things did not go to plan. They kicked off the season with a 0-0 draw at Torquay on August 5th and finished the match with nine men because Steve McNulty, now the club captain after Steven Jennings' departure, and James Norwood were sent off.

It did not take them long to chalk up a first victory of the campaign though as Woking were hammered at Prenton Park just a few days later. Andy Cook, restored to the starting line up after James Alabi was favoured at Plainmoor, got the first early on as Tranmere won 3-1, with Ollie Norburn and Jay McEveley also on target.

It was a huge improvement on the opening day action. Rovers were clinical and despite conceding just before half-time, they sauntered clear of their opponents after the break to seal the three points.

"We played well with and without the ball," said Mellon afterwards. "We looked fit and sharp. At this time of the season, I still expect us to improve. They've played very, very well and it's a good result.

"We want to go out and pass the ball and run hard to get it back. That's what the demands are here at Tranmere. Of course, now the standards have been set. We need to maintain them and try and get better all the time. But we won't get carried away. It was a hard game and we fought hard. We deserved to get the result."

The manager meanwhile also had some special praise for Cook, who took his goal in a tidy manner. The striker got lucky when the ball bounced off his chest and landed fortuitously in his path, but it was all class from then on as he waited for the precise moment to pass into the back of the net, urging the 'keeper to make his move before picking his spot.

"Andy Cook has worked really hard in pre-season," Mellon continued. "He's arguably as fit as he's ever been and you can see that in the way he plays. He's looking in great shape. He's obviously very determined and he loves scoring goals. I'm pleased to see him score."

Four points from two games was a decent enough start to the season. Most fans would have taken that if they had been offered it just before the fixture at Torquay kicked off. But unfortunately, things went downhill remarkably quickly as the wheels started to fall off Tranmere's promotion push.

A 1-0 defeat at Sutton followed, and then a 0-0 draw at Guiseley where Tranmere somehow failed to hit the back of the net. They had plenty of chances to win it, with Cook missing an open goal and Jack Dunn firing straight at the 'keeper when Cook put the ball on a plate for him in the closing stages.

They had now only scored in one of their opening four matches, and Mellon is just as exasperated when he looks back on the latter of those matches now as he was at full time.

"Chances can change a season," he said. "I don't want to name people, but Jack Dunn had a one v one with the goalkeeper and puts it straight at him. He ran down the middle from the half way line and missed it. Nobody could believe it.

"I was just thinking 'what is going on here?' That's the way the season was going. We just kept saying that our luck would change but it was the players' mentality to the chances that changed. They just knew the responsibility that they had and concentrated on things more."

Next came a 2-0 defeat away to Eastleigh, another fixture without scoring, and things were looking pretty bleak against Boreham Wood a week later when Tranmere were trailing 2-0 with just 10 minutes left.

On came Cook, replacing James Alabi who had been preferred up front, and Andy Mangan. They both scored as the hosts picked up a 2-2 draw. It looked like a turning point. Rovers were finally scoring and the hope was that they would now kick on.

"From the position we were in, to get something out of it, we're pleased with that," said Mellon. "But overall, having to score three goals at home to win a game leaves us with an awful lot to do.

"We know that we have to dig out a result when you're in the situation we're in. At a club like Tranmere, the expectancy levels are so high. Hopefully that's a turning point. To come from 2-0 down so late in the game and to get something out of the game, the lads deserve a lot of credit for that."

At last Rovers had some momentum behind them. Next up was a trip to Solihull, the team they had battered 9-0 just a handful of months earlier, on the August Bank Holiday Monday. In true National League fashion, kick off was delayed when Scott Davies noticed the net in his goal had not been put up correctly. Jay McEveley jumped on his shoulders to fix it, much to the amusement of the fans in attendance.

When the match eventually got underway, there was an immediate improvement. Tranmere had a bit of swagger and confidence about them and they ran out 2-0 winners. Cook was again on target, grabbing his third of the season, whilst Ollie Norburn opened the scoring in the first half.

It was just what the doctor ordered. Finally, Rovers were moving up the National League table. "It's a very important win," Mellon admitted at full time. "We came here to get a result. We'd have to say, to be fair to us as a group, that we've played much, much better, even this season, and got nothing.

"We had some one v ones with the goalkeepers that on another day we will need to take. But I've been through it myself in these situations. We need to win games. We need to get going again. When you get your nose in front, you're looking for the finishing line. That's what we did.

"I think we comfortably saw it out defensively in the end. I don't really remember Scott having a save to make. So every credit to them. They did what they needed to do and got us over the line and got us a really valuable three points that gives us four from the weekend."

The win at Solihull proved to be a false dawn. Dover were the next team to come to Prenton Park and Tranmere again failed to score as they were beaten 1-0 thanks to Ryan Bird netting the winner deep into the second half.

The tables were turned a week later when Barrow visited the Wirral. This time it was Rovers who left it late as James Norwood bagged his first goal of the campaign in the 90th minute. The hosts won 1-0 and again had some momentum to capitalise on.

Unfortunately, however, they once more failed to seize that chance. Harry Pritchard scored an 88th minute goal to earn Maidenhead a 1-0 win over Micky Mellon's side three days later, and that was followed by a 0-0 draw at Ebbsfleet, a match in which Jay McEveley was sent off. The latter of those fixtures was Tranmere's 11th of the season. They had already failed to score in seven games.

"People say there was a hangover from Wembley," says James Norwood. "Maybe there was subconsciously. I watch the highlights all the time and this is no disrespect to the gaffer whatsoever, but we didn't have a settled team or formation. Myself and Cooky only started three of the first fifteen games together.

"The team that started our run in the autumn would have beaten the team that started the season 5 or 6-0. They wouldn't have had a prayer. That wasn't down to confidence or anything. It was finding a way to play to our strengths. Once we did that, we won games. It was just finding a way that nobody could stop."

Mellon on the other hand insists there was no hangover from losing to Forest Green just a handful of months earlier. Indeed, he knows exactly why things were not going their way in terms of points.

"I just think we didn't take our chances," he argues. "We had more chances in those first ten or so games than at any other stage of the season. We've got the statistics to back that up. We missed too many chances. I'm not just talking half chances or making excuses. I'm talking one v ones with goalkeepers, side footers in front of goal and all the rest of it.

"We had a meeting after ten games and we said 'right, come on, shut the doors. What's going on?' There was a lot of frustration and anger. The answer was 'we're not scoring goals and we're not taking our chances'. It was nothing to do with anything else other than that.

"We were probably, I think, over playing. We were passing it too much and we weren't making teams defend enough. When we had the opportunity to take on a risky pass, we weren't taking it. We tweaked that a little bit and decided that we were going to tweak the way we were playing. But believe it or not, we didn't have as much control in the games.

"We weren't passing the ball as many times or defending by keeping the ball under control. There were a lot more turnovers because we were going forward a lot quicker.

"The chances to goal ratio went right down though, ridiculously down. The two strikers started to score, and between the two of them, at least one of them scored in nearly every game. If you're going to do that in a game of football, you're going to have a chance. That's all that changed.

"Was there a hangover? I think we were devastated or gutted or whatever about being back in the league, but we were determined to make it right the following season. There was no doubt about that. But we were getting angrier and angrier about the chances we were missing.

"People have got short memories but I can remember being in games and having interviews with the media and we were laughing at the chances we were missing. It was getting to a point where the crowd were in disbelief at the amount of chances we missed."

Norwood was one of the people not finding the back of the net. Indeed, his goal against Barrow was his sole strike in the opening eight weeks of the season, although the suspension resulting from his sending off at Torquay had given him a stuttering start to the campaign.

The striker is not totally convinced that they were getting enough chances in front of goal though. There was a lot of pressure on him, Cook and Alabi to be finishing things off, but he says the supply line was the problem.

"Cooky and I travelled in together and we are really good friends," he says. "We were talking all the time and we didn't think we were getting enough chances. We were getting some good ones, but not as many as we should have been.

"That's when pressure mounts. You're the ones who get blamed. Even if you lose 2-0, it's because the striker didn't score. You could have made the game easier by scoring a chance. Us strikers are just saying 'keep the ball out of the back of the net, it's not difficult!'

"You start to get that divide between the attackers and defenders. Then we found a way. From November, after a game against Gateshead, we scored in every league game. It's a club record run and it's still going."

The disappointment of the previous year was always going to impact

Tranmere somehow though, and Ben Harrison points out that they are not the only team to struggle in a new campaign, just months after missing out on promotion.

"One of the Wrexham directors said to us that when they went neck and neck with Fleetwood a few years earlier and missed out, they were garbage at the start of the next season," he says. "We weren't garbage. We just weren't picking up results. Mark Palios jokingly said to me 'I'm glad they extended the play-offs to seventh place!'

"They were unlucky though. There was a 1-0 defeat at Maidenhead and that was the only time they didn't turn up. Sometimes you just go through those periods and you have to stick with it. I'm not a tactical genius, but we were narrow. You need width in the National League.

"The lack of goals was frightening. At times, you've seen plenty of teams carry that form on through the season and end up in mid-table. There was never a stage where the fans turned on Micky Mellon though. The majority didn't want to get rid of him."

Chapter Twenty One
Another Wrexham Defeat

The pressure by now was cranking up on Micky Mellon. Drawing with Ebbsfleet had left Tranmere in 17th place in the National League, only five points off the top seven, but also the same distance from the final relegation spot, occupied by Chester.

If Rovers could take any consolation from their poor start, it was the fact that nobody was running away with the division. In previous years, somebody had often pulled away from the pack by now. For example, Forest Green won their opening ten games in the 2015/16 campaign, whilst Tranmere had been amongst the pace setters twelve months later.

This year, nobody had pulled away. Aldershot and Dover topped the table on 20 points, but they were only one win ahead of Boreham Wood and Macclesfield who sat in 11th and 12th. It was incredibly compact, and highlighted how even the division would be over the course of the season.

Given their form, the last thing Rovers needed was the visit of a high flying local rival. That is exactly what their next game was though, as Wrexham arrived at Prenton Park looking to close the two point gap between themselves and top spot.

Mellon needed a win. He needed Tranmere's season to finally kick on. He needed his players to start finding the back of the net. James Alabi started up front instead of Andy Cook, but it was partner James Norwood who had the first chance, finding the side netting with a cheeky back heel.

It was a positive start for the hosts, who soon had a one man advantage after Wrexham's Sam Wedgbury, who had played against them for Forest Green at Wembley, was sent off. Inexplicably, the midfielder picked up his second yellow card in just the 13th minute for a senseless tackle on Jay Harris.

Being reduced to ten men made Wrexham much more compact. It did not seem to be a disadvantage to them. Sure, Tranmere had chances, with Harris smashing against the post and Alabi having a shot saved, but it was the same old story for Rovers. They were not clinical enough in front of goal. Connor Jennings headed wide after the break and then Alabi actually found the back of the net, only for the strike to be ruled out for offside.

With each chance Rovers missed, the visitors were growing in confidence, and they duly delivered a hammer blow by taking the lead on the hour mark. They got a corner that was poorly defended, and the ball eventually fell to Chris Holroyd who slammed past Scott Davies.

1-0. Game over. Wrexham were never losing from that position. Tranmere's heads had dropped. The home crowd were getting angrier and angrier, much to the delight of the 1,000 fans who had made the trip over the Welsh border.

It was a tough day for Mellon. Even now he cannot believe his side lost, questioning: "How many chances did we miss that day? We had total domination. They went down to ten men and I thought we had to score, but we were in control. You couldn't tell me that we weren't. We were in complete control.

"We had the ball all the time with chance after chance. The 'keeper has made some brilliant saves, fair play to him, and they're getting blocks in, but it's like The Alamo. It was just the story of what was happening in those first ten games.

"They then got a set play and we looked nervy, because when you're a footballer or a fan, you think you're going to get sucker punched. If you don't take your chances, you're going to give the opposition hope. You're going to get sucker punched.

"It came midway through the second half and it was scrappy. It goes in and I just couldn't believe what was happening. I couldn't catch my breath. But we never really got carried away and the owner has to take an awful lot of credit. He had seen what we were seeing. We highlighted it and said 'watch the chances' and he replied 'I see it'. It got him more frustrated because he could see everything else that we were doing. That typified it."

The full time whistle was met with a cacophony of boos. Some supporters called for Mellon to be sacked. Tranmere had sunk to 18th place in the table and were only a couple of points above the relegation zone. This was not the position anybody had expected them to be in.

Mark Palios, however, was not about to make another managerial change. Twelve months earlier, he had decided to sack Gary Brabin, who had a much better start to the season. But he could see what was happening on the pitch. Rovers were having chances, but their finishing was truly awful. All they needed to do was start putting the ball in the back of the net.

"The 1-0 defeat to Wrexham was probably the nadir of the season for me," he admits. "Partly because it was Wrexham, but then secondly because it was a replication of the result two seasons earlier at Prenton Park. To lose against ten men worried me, because although we created chances and should have won the game, we were missing them. That was a difficult time.

"Micky's position wasn't under threat after that though. We were creating chances and there wasn't a massive gap appearing at the top. Plus, you don't become a bad manager overnight. I work with managers, rather than just say 'oh, there's a bit of pressure, throw him to the fans', because the fans would have wanted him out.

"My view is who do you bring in? The new man might say 'there are certain players I don't want in my team'. We were creating chances but not scoring them. We were playing some good stuff. That to me was the bright spot in it.

"So my view was don't turn a disappointment into a crisis. Yes, it was a disappointment for everybody because the expectation was so high, but we didn't want to turn it into a crisis. So I worked with Micky. We spent hours on the phone and talked things through. He needed support.

"I think he is one of the best managers around when it comes to tactics and he works very hard. Of those I've seen, he's probably the hardest working. All of his staff stay behind and they look at this and that and ways to get edges and stuff. They think about things quite deeply.

"Yes, I can probably get lots of fans who'd do that. Lots of managers can pick a player, but then lots of fans can pick a player too. Can you put it together as a team? Not necessarily. Micky can do that. What his real strength is, I felt, is he can change things tactically at the right time in a game.

"The biggest thing for me was that I thought he was a good manager as he could tactically change things. It was just a question of working with him. I wasn't giving him deadlines and saying 'you've got to do this by then' because they're pointless. The guy's already motivated.

"You're asking how you can fix it and help it. You look at all the things you can do in a holistic way. I considered a psychologist, and I am a psychologist originally by training, so I'm more cautious about them than most, but from that you're thinking about getting people's attitudes right, focusing on the next goal, the one after that and stuff like that. We worked on a lot of things like that together. We chatted through things, such as the shape of the team and the players we had."

Mellon did not feel as if there was a threat to his job either. Despite the shocking start - just three wins in twelve matches, eight of which Tranmere had failed to score in - he believed the chairman was content with the job he was doing. It would all turn around soon.

"I don't really feel under pressure," he insists. "I just feel the responsibility of fixing and making sure I know what it is. I never feel pressure, because if you're not good enough, you get what you deserve in football. As long as I know what it is that we have to get better at, or the mistakes that are getting made, I wouldn't say I'm comfortable with it but that's what you've got to do.

"'Just put the ball in the net'. That's all we were saying. It got to a point where we thought 'stop talking all the shit and just do us a favour. Put the ball in the fucking net. When the chance comes, just put it in. That's it! You're doing everything else right!'

"That was it. Because then everybody started questioning everything else. We were doing everything else. It was functioning well and we were creating the chances. It was just putting it in the net. Give yourself a chance. Score first, change the game and then we'll move forward from there."

When mentioning the Wrexham game to James Norwood, a smile of disbelief spreads across his face. With each passing moment, he remembers another incident in a match that his side should have won, but ultimately summed up the start to the campaign perfectly.

"That game - Oh my God," he says. "It was a disgrace. I've never seen that many shots on an opposition goal and they just didn't go in. It was getting to a point where it was stupid. It wasn't even bad finishing. It was good finishing but a great save. It was a disgrace.

"I came off after the Wrexham game thinking I should have scored five, and the 'keeper is wondering how he's kept a clean sheet. Chris Holroyd scored with a left footed shot and it was the biggest smash and grab ever. There was a lot of pressure on the manager after that game."

It was another strong call from Palios to stand alongside Mellon. The fans are eternally grateful now, but some would have been quite happy to have seen the back of him. Not Ben Harrison though, who is thankful that the chairman decided to stick instead of twist.

"Mark and Nicola were brave," he admits. "They came into the fan park after the Wrexham game and Mark needed a chaperon to tell him when to leave. Some of the fans were very disappointed after being beaten by our rivals, who only had ten men. But sometimes that can work in your favour - look at us against Boreham Wood. It galvanised Wrexham in that game.

"There were flashes of the Gary Brabin FA Trophy defeat, but it comes back to the loyalty. Sometimes you stick by people. It's been proven correct. We just hadn't clicked and had players who weren't performing.

"The Wrexham directors were having a party. I know one of them, who lives in Birkenhead, and she said 'what a great day'. I reminded her of that comment when they didn't even make the play-offs.

"We didn't speak to Mark or Nicola about Micky's position. We got to know each other well enough to know it wasn't a crisis. If it had carried on then yes, it would have been as we wouldn't have made the play-offs. Maybe it was a turning point because it got them out of feeling sorry for themselves."

***

When things are not going well in football, rumours start to spread like wildfire. Usually it is about the manager's position, but, oddly, that was not the case after Tranmere's start to the season.

Instead, supporters were beginning to question who the club had signed in the summer. Of the pre-season arrivals, only Ollie Norburn had proved to be a success, grabbing crucial goals against Solihull and Woking, two of the three victories so far.

Jay McEveley had struggled to settle in defence and did not really get back into the team after his sending off at Ebbsfleet whilst James Alabi on the other hand was in and out of the side and would eventually be shipped out on loan to Dover in mid-October having failed to break his goalscoring duck.

Speculation was growing that the players who had been signed were not brought in by Mellon. Palios though has moved to quash such rumours. "For me, there are various things I do around the club," he says. "If we've got the football side of things right, I can leave it alone, leave that plate spinning and get on to something else, such as international business which is something I have to spend a lot of time on.

"But then we get into August and we're 19th. By September we were 18th. I spent a lot of time with Micky talking things through and I'll scotch the rumours, I don't sign players. Whether I agree with a player, technically or not, I'll put my comments in, but Micky signs all his players and he picks his players.

"I'll make a point of not ringing him the day before a game at all. I never ask him what his team is. He may tell me, but I never ask him and I rarely ring him straight after a game. I leave that period to him. Then we'll talk about issues technically and so forth, because everybody's got an opinion.

"I've got 400 games under my belt, so I know the dressing room. We do have conversations like that, and I just challenge him. He makes the final decision though. It's like any business. If I had an engineering business, I'd talk to the director, but if that was his competency, at the end of the day, he makes the decision. That's the technical aspect of the business."

Mellon, meanwhile, always believed that he had the required tools available to mount a promotion push, despite where they were languishing in the table. Following the Wrexham defeat, he was asked whether his squad was capable of turning things around, and it was an easy answer.

"I believe in them," he said. "I believe in the group. There isn't a lot different from last season, the team that was so rampant last year.

There haven't been many or any changes to that. I think it's just a team lacking heavily in confidence at the minute. I think that shows when the first little bit of disappointment goes against us or frustration creeps in.

"That's what happens to human beings. It's frustrating for us all, especially us standing on the sidelines. The players need support at the minute and that's the only way to get through it; fight and battle hard and keep believing."

Chapter Twenty Two
The Recovery

Tranmere's next game was another potential banana skin as they travelled to Bromley, who play on a 4G pitch instead of grass. The hosts were one of those teams sitting just outside the play-off places, whilst Rovers had to make do without Andy Cook.

It was not the best of games. In fact, neither team had too many chances, with Connor Jennings and Adam Buxton coming closest for the visitors after the break, whilst James Norwood had a strong penalty appeal turned down in the first half.

The game was fizzling out for a draw when, deep into injury time, Liam Ridehalgh slid a pass into the box towards James Alabi. The striker fell over, but thankfully the ball found Norwood, who managed to find the bottom corner, firing across the goalkeeper from an incredibly tight angle.

It was a terrific finish that earned Rovers a hugely important 1-0 win. "It was always going to be difficult for a whole host of reasons," reacted Mellon. "We set them to have a certain mentality and we were determined as a group that we were going to dig in and give nothing away.

"I would like to see Tranmere teams playing a lot more slicker with their attacking football, but in terms of determination and character and fighting for that three points, it was great. We now have to kick on from this and take the lessons that we've learned from the games before."

It was an honest and refreshing assessment from the manager. He has extremely high standards for his team and knew they were still nowhere near their best. However, that did not matter at that stage.

Getting three points did.

"It was a big relief," admits Mellon, who's opinion on the performance has not altered. "It was on 4G and it was a crap game. It was as poor as we played, certainly on the eye. Well, we were poor in what I want to see in a game of football but great in what the game asked us.

"What we did, like we say all the time, is answer the questions that the game asked us. We had to be tough and accept that we were playing on 4G, so the ball was going to bounce high and things like that. We accepted that was what we had to be good at and if we kept a clean sheet, we'd have a chance. It just felt fair that we scored the goal, considering everything that had gone on before us. It felt fair that at last we had got what we deserved.

"I don't know if it was a turning point, but it does look like that. We weren't playing poorly before that though. I can show anybody the games. I'm not somebody who gets carried away with it. If we were shit for 25 minutes, I'll say it. I won't waste people's time. I'll say if we were crap, or we created one chance. I'm always like that. But that result felt fair."

The win, and what followed, justified the faith that Mark Palios had shown in Mellon. He was as delighted as anyone with the result. Yes, Rovers were not perfect, but it meant the pressure on the manager and the players started to lift.

"I always look at the players when a game's finished and when they've scored a goal," he says. "You could see that win at Bromley meant a lot to them. There was no question of motivation for the players. Everybody was focused on the same thing. They were all as frustrated as everybody else and you just have to have faith at that time.

"If you believe that you've got the right people, you might want to tweak this and that. You may look at everybody's reasons for failure rather than making excuses and if they're honest about the

193

assessment, then you've got a great chance. That's what we did.

"There was no massive gap and we just dogged it down. I didn't look at the table. All I knew was that we needed to win more games than anybody else and then we'd move up the table. Then you just literally knock them off. We pegged them off and had a great late autumn."

It felt fitting that Norwood was the man who got the goal. If anybody would have been feeling the pain of what was going wrong, it was him. The striker felt at home at Tranmere, they were now his club, and he was working his backside off to get results for the team.

Until then, things just had not been working out for him. Goalkeepers had been making stunning saves or he had been putting the ball just the wrong side of the post. Indeed, he had only scored one goal in the entire campaign up to this point. The second, like the first, that late winner at Barrow, gave Rovers a platform to build on.

"It was a massive goal," admits Norwood. "I didn't play well and we didn't create many chances. It just happened. That's a testament to the team. The gaffer doesn't panic.

"We could have just lumped it forward but we played some football. I had a snap shot and it goes in. After that we beat Leyton Orient and it changed the whole season."

The Leyton Orient game came a few days later, and it saw Ben Tollitt return from injury. The winger had been out since February and there was much excitement about his return to the team. Arguably too much pressure was being put on his comeback, with the fans hoping he could be the person to kick the club up the table.

Unfortunately, it did not go to plan. Just 40 minutes into the game, the winger limped off with another knee injury. The initial diagnosis was that after such a lengthy spell on the sidelines, it was just a reaction to playing his first competitive match. However, it turned out to be much worse. Tollitt had fractured his knee cap and would not play again until February.

Fortunately, a day earlier Tranmere had confirmed the signing of 19-year old Dylan Mottley-Henry on loan from Barnsley. The winger had bags of energy and pace and gave Rovers the lift that they needed on the flanks. He replaced Tollitt and made an immediate impact.

The hosts went on to win 2-1, and came from behind to do so after Matt Harrold had given Leyton Orient the lead. Thankfully, Andy Cook equalised just three minutes later and James Norwood earned the win in the second half when he headed home Mottley-Henry's powerful cross at the back post.

That meant Tranmere had picked up back to back wins for the first time in the season, and Mellon was delighted to see both his strikers on the scoresheet. "We always talk about scoring goals," he said. "We know that we had many opportunities to take more chances. They maybe feel it a bit more than most because when you speak about getting goals, people always think about strikers.

"We know that they're very, very capable. We know that if we give them the service, they'll turn those chances into goals. We never doubted them. We've still got a lot of work to do, but certainly we're moving again in the right direction."

A few days after beating Leyton Orient, Rovers had another one of those unbelievable games as they drew 0-0 with Chester at Prenton Park. They were completely dominant and had chance after chance after chance, but Alex Lynch put in a man of the match performance in the visiting goal. Can double book's again

"I've never had as many chances, clear cut ones, in a game in my career," laughs Mellon. "Never. I think we had as many in that game as we did in the 9-0 win over Solihull.

"I have to think back realistically. People will look at these games and say we didn't do very well. Anybody who was at the game, or if I showed you the DVD, they would say 'what is going on there?' There you go. That's your reply. It was either an inspired goalkeeping performance or poor finishing. It was ridiculous that game. Crazy. We had the chances and didn't take them."

That game was on October 7th. From then on, Tranmere scored in every single home league fixture. A corner had been turned. They were started to find the back of the net, so now it was a case of making sure the ball stayed out at the other end too.

"There's one person who was the difference, and that's Andy Cook," says Ben Harrison. "He came back into the fold and I think the arm went around the shoulder. We got a couple of wingers in and Cook started scoring.

"James Norwood and Cook played really well together too. They scored 52 goals between them. Staggering. I haven't seen a partnership that good since Colin Clarke and John Clayton, or maybe Jim Steel and Ian Muir or John Aldridge and Chris Malkin. They were playing at the highest level, but these two were great.

"I don't know why they just clicked, but there was just something about them. They had a really good understanding. I think the Chester game the previous season might have been the start of it. They were warming up in front of the fans and getting loads of abuse, then when they scored, they both ran over and gave it back.

"Dylan Mottley-Henry was a great addition, and Ollie Banks came in on loan in November and made a difference too. He was very solid. Playing with a bit of width helped, as did Eddie Clarke when Liam Ridehalgh was injured. He was going down the wing and putting it on a plate for Cook. They just got re-energised. Eddie Clarke did that to a point. He played a few games and was fearless."

After the draw with Chester, Rovers beat Halifax 3-1 in the FA Cup before losing 2-1 to Aldershot at The Recreation Ground. It was a tough game. They had to battle a fierce wind in the second half and ended up getting pinned back on their 18-yard line after the break.

Steve McNulty had given his side the lead in the opening 45 minutes, but it seemed inevitable that the hosts would get back in it. Eventually Fabien Robert and Scott Rendell scored in the last ten minutes to turn the match around.

A few days later, Jay McEveley earned Rovers a point as his second half header secured a 1-1 draw at Hartlepool. It left them in sixteenth place in the National League. Over one third of the season had now passed, but they were still languishing in the bottom half of the table, six points behind Dagenham, who were seventh, and 11 behind leaders Dover.

The players always remained confident that they could still mount a promotion challenge though. Time and again they were asked whether it was too late to make a push for the title, but the answer was always the same.

"I've played at this level and levels above and you find that the league's not won in August or September," said Scott Davies before the Aldershot game. "It's won when the weather turns and the cold nights come in. That's when you really find out about people.

"We've got many in this group who've been there and done it and I've got no doubt we'll be there where we need to be. If you look around the dressing room, you're looking at big characters. We're confident but our feet are on the ground. You don't win the league in October, you win it in May, so we know what the end goal is."

A couple of weeks later, James Norwood revealed his confidence in Tranmere's ability to play catch up - even if they left it as late as the new year. "Since I've been here, the results we've picked up after January have been phenomenal," he said.

"We've taken near enough every point available. So if we're in and around it at Christmas and can cut that gap down a little bit, if not be at the top of it, then we know within ourselves what Tranmere do after January.

"If people are ahead of us, we'll have to play them and we'll be looking to take points off them. Three points makes a massive difference. If you can grab six in a week, it could mean moving five places up the table. So if we can keep picking up wins at every possible opportunity, or a point as a minimum, then we should be okay by the end of the season."

Tranmere's next game was in the FA Cup. They had reached the first round for the first time in three years and had been handed a tough assignment - League One side Peterborough away from home.

Rovers were fearless and they were terrific. They drew 1-1, with Andy Cook coming on to replace Gerry McDonagh, on loan from Nottingham Forest, to score a second half equaliser, but they were by far the better team. Indeed, they should have won, but once again failed to take their chances as Ollie Norburn and Jay McEveley came close.

The team had grasped their chance to play against Football League opposition with both hands though, and James Norwood says they took a huge amount of confidence out of their performance.

"The Peterborough game was weird because we played a completely different way to normal," he recalls. "The way we played this season was to get it to the front as quickly as possible. Not by going long, but by finding a way to get it through gaps and into the front two. The wide men roll in and out. Get it wide and get it to the front two to let them do their thing.

"Against Peterborough, we played football, and I mean serious football. We were patient. Usually we played football to get to mine and Cooky's feet and we would also hit the channels sometimes. We hit the channels twice in the Peterborough game.

"It was total soccer. It proved how good our players are. League One standard. It wasn't a turning point, but we knew we were capable of it. Also, if anybody wanted to call us a long ball team, we shoved it down their throat. We can play soccer. If we're on a good pitch, we'll play you off the park."

As good a result as the 1-1 draw at London Road was, Tranmere were hopeless in the return game. Jay Harris got sent off for a horrific tackle, whilst McEveley's shocking and wild back pass put Scott Davies in all kinds of trouble and led to the first goal.

On top of losing Harris to suspension, Rovers, already without Mitch Duggan and Jeff Hughes due to injury, saw Connor Jennings pick up a fifth yellow card of the season. He would be banned for their next match, at Gateshead, and Ollie Norburn was struggling with his fitness. Mellon had a whole host of problems in his midfield.

"The game at Peterborough was fantastic," says Mark Palios. "The fans were fantastic too. I watched them for most of the game! We played really well and in my opinion we deserved to win it.

"When they came back to our place, we had the disastrous incidents with the goal we basically gave away and Jay Harris getting sent off, so we didn't perform. But at that point, I went down to Micky straight after the game because we didn't have any midfield players. Ollie Norburn was the only one.

"I know I don't normally speak to him straight after game, but I said that to him and he knew it. I just wanted to say it so we could get it done. We then brought in two loans who not only helped keep the momentum, but added to it a little bit as well.

"Ollie Banks was one of them, from Oldham, and he made a big difference. He fitted really well into the way we were playing. It kept the momentum going and that was the important thing to do. People decry loans, and I don't like loan players too much, but there's a massive place for them where we are. You can supplement your squad at the right time. That was good work."

After Peterborough, Tranmere had to travel to Gateshead on a fiercely cold November day. The game was dour, but the visitors should have been ahead at half time after Larnell Cole was sent through one on one only to fire too close the to 'keeper. The inevitable sucker punch came deep into injury time when Ritchie Sutton netted an own goal.

There have been 28 league games since that one. Rovers have scored in each and every one of them, a club record, including a 2-2 draw at Macclesfield in their next game. Once more, they should have won, and even led twice through goals from Cook and Cole.

"We had that many chances that we were showboating at the end and still missing them," says Mellon. "I was standing there thinking 'this is ridiculous, we need to be more clinical'. We end up conceding a last minute equaliser."

They were now up to 14th in the National League, five points off the race for the play-offs. The gap was starting to close and although the results had been inconsistent, some kind of momentum was being forged. The goals were coming and the points were trickling in.

One of the reasons behind the improved form in front of goal was Cook cementing his place in the team. Mellon had tinkered around with things up front. James Alabi and, albeit sparingly, George Waring and McDonagh, were used as partners for Norwood. But from October onwards, Cook started near enough every game when available.

"He got fitter," explains Mellon. "The way that I look at my football team is that there have to be jobs that are done with and without the ball. I don't know many teams who are winning leagues or getting promotions if they are not doing both sides of the game. They have to be aggressive in both sides of the game.

"We are always realistic with the targets that the players have for what we want to try and achieve in order to be a good team. We don't ask them to be Lionel Messi! When we're not getting those targets, we work very hard on making sure the players understand that that's what we've got to get.

"In all fairness, Andy Cook did play 43 times in 46 league games, plus both play-off matches. It wasn't like we left him out. We were just trying to find a formula that would suit both sides of the game.

"Then when you're not scoring goals, you're just thinking that we need to try and jolt or kick start somebody here and make sure that they know nobody's nailed on for a place in the team. We will find a way of scoring goals here. It was just a bit of that.

"It would be difficult for me say that I changed that, but he did play most or all of the games. The same applies to James Norwood and Connor Jennings, except for when he was ill. The team didn't change a lot. We just had to score goals and they did in the end."

Tranmere were presented with the perfect chance to keep climbing the table by the fixture list, which had handed them four home matches out of five games due to postponements for the FA Cup. They started with a 4-0 demolition of Maidstone before beating Torquay 3-0.

Fylde and Guiseley were also hammered 4-1 and 4-0 respectively, with Connor Jennings scoring in both fixtures. He would eventually be crowned the division's player of the month for December. But it was a game down at Sutton just two days before Christmas that showed Tranmere had truly turned the corner as they beat a top seven rival for the first time in the campaign.

Adam Buxton handed his side the lead after just ten minutes at Gander Green Lane when he converted a superb free kick from 20-yards out. Kenny Davis levelled with a close range header, but Jennings put Rovers ahead again before half-time with a quite sublime bit of skill.

A ball into the danger zone was poorly dealt with and landed invitingly for the winger who was on the corner of the box. He watched it perfectly on to his right foot before volleying into the far corner. It was a contender for goal of the season and gave the visitors the lift they needed going into the break.

Andy Cook completed the scoring late on when he surged into the penalty area and fired past the goalkeeper after being picked out by Ollie Banks. It was a superb performance and an even more important victory.

"Connor Jennings and Adam Buxton are both very capable of that," reflects Mellon. "I was really pleased with that one. We knew that it was a good performance. Beating top seven and all that stuff doesn't bother me - it's just points at the end of the season. But it was the performance - one of those times when we got a whole performance.

"It was on 4G as well! People started to understand what I keep going on about - doing what the game's asking you. You can't play every game of football the way you want to play it. We just accepted as a group that this was going to happen and that's what we had to be good at.

"On that day at Sutton, they were brilliant. We were brilliant with the ball and scored some outstanding goals. Some of the defending was mega and the set plays were brilliant, plus our counter attacks were great. We closed them down brilliantly and when we had to be a block in our own third, we pressed at the right times. When we got the ball back, we were really good with it. Our game management was superb. It was an all round brilliant performance."

James Norwood adds: "That game was big. They were above us in the table and we got them in good form. We weren't scared of them. We thought why can't we beat them? The 4G pitch is a leveller. At home, we'd batter them. But not on 4G.

"Even when it went 1-1, I thought 'this won't be a problem'. Connor put us ahead and what a strike it was. It's a wonder goal. Cooky then seals it in the second half. Buxton's free-kick was brilliant too.

"They can come off the pitch thinking 'that won't happen again. If we play them again, they aren't scoring a 20-yard free-kick or plucking a 25-yard volley out of the sky'. But it just shows how good they are as players. When you need players to step up, sometimes you have one or two match winners in your side. We had six. What are you going to do?"

The result left Tranmere on the verge of the play-offs. They were just two points outside of the top seven after winning three games in a row. Everything was steadily building in the right direction.

"I did really enjoy watching that game," smiles Mark Palios. "They got stuck in. You can go and be a great footballing side who get bullied. Our lads weren't going to be bullied that day. I'd go a million miles for a team like that.

"It also felt like a big moment. It was partly because it was going into the Christmas period and partly because it topped off a great late autumn, but also because it was against a top side who were physical bullies. They tried to intimidate us on a plastic pitch. We showed great character and scored some great goals. When I came away from that, I was thinking 'game on'."

Wins over Fylde and Guiseley in the week between Christmas and New Year meant Tranmere sneaked into the play-offs before the start of 2018. They were looking up the table and the faith of the players that they could mount a promotion challenge had been justified.

"If you trained with us every day, you'd know why we had belief," says Norwood. "We knew it just needed to click because we have got the best players in the league. We picked up 177 points over two years. We scored the most goals. Who can stop us? Nobody.

"If we hadn't had the start we had, we'd have won with about 110 points. Why wouldn't you believe? We knew that at any point we were capable of winning 10 on the spin, or 15 or 20. We knew we were capable of never losing another game at that level.

"So you never think the title race is over. You can prepare and get an inkling that it's over, but as soon as you start believing, it's over. If you don't win the league, you've got to come second or third."

Chapter Twenty Three
Macclesfield and Maidstone

Tranmere's promotion challenge continued to build in 2018, despite a 5-2 defeat to Fylde, the heaviest of Micky Mellon's tenure, on New Year's Day. Scott Davies pulled a muscle in that game, meaning he would miss the next six weeks. Rhys Taylor subsequently arrived on loan until the end of the season from Fylde and made his debut in a 1-1 draw against Barrow a few days later.

Rovers then picked up a 1-0 win away to Woking, just their third away victory of the season, as they started to build up a head of steam. Andy Cook scored the only goal of the game in the first half, but only after Rovers had lost Steve McNulty when he was on the wrong end of a horror tackle by Declan Appau in the first minute.

The defender was left with a huge cut on his leg when he was caught by a recklessly high boot when the two players challenged for a ball and was rushed home to Arrowe Park Hospital. Somehow, the Woking man escaped with only a yellow card.

Cook would be sent off in this fixture too. He picked up a second caution when charging back to defend as Tranmere tried to see out the game. Afterwards, Mellon joked: "I think he's just pretty crap being there to be honest. Has he made a foul? Come on! We're booking everybody for every bit of contact now.

"I actually think that might have been a striker, lumbering at the right-back position, trying to play the ball. He's just not very good there and he's just caught him. Let's be honest, I don't think there's any malice and he's found himself sent off."

Cook was therefore suspended for a 3-2 win over Maidenhead, a game in which Josh Ginnelly, a loan signing from Burnley until the end of the campaign, made his debut and scored. James Norwood and Jeff Hughes were also on target as the hosts survived a late scare to get the points.

Next up was a trip across the Welsh border to take on Wrexham, who at the time were just above Tranmere in the table and still challenging for promotion. It was a topsy turvy contest in which both teams held the lead as Ritchie Sutton fired the visitors ahead early on before Scott Quigley and Chris Holroyd hit back to put Dean Keates' side 2-1 up after just 16 minutes.

Thankfully, the returning Cook levelled in front of the Rovers fans before half time with a trademark bullet header. That goal was even more fitting because Wrexham had tried to sign the striker in the summer, but their approaches had been quickly rebuffed.

Two more home wins were registered, against Ebbsfleet and Bromley, either side of a solid 1-1 draw away to Leyton Orient, before league leaders Macclesfield came to Prenton Park in what was being billed as a huge fixture in the title race.

By this point, Tranmere had soared up to second spot in the National League. Their promotion challenge was well and truly on. The Silkmen were four points clear, but also had a game in hand. A draw would be a good result for them. They just needed to keep Rovers at bay.

Over 7,000 supporters came through the turnstiles to see this one. There was so much anticipation and excitement surrounding it. The hosts knew that if they could somehow pick up three points, they were realistic contenders for the title.

And they started brightly enough as Ben Tollitt made his first start since picking up that second serious knee injury against Leyton Orient in October. He replaced Ginnelly in the starting line up.

Cook and Connor Jennings had early opportunities but failed to hit the target from distance, whilst the former would go on to miss a hat-trick of good chances, including heading wide from Liam Ridehalgh's enticing cross.

It looked like it was turning into another one of those days for Rovers. They were by far the better team but had nothing to show for it. Macclesfield on the other hand had barely landed a blow on their opponents, yet went in 1-0 up at half-time thanks to Danny Whitaker's strike.

"I always want to do well when the big crowds come to Prenton Park for the big games," says Micky Mellon. "I think it gets the momentum going. It reminded me of a game that we played against Forest Green in my first season. We were so, so good. Everything that we did with the ball was great. I just thought 'score'. It would have settled us down. But we couldn't score.

"We missed a couple of chances. And then, with all due respect to Macclesfield, right of the blue they scored. I thought, again, what's happened there? I couldn't believe it. I don't think they could. I don't honestly think that they could believe that they were in front.

"I got them in at half time and the players couldn't believe it either. You look around you and they're devastated that they're not in front. They're absolutely gutted. So you then have to speak to them from that place, knowing that that's where they are as a team.

"We just said 'look, keep doing what you're doing, don't change that. The chances will come because you're just so in control. But don't start trying to be a hero and thinking you need to do any more. Just keep doing what you're doing. Keep the shape and all the rest of it.' That was the message."

It seemed to work, because Cook equalised straight after the break when he nodded home a beautiful cross from James Norwood. Game on. Tranmere were in the ascendancy.

However, Macclesfield struck back ten minutes later when Elliott Durrell flashed a long range shot past Scott Davies, who would then be beaten from the penalty spot when the referee harshly judged Liam Ridehalgh to have intentionally handled the ball in the area.

Durrell killed the game off when he netted his second and the visitors' fourth by finding the bottom corner from 25-yards after a rapid counter attack as Tranmere threw men forward. 4-1. Game over.

"After we equalised, we were on top," continues Mellon. "It was just a matter of time. But they get a throw in on the far side, out of nothing really, and we were a bit slow to get organised. We work hard on that - getting organised quickly and getting ready to go again - but we were slow. I think some of them were having an argument with each other about how they got the throw.

"Macclesfield take it, throw it inside and somebody doesn't do their job and somebody comes out a bit slow. Their lad has then hit it from far out and from where he hit it, I actually thought 'thank God he hit it from there'.

"Next thing, I've seen people cheering. I said to Eric Nixon 'has that gone in?' He said yes. I just thought 'for fuck's sake. What is this all about?' I couldn't believe it. Then quickly after that they got another one. I just don't get football sometimes! I just do not get it! That was one of those moments that I didn't get.

"Their lads had shown the ability to score the goals and goals win games, I know all that, but my opinion and emotion was that I just couldn't believe it. I looked on the pitch and I knew the players couldn't believe it either.

"At that moment, I couldn't stop the game like Sky+ and get their heads going and get them back in it. I'm not in control. It's gone. I can try and shout things that we've worked on and I can hope. I can say something like 'when that happens again, just sit in your shape, we've spoken about it', but we lost our shape a little bit.

"We started running around because we're all frustrated. The crowd are going bananas and people are leaving and you just go 'fuck it'. It was one of those nights."

It was a tough result for Tranmere to take. They had won nine successive home games up to that point, throwing themselves back into the title race. But this was the match that mattered more than any other, and they had lost.

"It was so frustrating, but that's football," says Norwood. "You're going to have those games. We got an equaliser when I crossed it for Andy Cook and we thought we could build on it.

"The 'keeper then makes another couple of good saves before we give some cheap goals away, plus the good strike from Durrell. They were in the position where they could draw or win. We had to win. There were just too many defensive errors, something that rarely happened.

"It was the first time we'd conceded four at home under Micky. I'm not used to it. I felt embarrassed when I came off the pitch. Nobody had ever dicked me like that before. Let's move on."

Mark Palios was equally in disbelief at the result. It was a carbon copy of some of those early season games - but also reminded him of a match he played in during his time at Prenton Park.

"It was one of those where you just don't know how it is how it is," he says. "How we were not 3-0 up at half time is ridiculous. The guy broke down the left and I just had a premonition. I thought 'oh no', and it screwed in. It was one of those scrawny goals.

"I played in that game where the goalkeeper got slapped on the backside by the fan with the walking stick. We lost 5-0 to Bournemouth, it was my last game at Tranmere before I went to Crewe. In that game, I don't know how we were 5-0 down. It was like that against Macclesfield. How are we 1-0 down at half-time? We should be 3-0 up.

"We come out after half-time and Andy Cook scores an equaliser and I thought 'that's it'. They knew that they didn't deserve to be level pegging with us. But we gave away a stupid goal and we could have actually pulled it back straight away. We broke away again, but the 'keeper makes a great save. They go down the other end, get a penalty and it's 3-1 all of a sudden and you're chasing the game. That was massively disappointing."

Unfortunately, to a certain percentage of people the result did not come as a surprise. There is a consensus amongst some that the club regularly slip up in the games that matter most, especially when there is a swelled attendance at Prenton Park.

"It was typical Tranmere," says Ben Harrison. "We had a good crowd behind us. The Macclesfield guys were a good bunch. One of them said to me at half-time 'you'll win this'. Then at full-time he said 'Elliott Durrell will do that one in every fifteen games, it just so happens that tonight he's scored two wonder goals'.

"Our home form had been so good ahead of that, and then that word comes out in the fan park afterwards - bottlers. I don't always blindly defend the club but I kept quiet after that one. It was the kind of result and performance we've seen from a lot of Tranmere teams before. Macclesfield played really well though to be fair."

The result left Rovers seven points behind Macclesfield in the title race, whilst the Silkmen still had that game in hand. Tranmere also plummeted to sixth in the table, and with just 11 fixtures remaining, Mellon admits that that was the night when their hopes of lifting the title evaporated.

"That was massive in the battle for top spot," he concedes. "That was it. When you look back on it, that was the moment. If we had won that night, there was still a lot of work to be done, but it would have been a massive blow to Macclesfield.

"They would have been thinking 'Tranmere are a good side. There's something big happening there'. I think it gave them a lift to know that they could dig in and stay in a game and still get results. It's only my opinion. Macclesfield might not feel the same. I'm entitled to my opinion. That's what happened that night in my opinion. It was a tough one, it hurt badly."

***

Football managers and players often say they want the next game to come as quickly as possible after a disappointing defeat. Thankfully, that was the case for Tranmere as they made the long trip to Maidstone just a handful of days after losing to Macclesfield.

Mellon had somewhat of a selection dilemma on his hands once again though. Liam Ridehalgh was unavailable due to a neck problem, whilst Eddie Clarke was still recovering from illness. That meant midfielder Jeff Hughes had to start out of position at left-back.

On top of that, Maidstone play on a 4G pitch, and that made Steve McNulty unavailable as his body takes longer to recover from 90 minutes on a plastic surface. As such, new signing Manny Monthe, on loan from Forest Green, made his debut.

When the game got underway, Tranmere were hopeless. There appeared to be a hangover from the Macclesfield fixture just four days earlier. Their opponents had not won in the league since mid-November, 16 games ago, but they were by far the more threatening team and came close early on when Delano Sam-Yorke lobbed wide.

The visitors were behind before the half hour mark though as Scott Davies came out to punch clear a free kick and made a bit of a hash of it. His weak clearance eventually fell to Alex Finney who hooked into the back of the net.

Andy Cook equalised for the visitors, tapping home from close range after a defender had missed Adam Buxton's cross, but Maidstone had retaken the lead by half time through Ross Lafayette from the penalty spot.

It was a dreadful opening 45 minutes for Rovers. They could barely string three passes together and were struggling to get to grips with the plastic pitch. Mellon tried to change things around, with Ben Tollitt even coming on at wing back in an attempt to shake things up.

It looked like they were heading for a second successive defeat when suddenly Andy Mangan made a nuisance of himself in the box as he tried to get on the end of Jack Dunn's low cross. The ball eventually took a deflection off a defender and dribbled into the back of the net. 2-2; five minutes left. Surely not?

Sensing the most unlikely of victories, Tranmere moved in for the kill. It duly arrived when Connor Jennings was chopped down in the box a few moments later, allowing Buxton to step up and convert from the penalty spot.

"I'm pleased with the character," said Mellon at full time. "The quality can be better. I'm not a manager who'll stand here and try and bluff people. But in terms of fight and desire to pick up a valuable three points, it's an absolute ten out of ten.

"They kept going right until the very end. It's a massive, important result for us. The way the game went, from 2-1 down, to dig a result out of it, we're obviously delighted with that.

"The conditions were very difficult and they were made more difficult by the officials. Let's get that right. I don't think the game went longer than 30 seconds (without a whistle), which made it difficult to get any kind of flow."

It was such a strange match. Rarely, if ever, has a Tranmere team played so badly and yet still picked up three points. It was a great escape and it was so important. They were back up to third and had some momentum again.

"It wasn't a good game," admits Micky Mellon. "We changed the shape after the break to try and create some one v ones. We didn't want to play Ben Tollitt on the 4G, but we had to stick him at wing back and told him to just go and play against their full-back.

We said 'go and play against him. Don't worry about getting back. We'll get the ball to you.' We had Jack Dunn on the other side. The instructions were to play through Ollie Norburn and to make sure we got it out early to the wide men.

"We knew that they would create chances, but through overloading them or playing through them. Gradually, we could see something was going to happen because we were getting some joy out of it. We were better than them at the one v ones in the wide areas. We just let Tollitt get on with it, the same with Dunn.

"We got a last minute penalty and it was about sheer desire and guts to get over the line. I was really pleased, because they adjusted and adapted to the change at half time and did what we said we wanted to do. That's always good for player-coaching staff relationship."

James Norwood also recalls that game, although not particularly fondly. The striker was hooked off with ten minutes left, Mangan coming on as his replacement, after a fairly anonymous game.

"I was warming up and heard a call from the crowd," he says. "I wouldn't normally look, but it was my old business teacher from school! I thought 'please don't play crap'. After 80 minutes, having had the worst game I've had in a Tranmere shirt, I got dragged off.

"Oh my word. What has gone on here? We just could not play football. I couldn't tell you what it was. The lads must have had food poisoning or something. It was just terrible. When we got the equaliser, I just thought 'thank God for that'. Then Buxton scores the penalty and we just laughed!

"We played about 17 minutes of injury time and they got a free-kick towards then end, when the referee made the wall stand about 27 yards back! Ollie Norburn picks up a tenth yellow card and misses the next two matches. It was ridiculous. I just wanted it to end. We won and nobody could believe it.

"The gaffer went mad at the end. He couldn't believe that we'd won. He was shouting 'don't you ever play like that again. It's embarrassing for everyone'. If Wrexham did a smash and grab on us earlier in the season, that was the biggest robbery I've seen. We only had three shots and one was an own goal! So we only had two and scored three goals!"

Mellon's take on what happened in the dressing room after the game is slightly different though. "The way that we got it in the last minute gives you a wee lift," he continues. "But the players weren't happy at the end. Sometimes when you go in, they've already started. They were all standing up and there was a lot of shouting and aggression towards the performance.

"I liked that. They were giving a shit. They're weren't whooping and cheering because they'd scored a last minute winner. That wasn't what was happening. I was pleased. I didn't really have to say anything.

"I just let them say their bit, calmed them down and said 'you're right. You don't need me for this now. You've sorted that out! But be respectful to each other, listen to what's being said and learn from it.'

"But it was important an important win, because we got the Macclesfield defeat out of the system straight away. We had to win the next game. We had to get a positive result. With all due respect, it needed to be a win, and we got it."

The Maidstone victory was the only game in the entire season that Mark Palios missed. He was listening to the game on the radio though and he did not like what was coming through his speakers.

"I was very down because what was coming across on the radio did not sound good," he says. "We were playing badly, but we nick it with two goals at the end."

Ben Harrison had not made the long trip to the Gallagher Stadium either, but adds: "It was a bit of a turning point. There was only one person from the Trust board who went. When it was 2-1, I was in a bar in Oxton and I couldn't believe it.

"I didn't know what to expect really, but I looked at my phone and we'd scored an own goal, which probably should have been offside, so it was 2-2. Then I looked again and we had a penalty. Adam Buxton scored it and we won 3-2. It was another defining Tranmere moment, with a makeshift team too."

Chapter Twenty Four
The Run In

There were ten games left following the win over Maidstone, and that period was punctuated by some seriously impressive victories. Tranmere actually had to wait two weeks for their next outing after a fixture against Gateshead was postponed due to a frozen pitch, but they turned on the style when they finally kick-started the campaign down at Dagenham.

The game was goalless at half time and the visitors had ridden their luck a little bit with one or two scares, but Andy Cook and James Norwood both bagged braces after the break in what would be Rovers' biggest away victory of the National League era.

"That was such a complete performance," says Norwood. "We kept a clean sheet and they had a couple of opportunities, but in terms of keeping the ball, going forwards and being disruptive and staying tight at the back, we were brilliant.

"The way we played over the last quarter of the season, that was the most complete team that I've been involved in. Nobody could stop us. I never wanted to say that in the press, because if we didn't catch Macclesfield, I'd have looked stupid.

"We reverted back to the team that in the second year became unbeatable. Cooky and I knew we were going to score week in, week out. We knew Josh Ginnelly and Connor Jennings would work their balls off for the team and create chances for us.

"We knew Ollie Norburn, Jeff Hughes and Jay Harris were just going to run the midfield and that the back four would keep it tight. Even if they didn't, Cooky and I were going to score three. Everybody knew their job and everybody executed it. Dagenham was a culmination of that."

Tranmere actually lost their next game at Boreham Wood. It was a bitterly cold day, with snow swirling around the stadium and settling on the pitch. Norwood scored a second half equaliser, but it was not enough as the hosts picked up a 2-1 win.

"I think Drissa Traore didn't fancy it that day and they went right through our midfield," says Ben Harrison. "That was the game when I thought we won't win the league. We were still seven points behind Macclesfield, but they lost that day.

"It was a defining day for me too. We were going to London to scatter my mum's Ashes. We took them with us in the car. We didn't know if the game would be on but got into the ground and it was very open. The snow was going sideways into the Tranmere end. The kit hadn't arrived, so the players were in short sleeved shirts with no numbers on the back.

"There was something about that game. Boreham Wood probably deserved to win, but at the very end their goalkeeper was making gestures to the Tranmere fans. I was just thinking 'hang on, there are 300 or 400 people here who are covered in snow. You should appreciate the fans for being there'.

"A lot of the Tranmere players wanted to get off the pitch, but he was giving it large. I said to my friends that it's just a shame we can't play them again, because the goalkeeper was out of order."

Norwood adds: "It was such an odd game. We were up for it but pre-match we were told they weren't. They were trying to get it called off. So we relaxed a little bit. They came out like they'd been in the Bahamas and they came out of the traps flying. It was like the Red Arrows upfront.

"Cooky and I couldn't get the ball and we couldn't get close to the goal. Anything that did come to us was bouncing off us. We came in at half time and we got roasted by the gaffer.

"We came out in the second half and I equalised. We gave it a go, but conceded another crappy goal. They leap frogged us in the table after that and you just thought 'oh no'. We were going for the title. We needed to be beating teams like that, and Macclesfield dropped points too.

"It was a massive opportunity for us. Not only did we have frostbite, not only did we get hammered by the gaffer and have to drive back from London, but we missed an opportunity to get closer to Macclesfield. It was a bad week."

Tranmere did not lose another important game after that. They soon beat Eastleigh 3-1, before the weather put paid to a couple of fixtures over the Easter Weekend. Firstly, Rovers made a long and pointless trip down to Dover on Good Friday, only for the match to be postponed an hour and a half before kick off, just as the fans turned up at the Crabble, because of a waterlogged pitch. That was also the reason behind the Monday clash with Solihull being pushed back a few weeks.

"It meant we had a week or two off when everybody else played fixtures," adds Norwood. "We put in a rusty performance in our next game, but I said to the lads that the break was the best thing that could happen to us.

"The year before, people were burning out. We didn't change personnel. The manager never changed me and Cooky, Connor played every game, so did Steve McNulty, Ritchie Sutton and Liam Ridehalgh. We had two weeks off and we were rusty, but after that, we caught fire."

The next game was Tranmere's final local derby of the National League era. They went away to Chester and won 2-0, with Norwood scoring at the Deva Stadium for the third year running. The result also meant that Rovers' bitter rivals were relegated to the National League North.

"I'll miss those derby games," he continues. "I remember the first time we played Chester and somebody sent me a picture on Twitter - he was wearing a balaclava and had a big knife. I was like what the hell have I joined here!

"I'll miss them because our crowd outweighs Wrexham 5 to 1, and Chester 10 to 1. When you score against them, that's when you do a stupid celebration and the fans love it. They remember people who have scored in big games and people who do rivals. Score a 90th minute winner against a rival and you're a hero. Score a 90th minute winner against Guiseley and it's nothing.

"Those Chester and Wrexham games are remembered and it's bragging rights for six months. When we relegated Chester, all our fans now know that when they're playing in the National League North, we did that to them. That's what they can say. It's bragging rights. If they never come up and we don't go down, we've got that for a lifetime."

Gateshead came next, a match in which Tranmere were 2-0 down approaching half time, but Cook turned the game on its head just before the break. He scored all four in a 4-2 win, becoming the first person to do so for Rovers since John Aldridge 24 years earlier.

"That was a mad game," laughs Norwood. "Even when we were 2-0 down just before half time, nobody was panicking, which was odd. Usually we would be by that point - the way we played would have been a bit sharper.

"Somebody put a cross in to me which I slid for, got my toe on and somehow diverted it away from goal! Cooky tapped it in though, 2-1, and it changed the whole complexion of the game. The chat would have been 'you lot are a disgrace', but now it's 'you're in this game'.

"Cooky's second goal is from a Liam Ridehalgh cross and he hits it with his left foot. It is an unbelievable finish. Unless you try that, you will never know how hard it is to do at that pace. The third one for the hat-trick is a header. Game over as far as we're concerned.

"Then Ollie Norburn hits one that hits Cooky who's stood miles offside and in it goes. Four. How do you like them Andy? You're good at heading so have one on your head. Have a tap in from three yards as well and have one hit you too.

"He doesn't get the credit he deserves though. He's scored a lot of long range volleys for Tranmere. I don't think people quite remember all of them. Braintree, Barrow, Ebbsfleet - he hits them from distance and kicks it so hard.

"Playing with Cooky is my best partnership. I've been fortunate enough to play with Gary Taylor-Fletcher, who understood my game and was a completely different player. I'd make a run and he wouldn't see me, but he'd know where I'd be.

"I was also fortunate enough to play with Lee Hughes, who's the best player I've played with. He could find space in a phone box. Be it a free kick or a corner, he'd always end up having a free header. He showed me how and I learned to get into positions and make runs in behind. Then there's Marcus Stewart at Exeter, a former Premier League top scorer. Movement again.

"I played with two people who helped my movement, Fletch who knew exactly where I was, and Cooky, who meant that I never got touched and he got battered. We scored 52 goals that season. It's a partnership that. The best I've been involved in."

Tranmere reeled off a further three wins before the end of the season, beating play-off rivals Aldershot 2-0 and winning the rearranged game at Dover 1-0. Finally came a 2-0 victory at Halifax on the same day that Macclesfield sealed the title. It also confirmed that Rovers would finish in second place in the division for the second season in a row.

Two games still remained at this point. One was against Solihull on a Tuesday night, a match where, like Maidstone the previous season, Micky Mellon rested his first team squad. The likes of Jack Dunn, Devarn Green and Andy Mangan were given a chance to show what they could do but could not prevent a 2-1 defeat.

It was objective achieved for the manager though. He got some minutes into the legs of the players who, if an injury crisis occurred similar to the one twelve months earlier, could be needed in the play-offs. He also managed to wrap his first choice players in cotton wool.

A few days later came the final game of the league season. Tranmere lost 2-1 to Hartlepool in a match where Mellon went with his strongest team, bar Connor Jennings who was in hospital with a serious illness that threatened to end his season.

In his absence, the remaining players pretty much coasted through the 90 minutes. This was just a case of keeping them ticking over ahead of the play-off semi-final that was due to take place a week later. All that Mellon wanted was for his players to get through without any injuries. The result did not matter. Job done.

Chapter Twenty Five
Ebbsfleet

Great day. Paulaner, Cormac + Steeeve. Bal absent again.... Red hot... day ;-)

There was a change to the format of the play-offs for the 2017/18 season. National League clubs had voted in favour of the sixth and seventh placed clubs qualifying as well. They would have to play a one legged quarter-final against fourth and fifth, at the ground of the higher placed team, to reach the semis.

When the final four had been decided, it would once again be a one off match to decide who reached Wembley, hosted by the teams who finished second and third.

It looked like a ridiculous idea when it was first implemented. Taking the previous campaign as an example, Barrow, who ended up in seventh, finished 20 points behind Tranmere in the table, and it would have been an injustice if they had somehow sneaked through to the final and then made it to the Football League.

In actual fact, however, the new system strongly favoured the teams who were higher up the league. Rovers only had to win one match to get to Wembley, instead of coming through a double legged tie. It would be on home soil, where they had been in terrific form, and it would be against a team who had been in action less than 72 hours earlier in the quarter-finals.

Their eventual opponents were Ebbsfleet, who had finished the season in sixth. They qualified for the semi-finals by sneaking past Aldershot in a topsy turvy game that went all the way to penalties after Dave Winfield scored a last minute equaliser in extra time.

Daryl McMahon's side then made the long trip up to the Wirral having had little time to recover or prepare for the match, but they were on the crest of a wave after the win at the Recreation Ground.

They came out of the blocks quickly and took the lead after just 16 minutes at Prenton Park as Luke Coulson brilliantly headed home from near the penalty spot. Thankfully for Tranmere, James Norwood equalised before half time, weaving his way past a couple of tackles before unleashing a vicious shot that beat Nathan Ashmore.

It remained 1-1 until the break, but a defensive mix up in the 51st minute allowed Ebbsfleet to take the lead for a second time as Scott Davies and Ritchie Sutton left a long hoof up field to each other. Eventually, the ball found its way to Myles Weston, who prodded into an empty net.

"I was quite relaxed about the Ebbsfleet game," says James Norwood. "Again, if I was doing an American interview I'd have said 'they can't touch us. I'm not scared of them at all. Cooky and I will score three against them. They can't stop us. They know that'.

"We started well, really well, but gave a really cheap goal away that should have been stopped. When I equalised, I thought there was only one team in it. And then we gave an even cheaper goal away. Oh my God. This is going to happen to us again isn't it? We're going to shoot ourselves in the foot. It's like we'd bet on ourselves to lose."

Thankfully for Tranmere, Josh Ginnelly had other ideas. The winger was having the best game of his short stint at Prenton Park and equalised only five minutes later with a splendid finish, firing powerfully across goal and into the far corner.

"That was one of those that we needed to score then," admits Micky Mellon. "The way that he scored was great. It was a magic time and I thought 'here we go'. In the season or through certain games, you can score goals at brilliant times and you can score goals at not so brilliant times.

"In certain situations or parts of games, there is a brilliant time to score a goal. In big games, anybody who's ever played in them, if you ask when was the best time to score that goal, they will point to a certain moment. That was one of those moments."

It gave Tranmere the lift they needed. There was only one team in it from then on, with Andy Cook and Ollie Norburn coming close, whilst Ashmore was forced into a couple of saves by Norwood. Nobody could score before the 90 minutes were up though, so extra time was needed to settle the tie.

By this point, the quarter-final clash with Aldershot was beginning to take its toll on Ebbsfleet. They were knackered. That game had also gone the distance, and they had not had much time to recover. This was another emotionally absorbing and energy sapping fixture; even the spectators were exhausted! Adrenaline would not be able to save them now.

Rovers took the lead for the first time in the match with 102 minutes on the clock as Norwood curled home a majestic free-kick. The striker, who does not often find himself over set pieces, found the top corner from 25-yards, with Ashmore getting a finger tip on it but unable to keep the ball out.

"I think it's only the third I've taken a free-kick for Tranmere," he laughs. "One of them I scored and another hit the wall for Connor Jennings to tap in. I only take them if I know I can score! For me that's usually when I'm having a decent game! I just fancied it.

"I looked up midway through my run and saw the 'keeper take a step, so I went to his side. I caught it well and the good thing about Conference balls is they don't bend! If it had, it would have finished in the middle of the goal!

"From then on, the game is dead. They weren't getting back in it. I genuinely think I could have walked around for the rest of the game. That's no disrespect to them, we were just in that mood."

Larnell Cole made it 4-2 to Tranmere moments into the second half of extra time, battering a long distance effort towards goal that took

Ashmore by surprise and cannoned off his shoulder before hitting the back of the net.

Prenton Park exploded. After a crazy game of football, coming on the back of an exhausting season, twelve months after the heartbreak of the defeat to Forest Green, Wembley was beckoning again.

And if having a two goal advantage was not enough already, Ebbsfleet's hero from their quarter-final against Dagenham, Winfield, was sent off moments after Cole's goal following an altercation with Jay Harris. There was no chance of them mounting a comeback now, not with ten men. Rovers practically strolled through the remaining minutes.

"It's great to get to the big house and to go and contest the play-off final," said Mellon afterwards. "But we know that we've still got to go down there and do a job. We'll get the players dusted down, recovered and ready to go and we'll certainly go down there knowing a little bit more about what we're going into to.

"That experience can only help, but we've still got to do the business on the pitch. As you've seen today, there'll be no quarter given. We know that we're in for a tough game.

"We know that nothing's been achieved yet except for going down to Wembley and getting the opportunity. So we're not really celebrating anything at all. We've extended the season and given ourselves an opportunity to do what we set out to do on the first game of the season, and that was try and get promotion.

"The strike for Josh Ginnelly's goal is terrific and it comes at the right time for us. To get the momentum back and hit a shot like that is brilliant. I thought he was terrific all game. He stood up and was counted all game. He enjoyed it and showed us the player that we all know he's capable of being, so I'm really pleased for him.

"Norwood's second is a great goal, past a very, very good goalkeeper who we know a lot about. He is so valuable to us, so I'm pleased that he did it on the big stage today. And then Larnell Cole's goal was the icing on the cake."

The manager was quite rightly trying to keep a lid on celebrations. Some people had criticised the reaction to winning against Aldershot a year earlier. This time, they knew the job was far from complete.

Even the fans were not partying quite as hard as they had done twelve months earlier. There was no pitch invasion or anything like that. They knew the importance of going up. After three long, hard years in the National League, a fourth season was unthinkable. But the fan tent was still the place to be after the game.

"We tried a mosaic on the Kop that day," says Ben Harrison. "People started throwing the paper at the goalkeeper when he was time wasting from the fifth minute. The referee comes over and announces the game will be abandoned and Tranmere will forfeit it if this carries on. There would have been a riot if he'd done that! Somebody at half time told me it was my fault!

"I was sitting next to Mark and Nicola and I could feel the tension, especially when the second goal went in. You don't say anything, but I was thinking 'surely our season cannot end on that mistake?'

"Josh Ginnelly pulled off a cracker thankfully and had a great game. He was an unexpected hero. We hadn't seen too much of him but he was great in that game. The goalkeeper had no chance with his strike. It was a shame that he cramped up at the end.

"Norwood's free-kick was a brilliant way to win a game. Ebbsfleet were out on their feet and as soon as he scored there would only be one winner. Jay Harris might have done something to their centre half to get him riled a little bit and see him sent off, but in that league, he's the type of player you need, especially in games like that.

"The celebrations were still crazy, but a bit more low key. We knew it was Sutton v Boreham Wood the next day in the other semi-final and we fancied our chances in the final. We weren't going to play a Forest Green or another ex-league team who were going to be tough.

"But people were still celebrating. Mark Palios was in there and somebody said to him 'I've got strong legs, do you want to get on my shoulders?' On one shoulder, he had the sensible ex-Chief Executive of the FA saying 'you can't be doing that', on the other shoulder it said 'go head!'.

"As that Liverpool supporting friend of mine said the year before, enjoy it, because you can't go back next week if you lose. It was manic in there in the end, but this year we didn't run out of beer!"

Palios, who was just as knackered as everybody else in attendance, actually had some special visitors over for the game from Asia. The latest cohort of coaches had landed in England that morning and they enjoyed the win as much as the other Rovers fans who came to Prenton Park.

"What a fantastic game it was," he says. "The atmosphere was electric. The Chinese coaches were here and they wanted to absorb the English culture as well as the training.

"They'd got off the plane at about 8am and by 12pm, they were in the ground watching a game like that. They then did their training all week and watched the Wembley game on the TV. They were all jumping up and down and screaming! A few days later, their leaving do was delayed because we had a civic reception with the council. They thought life at Tranmere was like this!"

He admits however that winning this game felt very different to the annihilation of Aldershot twelve months earlier. As well as going into the match at Prenton Park without a 3-0 advantage, everybody knew what was at stake. This was not just about getting back to Wembley. It was about earning a shot at redemption as well.

"The Aldershot win down there was fantastic," he continues. "But it wasn't quite the same because the job wasn't done. The Ebbsfleet game was different because the job was done there and then. It was a massive release of tension.

"The celebrations in the tent reflect the position of going back to Wembley and being one game away from the league, but also the game on the day. The game against Aldershot was a bit of an anti-climax a year earlier. They were winning 2-1, we scored a late goal to make it 2-2, we were expected to go through to a certain extent after the first leg.

"This was different. This was backs against the wall at 1-0 down and 2-1 down. At that point, I was just thinking 'I'm not lucky in football' again. I was feeling sick! But there was an element of me even then thinking that there was enough time left and we were playing well enough to get another goal. Thankfully, that's what happened. Josh Ginnelly scored a cracker. Then there's extra time and two more great goals."

A day after beating Ebbsfleet, Tranmere found out who they would be playing at Wembley as Boreham Wood won 3-2 away to Sutton, having already beaten Fylde 2-1 in the quarter-finals. Bring it on.

Chapter Twenty Six
Mellon's Mission Accomplished

So here we are. Tranmere's 143rd game in the National League, and it just happens to be against the team who inflicted their first defeat nearly 1,000 days earlier. The team are up for it. They are ready. The fans are up for it. They are ready. Wembley awaits.

Rovers had been through a lot in the three years leading up to this point. They had suffered a lot of hurt and disappointment. They had struggled against and lost to opponents to produce results that would have been considered unfathomable just a few seasons earlier.

Crucially, they had also lost out on a huge amount of money. The parachute payments had disappeared and, amongst other things, so had funding from the Football League for their youth set up. That led to a restructuring of the club's academy in March, just one of many tough decisions that were made.

Another year in Non League did not bear thinking about. The consequences would have been huge, particularly financially. The playing budget would have had to have been reassessed and jobs would have been at risk. All that considered, this was Rovers' biggest game since 1987, when a goal from Gary Williams earned a 1-0 win over Exeter and kept Johnny King's side in the Football League. Like then, they could not afford to lose.

However, the pressure did not seem to be weighing on the players like it had a year earlier. Although the fixture was much more important than the Forest Green game, the magnitude of the match appeared not to worry them. Indeed, they were just desperate for redemption after defeat twelve months earlier.

"We'd been to Wembley," explains Micky Mellon. "We'd done it all before. It wasn't new. We weren't going to play at Wembley for the first time in 17 years, or in our lives. Because then it all builds up on you, because you never know when you're going to get back. When you're going for a second time, that baggage is all gone. You've been there before and you've played there before. That had all gone.

"They were so keen to get back and get rid of the pain. We took the punishment for not getting Tranmere promoted heavily. A lot of things happened to us as playing and coaching staff that if I ever went through that again, I wouldn't allow to happen.

"I felt, probably the same as everybody else, that we deserved to be punished. I felt that because we didn't get promoted, we deserved to lose certain things that people looked at and thought were privileges. Possibly that had an impact on the group, thinking back now. We'd gone through all that and we'd got a crack at fixing it at Wembley."

That attitude was evident in the week leading up to the game. Whereas a year earlier, the party atmosphere from the semi-finals was carried right up until Wembley, the players knuckled straight back down. The Forest Green match had felt like a day out. This time, it was do or die.

Mark Palios noticed the difference in attitude. "There was a much more focused, business like approach," he says. "It was more a case of 'let's just get this done'. The focus was on the game. You sensed that, and that's a tribute to Micky and the lads. Whilst everybody has a right to get excited, they just went and started to do the job."

Mellon therefore did not need to motivate his players. But physiologically he needed to get them in the right frame of mind. The players were going to be up for it. Adrenaline would be flowing through their veins at kick off. It was his job to make sure it was channeled in the correct manner.

"The whole determination was focused on the 107 steps to picking up the trophy at Wembley," he reveals. "It's all I said to them. I sat them down in a meeting and said 'how many steps is it to the trophy?' None of them knew. I said 'there's 107 and you're fucking going up them. You're going up the steps. We have to.'

"It felt like we needed to go up them to leave the pain behind. I think I have to make it clear the pain that we were in. I can't tell you the depths I'd gone to myself, and probably the rest of the staff and players too. I felt the only way to get rid of that or deal with that was to go up those 107 steps.

"Emotionally, it was a case of going up those steps, lifting the trophy, leaving my shit at the top and walking to something new down the other side. That was where my mentality was. It was crazy how I was feeling.

"I spoke to the players and said 'under no uncertain terms, we are going up those steps'. It's all we spoke about. There was nothing else that was going to happen for us. We were doing it. We just knew that getting past Ebbsfleet and Boreham Wood was part of the process."

***

After a week of excitement, the day of reckoning finally arrived. May 12th 2018. A date that will live long in the memory of every Tranmere fan and also go down in the club's history.

The atmosphere was different at Wembley compared to the year before. Twelve months earlier, it built and built and built in the hour leading up to kick off. The supporters were boisterous and they were partying. This year, they almost reflected the mood of the players. They knew it was business and they were nervous.

It was the same outside the ground. Before the Forest Green game, people had been partying on Wembley Way or in the Fan Zone next door to Wembley Arena. Former players like Steve Mungall, Eddie Bishop and Eric Nixon had all been in there, but there was none of that this time around.

"There were fewer fans, but those who did go were the real deal," says Ben Harrison. "There was a lot of tension, much more than twelve months earlier. They were thinking 'surely we will do it this year'. Like Forest Green, Boreham Wood didn't bring many fans.

"It wasn't a sunny day and I quite like the idea that it was dampened down. Wembley wasn't the same. Mark and Nicola weren't happy because Tottenham were playing the next day, so there was no fan zone. There was no buzz outside. I think that was good for us in a way.

"I made a decision to go in the Royal Box this year, which I took a lot of stick for, but I met everyone in the pub up on the high street. I just wanted to do something different and also, if we got promoted, I didn't want to be in the pub for three hours. I wanted to appreciate it. I just went on my own and it felt a bit odd.

"I got friendly with some of the Boreham Wood guys and went over to their table. The owner had paid for all their hospitality, and they were partying just because they were there, like we were twelve months earlier. When their chairman walked in, he basically got a standing ovation, although mainly because he was paying for everyone's match ticket! On the Tranmere tables, people were confident but laying it back a little bit."

***

Micky Mellon was forced into one change from the play-off semi-final as Adam Buxton was unavailable due to a stomach injury. The complaint had been troubling him for several weeks, and he only returned against Ebbsfleet after limping off during the 2-0 win over Halifax a week before the end of the regular season.

Plenty of credit has to be heaped upon the defender though. He declared himself unfit for the game at Wembley. It takes a big person to admit they will not be able to play, especially in a final. The right-back put the team's best interests ahead of his own. He was replaced by Manny Monthe, a left footer who was playing out of position.

Meanwhile, the manager was able to call upon Connor Jennings, who was available again after his health scare. The winger had spent a week in hospital, most of it on a drip. There were serious fears for his future while he was treated for meningitis. However, he was not missing this occasion. He was desperate to play his part and help his team to promotion. As such, he was named amongst the substitutes, a huge boost for Mellon and his squad.

The teams emerged from the tunnel, walked down the red carpet and shook hands. They ran towards their respective fans and the 2018 National League play-off final got underway. And then, after 48 seconds, the game plan went out of the window as Tranmere suffered the worst possible start.

A loose ball fell to Liam Ridehalgh in midfield. He took a heavy touch and charged forward in pursuit of it, desperate not to give up possession so early in the match. Unfortunately, his eagerness saw him leap off the ground and crash into Ricky Shakes, wiping the man out and completely missing the ball. It was a poor tackle - and it resulted in the fastest red card at the new Wembley.

"I couldn't believe it, but it's football," says Micky Mellon. "It's still 0-0 and anything can happen. They just have to show character and dig in. We quickly reorganised the game plan because it became different then. All of a sudden after 48 games, the game was asking us a different question.

"It didn't matter what we'd practiced for a week, two weeks or a year before. I'm being asked if after 48 seconds, with ten men, can I get Tranmere promoted? Already I've got injuries in my back four as well!

"That's where we work hard on the mentality of the players and tell them to be good at what the game's asking you. So when we went out on the astroturf at Maidstone and Bromley, we had the mentality of being good at what the game asked us. They quickly flipped into that.

"The game is asking something different, the environment is different, and they'll sacrifice their own personal performance. They quickly settled into that and concentrated on being good at what was needed. They kept it simple and ground their way through."

It was a huge call from the referee to send Ridehalgh off, especially so early in the game. He could have let it go and just produced a yellow card. But in Mark Palios' opinion, the official was eager to make his mark early on.

"The referee has four or five big decisions to make and he's got to get most of those right," he explains. "It's then about game management. Everybody says technically it was a red card. Well technically it might have been, but his job is to manage the game fairly. It's not about influencing the game. I think it was more about him as a decision.

"I don't know what was in his mind, but I would suspect that it was 'I can make a big decision early on'. He was running towards it with his red card out, whereas if you'd looked at it, what would have happened if he'd have given a yellow?

"Take into account that the lad's come straight out of the dressing room and he was fired up for a massive game. He miss-controls the ball and flies in to try and retrieve it. There wasn't really any malice involved in it. What you should say is 'here's a yellow card', and then when he's on a caution, would he make a tackle like that again? No.

"So what have you done? Well you haven't actually influenced the game in the way that he did. As it happened, it worked out for us and it was almost as good as Dunkirk, without minimising Dunkirk! It was a fantastic, fantastic drama, but that isn't the referee's job. I feel badly about it and disagree with people who say it was a brave decision. Yes, it might have been a great decision, but you might make it for the wrong reasons."

Ben Harrison does not think the defender should have been sent off either. "If it had been against Tranmere, it would have been a yellow," he says. "I'm convinced it wouldn't have been a red. When it was, I couldn't believe it.

"Obviously I'm biased, but I didn't think it should have been one, especially because it was Liam. He's not that type of player. If it had been Jay Harris, it would have been different! I've seen it back and other fans say it was a red, but technically he didn't get him.

"The referee made his decision though and that meant Boreham Wood went from underdogs to favourites. We were underdogs and that suited us. It was like that Wrexham game earlier in the season, but reversed. Boreham Wood didn't know what to do. They passed the ball from left to right but not to each other."

***

The sending off had a massive influence on the game, but not in a way that you would expect it to. This Tranmere team had heart and desire. They had guts and team spirit beyond belief and they would fight for each other until the bitter end. They were not going to let being reduced to ten men shatter their Wembley dream.

The crowd on the other hand were fearing the worst. They had seen Rovers teams of the past mess things up before. Go back to the 2000 League Cup final, and they'd had a man sent off. But this was completely unchartered territory.

However, this team would make things work. Jeff Hughes, momentarily at left-back after Ridehalgh had been dismissed, took a quick throw-in, releasing James Norwood down the wing.

The striker allowed the ball to bounce twice, taking a quick look into the box after the first, before releasing a pinpoint cross towards the near post. His partner in crime is there, charging forwards like a man possessed. This was his moment. Bang. A trademark bullet header. Vintage Andy Cook. Grant Smith had no chance in the Boreham Wood goal as the ball fizzed past him. 1-0.

"I couldn't get excited," admits Mark Palios. "I was still fuming from the sending off. I knew we had to go 90 minutes with ten men. Being valiant losers wasn't something I wanted to end the day as."

After taking the lead, Mellon immediately turned to this substitutes. Larnell Cole was replaced by Eddie Clarke, who slotted in at left-back. The move allowed Hughes to push back into midfield, whilst Norwood would cover both the wing and his centre forward position.

Another issue was Josh Ginnelly, who was hit by a bottle thrown by a spectator in the Boreham Wood section during the goal celebrations. He required lengthy treatment to his head and was replaced after 34 minutes, partly due to the incident, but also because the manager wanted a more defensive option on the right wing.

The man Mellon turned to was Connor Jennings, one of Tranmere's most consistent players throughout the season. He had scored and created vital goals, and of course netted at Wembley twelve months earlier. There had, though, been those serious concerns about not only his health, but his future in football. Simply being in the squad was a miracle in itself.

"It was obviously in my mind that we were running out of substitutes," Mellon admits. "But I had to get somebody on the right hand side to help out Manny Monthe. We were getting exposed. It's that golf club analogy again - you've got a set of them behind you.

"So we're away from home, we've got ten men and we're 1-0 up. Who will give me the best chance of fixing that right hand side? Josh

Ginnelly was getting too far forward and they were getting in behind him. I looked behind me and Connor Jennings is there.

"I know what he's been through, but he's got balls the size of Birkenhead. He doesn't care what he's been through. He wants to play. I'd promised his mum, Debbie, and his brother, James, that I would only use him if I needed him because of what he's been through. She said 'thank you Micky, I appreciate that'.

"When she saw him coming on so early, she probably thought I had Alzheimer's or something and that I must have forgotten that conversation we had about sticking her son on at Wembley! I had no problem with it though. We knew he was ready. He goes into that right hand side.

"On the left, we had Eddie Clarke. People asked me if I was worried about putting a young boy on, but I wasn't. He's here to play football. We've worked all season. He knows the role and the principles of how you play in our back four. He could probably tell you now, even though the bugger's done one to Fleetwood! I asked him if he knew what to do and he told me. He just went on at left back and away we went. We were compact and strong."

In between the two substitutions, Boreham Wood created relatively little. Steve McNulty made one crucial block from Bruno Andrade at the near post, whilst Rovers also had Ritchie Sutton to thank for an inch perfect tackle on Michael Folivi after he burst into the box and was just about to release the trigger.

Unfortunately, that was to be the defender's last telling contribution. He too had to be replaced in first half injury time due to an Achilles injury. Jay Harris came on in his place, with Monthe moving across to partner McNulty at centre-half, but it was a nightmare situation for Mellon. He had had to make all three changes before the break - and had ten men.

At this point, he still had a 1-0 lead to protect as well. He just wanted to get his players into the dressing room. The six minutes of added time had elapsed and he was begging for the break, as were the Tranmere fans who were whistling and calling on the referee to bring a halt to proceedings.

It was all in vain though as Boreham Wood equalised out of the blue. Danny Woodards, who had six months at Prenton Park when Rovers were in League Two, was picked out on the left and he sent a skidding cross in towards the penalty spot.

It picked out Andrade, who fired through Monthe's legs and past Scott Davies, who had no chance of getting down to his right to keep the ball out. It was a tidy finish, but with eight minutes of added time having been played, Mellon was fuming. His assistant Mike Jackson was actually sent off when the break finally came for complaining too forcefully to the referee.

"When I saw the board going up for the injury time, I could not believe it," says Mellon. "I thought 'this is not happening'. We're already gutted about the injury time and we have ten men. I need to get the lads in.

"We would then be 1-0 up for the next fifteen minutes. I can then reset the group. But they scored at the worst possible time for us, best for them. Their tails are up and they're thinking 'here we go'. I'm looking at us and I knew I needed to get them in."

***

When the half-time whistle finally went, a strange atmosphere engulfed Wembley. Tranmere were devastated. Their chins were on the floor. Despite everything that had gone against them, they thought they would be heading to the break 1-0 up. But, with ten men, having lost a key centre-back to injury and made all three substitutes, they had conceded an equaliser in the eighth minute of added time.

Heads had dropped, for the players and the fans. Everybody was thinking the same thing. 'It's gone. Chance blown. Another season in the National League awaits.' Everybody, that is, apart from Micky Mellon.

"They got to the dressing room before me and they were all arguing," he reveals. "They're fighting and all the rest of it in there. It's just my job to go in and gauge what's going on. I wasn't interested in what they had to say.

"I said 'sit the fuck down and shut the fuck up. It's 1-1 and you're at Wembley. This can go one way or the other. We can leave now, or we can go out there and fight. What I will tell you is if you get over the line here and you keep believing, keep fighting and you stick to the game plan, you walk out of this stadium as a fucking legend.

"They will be talking about this game forever. You will be coming back to Prenton Park with your kids and grandkids and they'll be talking about the time you saved the football club. That's the gift and prize you're getting offered now. There it is. Be a fucking legend.

"You don't often get offered that. It's there for you. Go and grab it. Go and take the gift and the prize and be a legend. You will go up those 107 steps. When you walk out, have a little look back at them, because you're going up them. Fight to go up the steps.' And they did."

It was a slightly different half time break for Mark Palios. He was still riled by the sending off, but to add insult to injury, his team had conceded that late goal. He simply could not believe what he was watching.

"That as a player, I know, would have hit me hard," he says. "It would have hit your belief that we could actually hold out and win this. Having done so well for 45 minutes and taken the lead with 10 men, you know you've got to score, otherwise you're into 120 minutes with 10 men, or 130 or 140 minutes! That was a body blow.

"I went in at half time and I was just unsociable. I actually went back out and sat in the Royal Box on my own. Somebody came out and tried to talk to me and in the end I just said 'Do you not understand why I'm out here on my own?' I just thought it was one of those days where everything was conspiring against us."

*　*　*

Mellon's team talk worked. His players came out for the second half and they had a game plan. Whereas before the break it was a case of defending and then hoofing clear, they now tried to play around with possession and tried to pick holes in the Boreham Wood defence.

One opened up almost immediately as Jennings broke into the area and forced a solid save out of Smith at his near post, whilst Cook followed up on the rebound only for his effort to be deflected wide. James Norwood headed over the bar from the resulting corner.

Boreham Wood on the other hand grew into the half. They did not create too much to trouble Scott Davies though as they were restricted to efforts from distance. Andrade had one shot tipped around the post, whilst another weak free kick was easily claimed.

They were, however, having more and more possession. That in turn meant Tranmere started to sit deeper. They were camped in their own half. Tiredness was setting in, sapping the energy out of their legs. They had ten men. Mellon could not make any substitutions. These players were in for the long haul.

Sensing their team needed some assistance, the Super White Army lifted, man, woman and child, and created a cacophony of noise. From the hour mark onwards, Wembley was filled with chant after chance after chant. The fans were utterly remarkable.

Spurs have spent a year playing under the famous arch and even then, when the stadium is full, the atmosphere cannot be as effective as it was for those 30 minutes. The supporters were not going to allow their team to lose. They sucked the players forward. They gave them the energy they needed. Everybody at the club came together as one.

"I've never seen a crowd have as much of an influence on a performance as those fans," remarks Ben Harrison. "Give Eric Nixon and Micky Mellon credit because they were going to them and telling them they were the eleventh man.

"The noise levels just went up and up. A lot of people who watched on TV or listened on the radio have said they've been to Wembley before but, even when it's full, it's not that loud. It showed the unity between the fans and the club. We will see the benefit for years to come. It's the manager, the club and the fans all in a line."

Mark Palios has been through all of this as a player. He knows how much of a difference the crowd can make on you, whether the atmosphere is positive or negative. When in that first season in the National League there had been boos, now they were all working together. And it had such an impact.

"When the fans came into their own, you just don't know how much that does for you," he says. "When you're playing in a big game, the adrenaline can make your legs feel heavy, or it can work the other way. I don't know how it happens physiologically, but the energy from the fans transmitted to the pitch.

"I don't think I've ever seen a crowd have that much influence on a team's performance, to be honest. I'm sure it happens at Anfield and places like that, everybody will say that it does, but I think the biggest thing for me is the stark contrast in a short number of years.

"You can be churlish and say it's because we're near the top of the league, winning games at home and we're in a crap league and it'll all change once we go up. I'm sure there'll be a few who will fall away, but for me the best thing was to be able to get people to see it at the end of the day. To get them to see how good it is when everybody's together and focused in the same way."

***

With the fans behind them, Tranmere grew and grew. They did not look like the team with ten men. Scott Davies barely had a save to make in the next twenty minutes as Rovers started to push further and further up the pitch.

They were now getting into areas where they could hurt Boreham Wood and their opposition did not look like they knew how to break down a sturdy defence that was being well marshalled by captain Steve McNulty.

Tranmere just had to be patient. They had been the better team. They were using the ball in a tidy and effective manner and looked the far more likely to score. A chance would eventually come, it was just a case of when.

Jennings dragged one wide from distance, whilst his skidding ball in from the right hand corner of the box took a deflection and fizzed past the outstretched boot of Norwood. The striker also did well to get on the end of a corner from the right, but could only head wide of the post.

The moment of truth finally came with ten minutes to play. Cook laid the ball out to Jennings on the right wing, and his first touch was beautiful as he effortlessly glided past Danny Woodards before looking up and clipping a cross in towards Norwood who was near the penalty spot.

The Rovers number 10 had made a brilliant run. He had got in between two defenders and found himself in acres of space. For a moment, time stood still. The ball was hanging in the Wembley air. Smith did not know whether to come or go, and that left Norwood with plenty of time to pick his spot.

By the time he met the ball, he was basically on the six yard line, but the angle was tough. He was nearly past the front post. The striker had to crane his neck and, if possible, find the far corner.

Norwood's connection was perfect. There was not much pace on the cross, but he headed it as hard and as low as possible. Smith tried to keep it out, but despite getting his right glove to the ball, it still dribbled over the line and into the back of the net. Cue jubilation. Cue tears. Cue delirium.

"You see the lay off to Jennings and to be honest it's unbelievable that he's even on the pitch," says Ben Harrison. "You're thinking how is he going to last this game? Surely he'll just slump over soon. He crossed it and the guy didn't go with Norwood.

"There's a great shot from one side where Wembley is complete empty behind him but he's four foot off the ground heading that ball. I was in line with it and it had spin and I thought he'd saved it, but it goes in. The 'keeper had his head in his hands and I thought it was karma after the away game. It was almost like Boreham Wood, to a man, had just gone 'we've lost'.

"People weren't just smiling. They were crying, including myself. I was tearful. I'd lost my mum six months earlier, she was a Tranmere fan, and there were lots of different things that led to that moment. If you look at the footage, there were a lot of grown men crying."

Mark Palios adds: "After 70 minutes, I thought they weren't going to score. They didn't have a clue how to break us down. The sending off played right into our hands as there was no room behind our back four, which was their strength and our weak area.

"We were sitting there quite comfortably and looked more dangerous on the break. They actually looked scared of us on the break. I felt comfortable and thought it was either going to be penalties, or we were going to win it.

"Then just as Connor picks up the ball, I said to Nicky 'if we score, we're going to win this'. I couldn't have timed it better! The ball comes over, Norwood heads it and I thought it's not in! Then you see it hit the net, the net ripples, and it's an unbelievable feeling."

***

There were ten minutes left. Ten minutes for Tranmere to hold on. Ten minutes between Tranmere and the Football League. And it was the longest ten minutes in the life of everybody in the stadium. It dragged and dragged and dragged.

The fans continued to play their part. They viewed the remainder of the game through tear-filled eyes. They begged their team not to concede. They could not take another 30 minutes - and given Tranmere only had ten men and could not make another substitute, the players probably would not have lasted it either.

Boreham Wood threw the kitchen sink at them. Long balls were persistently pumped into the Rovers box and that led to some heart stopping moments. Scott Davies dropped a cross, creating plenty of panic before the clearance was eventually made, whilst huge penalty appeals against Jeff Hughes and Eddie Clarke were turned down.

In the dying seconds, Norwood conceded a free kick fifteen yards inside his own half. This was the last chance. Smith looped the ball into the box, but it was met on the 18-yard line by Hughes. He headed clear and moments later, the referee blew his whistle. It was over. Finally. Mellon's mission accomplished.

"When that final whistle went," says Mellon, "I just thought 'that's the end of the pain. It's gone'. I knew what was going to happen on both sides - whether we went up or not. If we didn't, I knew what the plan was and it wasn't a good place to be for Tranmere.

Bal darts home sber...

"Going up was a massive step forward, I knew that, in building the club back up again. When I heard that whistle, it was as clear as day. I can still hear it now. It was a real hard, sharp pitch. As soon as I heard it, I said 'that's it, it's done'. That was it.

"Those players managed the game and did their jobs with some heroic stuff. They didn't get caught up in any disappointment. They just kept going. We knew we'd get a chance. We knew that they would become desperate and we knew that we had pace, so we knew how we would catch them.

"When we scored to make it 2-1, there was delirium from us all, but we quickly settled down. I told them to stay there and celebrate because we needed to calm down again. We needed to get back to the half way line and reset.

"They were going to throw the kitchen sink at us and we needed to stand strong and do our jobs. If it was going to get booted into our 18 yard box, we had to win the first header and maybe score another, or stop the cross, or slow the game down when we could. Whatever it was, they knew the jobs and they did it.

"There's something that I always say to the players, and that is that it's harder to play for Tranmere than against them. I hope people understand what I mean when I say that. Tranmere have got to win every week, certainly at this level. We're a big club and a big favourite. To be able to go out and play under those conditions all the time is very satisfying to us.

"Like the pain of losing to Forest Green will stay with me forever, the feeling of success and the satisfaction of getting promoted will also be there. It's a day that I will remember for the rest of my life."

When the whistle went, the scenes inside Wembley were unbelievable. Players streamed across the pitch. Mellon ran at a speed he had never reached before, accelerating towards the Super White Army like a Formula 1 car. His momentum was halted when Ollie Norburn rugby tackled him to the ground.

In the stands, fans hugged strangers. This was pure, unbridled joy, the kind which is rarely witnessed. At times in your life, something so good happens that your brain switches off. You do not realise what you are doing. You have lost self control. Every Tranmere fan in that stadium went through that. They got lost in the moment. This had been 27 years in the making. A whole generation of supporters had never witnessed anything like this. It was the happiest day of their lives.

"A number of things were coming together all at one time," says Mark Palios. "One was the policy of trying to keep a consistent squad, which you don't get at the bottom end of the league. Tranmere used to clear out their squad most seasons.

"It takes you time to then build that team spirit. James Norwood, Jay Harris and Scott Davies, plus others, had been there for three years. Steve McNulty had been there for the thick end of three years. So this squad had built up a massive team spirit.

"You saw them digging in and you could sense it on the pitch. I just looked at that, and apart from when Scotty flapped at one, because you know there's always going to be one mistake but even that was cleared, I was comfortable.

"Then there is the manager. One of the main reasons I kept Micky, and it is something that makes him stand out from other managers, is that he really does make positive substitutions. He uses his squad well. That happened, quite clearly.

"The next thing that was coming together was the fans. Lots of the stuff we were doing in terms of communication, what we were trying to do and how we were trying to run the club, was there. But if you then look at the medium term strategy, how do you get kids back into the game? First of all you have to get them into the ground and secondly you have to make the experience good.

"You've got momentum in the fanbase but you've also got it closer to the team, because if they're helping you when you're down, it just creates a bond. I just sat there and thought 'yes'. So those three things came together at the final and nobody knew.

"There are so many guys who have come up to me and said 'I was crying'. It was a fantastic feeling. I've been in the game for years. I remember standing at the European Championships and I was badged up as the Chief Executive of the FA. The grounds are full and you're standing for the national anthem. There are crosses of St George and you think 'it doesn't get much better than this'. But it was by far and away surpassed by that day at Wembley.

"I'm a great believer in visualisation and I visualised that day. You wouldn't believe me, but I did. I'd always planned to go on the pitch and give Nicky a kiss in the centre circle, but she ran off, so I was left on my own! I was just walking around trying to absorb it all.

"Then I ended up with a fan's scarf and I started twirling it. All my partners at PWC would be saying 'what a knob!' It was a surreal experience, as was being on the supporter's shoulders in the tent after the Ebbsfleet game. I came back the next morning and thought 'oh shit'. People who don't like football won't understand it. It's such a unifying force for the community. It really has lifted the Wirral, and even Liverpool and Everton fans are quite pleased."

For Ben Harrison, the emotions were just as high. He had been there for the glory years under Johnny King and had devoted so much of his life towards championing the cause of Tranmere Rovers. In terms of success on the pitch, they had given nothing back since the turn of the century. Now, though, he had something to celebrate, and it was worth the wait.

"We performed so heroically," he says, eyes twinkling as he recalls the feeling that the final whistle gave him. "I've never seen anything like it from a Tranmere team. There are a couple of other games that come to mind, like when we beat Exeter to stay in the league and the play-off final win over Bolton, but that was different. Nothing was like this.

"Forest Green got the trophy on the pitch the year before. We came up the steps and I stood there thinking 'what a place to be'. I said to Mark 'this is just the start'. We hugged each other and I'm excited to see what happens next.

"It meant so much because it was some kind of escape act. Look at that league next year - with Salford, Chesterfield and Fylde and so much more in it. We could have injuries again and not go up. So it was relief. But also Tranmere are back where they should be.

"I've never been more proud to be a Tranmere fan. I saw all three promotions under Johnny King and this one was sweeter, certainly more significant. Mark or Nicola could have questioned how much longer they could go on if we didn't win. It's given them such a boost and some pride. The same goes for the fans.

"It's relief, but with massive optimism. We got back to the bar in Oxton and my friends and family were there. The atmosphere was unreal. There was such a buzz.

"Birkenhead has been down on it's luck as a town. I always defend the place, I've got businesses here. The Football Club can be a catalyst. People who live here say it's a shit hole, but they've got a Football Club who are back in the Football League.

"Look at what Liverpool Football Club does for the city of Liverpool; it can start something off. All of a sudden the council have got a civic reception at the Town Hall to celebrate our promotion. It's huge and I don't think we've seen what could happen after this.

"But if Tranmere go up from League Two next year, nobody will cry, they will just celebrate. That's what we did with the other promotions. It wasn't life or death, but this meant so much."

Chapter Twenty Seven
Promotion Monologues

Everybody has their own story of Wembley. Each player had a different view of what happened on that pitch, or a particular moment that stands out more than any other. Here are the stories of some of the key figures, who describe their experiences and recollections from the day.

Scott Davies

The morning was quite relaxed. I'm quite close to the likes of Steve McNulty, Jay Harris, Andy Mangan and James Wallace and we all went out for a little walk. We even went around the outside of the ground.

The year before, we stayed a 40 minute drive from Wembley, but this time we stay at the Hilton right outside. There were some fans turning up and we met a few of them when we were sat in Costa.

The year before was different. We went down two days before and trained at Barnet the day before the game. Then we went to the Women's FA Cup final after training. They decided we should go and sample the stadium, so we did.

We got new tracksuits and polo shirts as well, with Wembley stuff stitched in. I think that things like that, without us knowing it, turned the game against Forest Green into a big who-ha. It was almost like a festival. Even with things like tickets, we were talking about them on the training ground. We needed this and that and to go here and there. The football side of it got lost. That will happen to a lot of teams because going to Wembley is such a big event.

This time, we trained at Tranmere on the Friday morning, as normal, and travelled after training, as we usually do for an away game. We got to the hotel, had some tea and massages and used the pool if we wanted to. This time we knew it was about business and getting the job done.

I think that because we'd been there the year before, we knew what it was all about. That was what we would normally do on an away trip and we treated it that way. It was a nice, relaxed morning. When we arrive at grounds, I don't really go on the pitches. But last year, with it being Wembley I did. We were taking photos. This time, that wasn't the case. It was all about business. The lads just got in there and did their usual routine.

In the dressing room it was calm and quiet, apart from the music that was playing. Adam Buxton had picked that, he always does. I'm not sure why, though. I've had the selection a few times but it always gets turned off because Eminem comes out! I've no idea what he put on. It's always this dance stuff that is meant to get you going, but I tend to block it out because it's not really my taste.

There seemed to be a confidence that we were going to do it. I think fate is a big thing in football and I think a lot of people felt that it was our destiny to do it, especially after the way the semi-final had gone.

Then we go out there and after less than a minute, Liam Ridehalgh got sent off. I didn't even see the referee pull his card out. I just remember turning around to the goal and thinking 'oh no, here we go'. It was harsh on him. We can all see why he did it. The emotion's obviously built up, a lot from what happened on his part the year before too.

We had to regroup, but even then there was no panic. I think the way the three years had gone, it was just another thing to come against us. Nothing was going to beat us that day.

Cooky's goal came close to the sending off. Whenever we've gone ahead, I've never felt like we were going to lose because we're always resolute when we take the lead. With Steve McNulty and myself and the experienced midfielders, we knew how to see out a game.

There was one moment in the game where belief dwindled from me, and that was when they scored. You look at the body language of the lads and you can see belief sap from us. Everything had gone against us. We had no subs left, Ritchie Sutton had gone and we had a centre midfielder playing left-back at one point. It was all over the show.

I give huge credit to Micky Mellon, Michael Jackson and Eric Nixon, because they knew what needed to be done. In football, sometimes if you just stick to the plan and do nothing more than that, you get your rewards. They didn't panic once. There were substitutions going on but they didn't rush any of them. They waited until they knew that that was what they needed to do.

Even at half time, straight after the equaliser, there was no panic. The gaffer just told us what needed to be done and we stuck to his word. The staff hadn't lost belief.

Connor Jennings was one of those substitutes. When he came on, he made a big difference. Straight after half time, he has a shot and Cooky follows it up. That's when I thought it was on. The gaffer had said to us 'stay in the game, don't let them score and you'll get a chance'. After that chance, the fans went up and I thought we can do this.

I don't really remember the goal. I remember all the lads celebrating and Steve McNulty turned round to me and we had a little hug and said 'come on, it's up to us two now to get us through'. It was a good moment. I've watched it back and it took an age from James Norwood's head to reach the back of the net.

I think the last ten minutes are more clear than that goal. I dropped that cross! Blame the weather because it was wet! There was another moment when Eddie Clarke hand balled it towards the end.

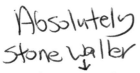

Absolutely
Stone Waller

It's a stone wall penalty, but it ended up in my hands thankfully. I looked up at the clock and it was nearly done. That was the moment when I thought we're going to do it now.

It was a strange game though, because I didn't have much to do. I give huge credit to Macca in front of me for that. He's been written off so many times over the years but that performance was a captain's performance. He led and saved me from doing a lot of work. Manny Monthe was the same.

When the final whistle went, I fell on my knees and I was almost in tears. I was very emotional. All the rest of the lads ran to the fans, but Macca turned to me because we've been through a lot together in our careers. It meant a lot to both of us. We've both been written off and we've both proved everyone wrong again. It was a great moment.

When I played at Wembley for Morecambe, I remember looking back at the celebrations and thinking 'I don't remember any of that'. My mates said to me 'it wasn't you, you were just away with it'. This time I tried to take it in a little bit more, but when I got up there and got hold of the trophy, emotions got hold of me. It had all built up over three years and it all came out that day.

My 48 seconds

We were all very excited on the morning of the game. We knew that we didn't want a repeat of twelve months earlier. The occasion had got to us then. We had struggled against the top sides and I personally believe that was in the back of our minds.

Having said that, I've watched the game back and I do think it could have gone either way. James Norwood has missed a one on one and there's a cross to Andy Mangan that he nearly tapped in too. It just wasn't meant to be.

I made the error when they scored the third. It was a pivotal moment in the game. It made it 3-1 just before half time and it was an awful time to concede. If we'd gone in 2-1 down at half-time, we might have had the belief that we could win it, but I think it was just too much.

So when we are in the tunnel before the Boreham Wood game, I am really hyped up. I really wanted to make up for that mistake the previous year. I wanted to put things right.

I was also thinking that we had a great chance because, and I mean no disrespect to them, but they were nowhere near the standard of Forest Green. They had a few good players, don't get me wrong, but if you take the front three out, they didn't really have much.

We get underway and when the ball landed to me, I took a touch because I saw a big space in front of me. I thought if I take the ball into that space, I'm running onto the back four. It was just too heavy but so early on, I didn't want to give it away. I lunged in and I think it was the correct decision from the referee to send me off, but it wasn't malicious.

I'm walking off and Eric Nixon puts his arm around when I get to the tunnel. I'm just thinking to myself 'what have I done?' I'd let everyone down – my teammates, the fans, the club, the manager, the chairman. Everybody.

We all fucking were pal!

253

I knew how important this season was for Tranmere to go up, for so many different reasons. Coming down into the National League was a big thing in terms of the club's finances. We needed to go up. I thought I'd messed that up.

Connor Jennings then came into the dressing room and said 'it's going to be all right – we're still going to win' but I was just saying 'no, Connor, we've messed it up'. He is a very good friend of mine and I'll never forget that.

I was taking my shin pads off and I was going to stay in the changing room. I was being a bit of a coward. I was thinking 'I can't go back out there'. Then John the coach driver ran in and told me Andy Cook had just scored. I said 'get away, no chance'.

Thankfully, I wasn't in there for long in the end. I didn't even need a shower! If it wasn't for John, though, I don't think I'd have gone back out. I'm glad he got me out there.

I go out to watch and it's all collapsing in front of me. Larnell Cole had come off and I felt so sorry for him because he didn't really play. If I hadn't been sent off he wouldn't have come off. He's another good friend of mine so I was upset for him.

Then Ritchie Sutton had to come off and I was thinking it wasn't our day again. I just couldn't believe it. Then they score just before half time. To be honest, I think half time came at a great time. They were on top for the ten or fifteen minutes before hand. Half time settled people down.

I didn't go into the dressing room during the break. I was thinking about it, but I was trying to put myself into the players' shoes. In a game of that magnitude, after I got sent off, I thought I'd better stay away. I just sat there with Elliot Rokka.

The second half got underway and when James Norwood scored, I thought there was a lot longer left. I don't know why, but I thought there were 20 or 25 minutes left.

Anyway, the ball hit the back of the net and I just burst into tears. I'm a bit of a pansy anyway, I do show my emotions! Every emotion that you could think of was going through my body. I was angry at getting sent off, but so relieved as well.

That was when I thought 'we're going to do this'. There were nine minutes left. We had done it before that season. I knew we could hang on. But the time that remained dragged. I just wanted the whistle to go. I had my fingers crossed and every time Boreham Wood put the ball into the box, my heart was in my mouth.

I thought if they had scored and it went to extra time, just having an extra man would have meant they punished us. I'm so grateful that they didn't!

It took me ages to get onto the pitch when the final whistle went because I hurt my knee in the tackle! I wanted to sprint on, I really did, but I had to hobble on. I've made a lot of friends at that Football Club, so I wanted to celebrate with them. I was as happy for them as I was for myself.

I was very emotional. I had signed for Tranmere when they were in League One and I never thought we'd end up in the National League. After having such disappointing times at Tranmere, to actually have a year of success was amazing.

When we were relegated, I said to myself that I was always going to stay to get them back into the Football League. I never wanted to leave them in the National League, never, as long as the contracts were available! I wouldn't have a choice if they weren't! But if I had a choice, I was always going to stay and get them up. I've done that now.

I'm very proud of what we have achieved over the last twelve months. It hasn't been easy at times because of the relegations. Other players would have crumbled with that. But from a personal point of view, you've just got to keep going. I'm really happy that we're back in the Football League now.

James Norwood

We stayed in a different hotel to the year before. The one ahead of the Forest Green final was much further away and there wasn't really a communal place where we could chill out.

This time, we had the physio room and everybody was in there watching football. We were having a laugh and chilling. On the morning of the game, I ended up going to Liam Ridehalgh and Ollie Norburn's room and it was so relaxed, because we were only two minutes from Wembley. It was a nice hotel.

I wasn't nervous in the morning. I can only speak for myself and not the other lads, but games don't phase me. Why would I be nervous? I've been doing this for twenty years. It's a game of football. You're playing with some of your best mates against a team of other mates. You may as well be down the park.

If you can't enjoy massive occasions, why are you playing the game? If you can't be relaxed, why are you playing the game? You've got to trust your own ability. Unless you think you're crap, you can do it.

Whatever league I play in, I want to be the best player in the league. Why would I be scared of Boreham Wood? Why would I be scared of playing football? It's in my hands. If somebody passes me the ball, somebody isn't moving my legs or body for me, so why are you worried?

That was the difference this year. People had played there before, so nothing was new. There were no nerves. It was in the same changing room. We'd seen it all before.

We get underway and I was very close to Liam Ridehalgh when he made the tackle. I thought he'd kicked the ball on to him, that's why it ballooned out. So me and Cooky run over to the ref and tell him that. He slid for ages and kicked it on to him. I've seen it back now - it's a good decision.

Twelve months earlier, I had to sit next to Liam on the coach home and he just kept saying 'I've cost us' because of the third goal Forest Green scored. Of course he didn't. But genuinely, hand on my heart, my first thought when he got sent off was that I had to sit next to him on the way back.

I didn't care that he'd been sent off, because I knew that we could play with ten men. It's not the end of the world. I just thought if we lose, I had to sit next to him for four hours and I would say something, not to him, and he'd punch me in the face!

After the game finished, we're on the coach, all drinking and that, and Liam is very deadpan. He just says 'I can't play at Wembley me'. We were all laughing and saying 'You're right! You can't! If we get there again, you're not playing!' That's the sort of guy he is, he's very self-deprecating.

A few minutes after he's sent off, I get the ball on the left. As it bounces the first time, I have a look and see a white shirt near the centre of the goal. I knew it must be Cooky and he was making a near post run. Normally you wouldn't see him, he'd be behind someone.

I just put it in there and I've hit it so sweet. I thought I'd half looped it, but when you see the video it flies in with a bit of bend. You can't stop Cooky in those positions. He's getting his head to the ball. There's only one outcome. I just stand there with my arms outstretched.

That's a partnership - know where he is and know what he's going to do. He knew to get to the near stick. It took him 48 games to know that! But he made the run and he's got a goal at Wembley.

So we are 1-0 up, but they equalised just before half time. Honestly, I didn't think it was a problem. Tell me a centre forward who's going to bully Manny Monthe and Steve McNulty? I can't think of any.

Jay Harris is now at right back because Ritchie Sutton has come off.

He had done brilliantly there before - he sent Dagenham's winger into the stands! But a couple of times, we were overloaded on the right hand side because we had somebody there who wasn't a natural there. If you don't play there, you're going to over cover inside because that's seen as the danger.

It's a good cross that goes through Manny's legs and it's a good finish. Six minutes of injury time had originally been signalled but Sutton had gone down and needed treatment, so we played more than that. To be fair, the referee's got it right again. I can't complain.

However, all I'm feeling now is 'that's the game', because we spent the whole half just kicking it out. We didn't try and play football. That's what we were going to do for 90 minutes. Just whack it and soak it. They get the goal and it changes the whole complexion of the game.

After half time, we had a chance straight away. It falls to Connor and Cooky, and it goes out for a corner. That's when I started thinking that we're in the game. We can counter attack. We just dug in. With the team we've got, the players should be in the League. I don't know why they aren't. So why shouldn't we be in the game? Just wait for a chance.

That's when the fans came into it and they were massive, absolutely massive. There were more of them last year, but last year they didn't get behind us as well. They realised that we missed them last year. They were groaning and everything, but I don't hold it against them as it wasn't a good performance.

I've watched the whole game on television about 30 times. The volume has been on 75. About 60 or 61 minutes in it has to go down to 41 because I'm thinking I'm waking people up in the street! There was a challenge by Jay Harris, bang, welcome to the game, and the fans didn't stop for half an hour after that.

And then we get to my goal. Scotty lines up for a goal kick and the camera pans to their manager, who tries a bottle flip! The commentator says 'can they muster anything from these last ten minutes?' Cooky wins a header and then Jeff Hughes, going backwards, slightly puts his arm on their man, who heads it down.

Cooky then lays it off to Connor and his first touch is the best of the game. It goes forward and he takes it outside. He has a look and I point inside the defender. He crosses and it takes a massive deflection and spoons up in the air. If it had come normally, I could have glanced it, but there's no pace on the ball. I was just waiting for it to come down.

I look at the 'keeper who's thinking about coming but then backtracks. I'm at an angle where, with the ball coming down, there's no way the 'keeper thinks I'm going across goal. It shouldn't really be possible to get an angle on it. He's got to think I'm going near post or straight at him.

I just made sure I twisted everything and it came off my scar. If I headed it with the side of my head, I knew there was no way he'd save it. I got a good connection. On TV it looks slower than it is and people say the 'keeper should have saved it. But there's one angle where you see it at full pace and it's quick.

You see the 'keeper take a step and it bounces just before him. Because it looks like it's close to him and he gets a hand on it, it looks like he should save it. I genuinely don't think if you put him in that position again, or any other 'keeper in the league, that they'd save it. It was seven yards out and I got a good connection. I went exactly where he didn't think I was going to go. It bounced just before him and skidded. I just don't think they save it. I've looked at it in slow motion and the lot. You could see the way he dived. He just wasn't expecting it to go there.

It was absolute scenes. I love looking at the pictures of Ridehalgh in tears and the fans in tears. It shows the bond between us. We were all feeling the same emotion. They're crying and they just can't wait for the game to end. We're just grafting to make sure it happens.

I can't remember the next ten minutes. It was a mixture of fatigue, euphoria and adrenaline. That's why I've watched the game back so many times. I'm trying to trigger my brain into remembering feelings that I had. Hughes wins the header though and we should have stayed in the box because it was going to get hooked back in, but we're charging out. We're going to pressure the ball. Then the whistle goes and you see this wave of players.

There's an incident with me and the Boreham Wood manager too. Steve McNulty asked me what happened afterwards, because he was involved. Basically, their gaffer was unhappy that when the final whistle went, our gaffer didn't shake his hand straight away, he just took off.

So he said 'well played, your lads deserved it, congratulations and do well' and all that, 'but your manager's this for not shaking my hand'. I was saying 'he'll come and do it in a minute'. Macca, being the big daddy that he is, thought he was having a go at me because I was making all sorts of hand movements, and he just gripped him and lifted him up. You see their manager, who's not a small bloke, going up in the air! I pushed Macca off and gave him a hug and then when I told him on the coach what it was over, he just went 'oh no. Oh crap'.

Then I somehow manage to spot my family in the crowd. I don't know how I saw or heard them, but it was just special that I got to share that moment with them and hug them and kiss them.

Also it was so lucky that it got caught on TV. Somebody paused the TV screen and took a picture of it and now my mum has it printed on her mantelpiece. When I was 18, I won the National School's Championship out of 3000 schools at Aldershot. I went and hugged my mum and dad then. I got to do that again as a play-off final winner.

All it is is memories. You can't pass on memories. But every time somebody comes round to my mum's house, they'll see me wearing a Tranmere shirt - Norwood 10 - and my mum crying in a red jumper and they'll ask what it is. She can reply 'that's when my son hugged me after scoring the winner at Wembley'. It's such a good moment. The whole thing. I'm getting DVDs sent to my mum and dad so they can keep it and they can make a shrine to me because I've been away for so long!

After that, we get to go and lift the trophy. There are 107 steps at Wembley. It was all the gaffer talked about for two weeks. He said 'you as a group of players are going to walk those steps, I guarantee it'. There were over 20 of us there. At least 19 counted 107 steps. Some of them didn't because they're too stupid. They got lost at 10 and counted to 10 eleven times!

I counted every step and got emotional. I stood there just trying to take it all in. I was next to Connor and Liam and looked to my right where all our fans were. It was just a special moment. It's something I can never draw or take a picture of again, but I've got it in photo form in my head. Nobody can take that away from me. It's beautiful. I would give anything to have those three days back.

Connor Jennings

I took ill on the Friday, the day before the final game of the season against Hartlepool. I got home and I wasn't well at all. I was hallucinating and was going through hot and cold sweats, plus I had some really bad migraines. I got rushed into hospital at midnight and I was getting treated for meningitis in the end. I was on quite a few drips. I was there for just short of a week and it was quite a crazy time.

If I'm honest, I don't really remember the first few days. I was pretty out of it. My first thought when I came round was about missing the most important games of the season though. I was going to be out of the Ebbsfleet match and I wasn't very happy.

So I was thinking very short term - just about football. There's no worse feeling than not being able to help your teammates. I felt hopeless. It wasn't good. But my family were thinking it was a lot worse. It wasn't good for them.

Micky Mellon was in a lot of contact with my mum and my brother. He was great. He was always texting and asking my parents if I was okay. He wasn't rushing me back, although I was trying to rush back. He was taking it day by day. I can't fault anybody from the club. They were so supportive of me.

I got released from hospital and returned to light training the day before the Ebbsfleet game. I wasn't 100%, but by then I was gradually feeling a lot better and stronger, so I was just having a little walk around the pitch. Then I had the heartbreak of missing that match. Watching from the stands nearly put me back in hospital!

I knew when I left hospital that I would be involved at Wembley if we got there. I wasn't going to let that chance slip. I would do everything I could to get there, but I only wanted to be there if I could give 100%. There was no point being there only for myself. My dad wanted me to play. He understood I couldn't start. He just said 'make sure you're ready, enjoy it, and see what happens'.

I end up being on the bench. Obviously you want to start every game and I'm sure the gaffer lost a bit of hair thinking about it. It was so difficult. But I can't blame him for what he did. He didn't know if I'd be alright. Neither did I. I totally understand and respect his decision.

Also, we had a great squad, so it's not like missing out massively. Josh Ginnelly and Larnell Cole start on the wings, so it's not like we didn't have anybody else. That's the trust we all had.

Less than a minute into the game, Liam Ridehalgh gets sent off. Now I travel into training with him every day, so we're very close. I ran down the tunnel to speak to him because I was so gutted for him. You don't wish that on anybody. Everybody was really looking forward to the game and then something like that happens. So a friend is a friend; I had to go and see him to make sure he was alright. I knew he'd be upset so I just wanted to comfort him.

Thirty minutes later, Micky turns round and calls for me to come on. I was thinking 'oh no'! But it was just a case of going back to work. I didn't think too much about it or put too much pressure on myself. I knew that it was going to be a slog and that I'd have to concentrate a lot more on our shape and my positioning. It was tough, but it was certainly worth it.

Ritchie Sutton then comes off, and I couldn't believe it. Everything was going against us. But it was just another hurdle to get over. Five minutes later, they scored. That was another hurdle.

I think the most important thing was half time though. It gave the lads a chance to chill out and relax and get their heads focused on the second half. They did that really well. Everybody kept really calm. There was a lot of togetherness in there. We regrouped and had a chat. Conceding was gutting, but we knew we had another big 45 minutes coming up.

We knew we were always going to get chances, even with ten men. We had been creating so many all season, so we knew we'd get at least one. We would be in it to score, so it was just keeping the shape and being patient - the boring side of football! We had to stick together and when a chance came, we knew we had to take it.

I had a chance just after the restart. We played some good football and got in behind. The 'keeper saves my shot and then Cooky's rebound is blocked for a corner. We all sort of went 'we can push on for a goal here'. Obviously we only had ten men, but we still thought we could have a good go at it. We created a few chances after that, maybe not clear cut, but we started to believe.

Extra time was looming and in my head I was thinking 'I wouldn't be surprised if it did come!' But it would just be another hurdle to overcome. I don't think we were really thinking about it though. We thought we'd get that chance. Too many bad things had happened to Tranmere. I said it even at the start of the season. I knew something good would happen. It was written in the stars for us to go up at Wembley. I really believe that. It turned out to be the case!

Then the goal comes. Jeff Hughes heads it down and Andy Cook picks it up. He fed it to me first time and the defender tries to get tight to me. I just took a touch - some may say it came off my shin pad...I don't know!

I wouldn't say I'm a big dribbler, so I was never going to run the rest of the pitch. I had a look up and I can see Norwood in between the two defenders, so I play it a bit earlier before the centre-back drops back. I think it took a slight flick off the defender, which gave it the height, and then he heads it in.

The airtime from when it hit his head was forever - but it led to pure emotion. I just thought 'surely not! Surely not!' Hopefully I will feel like that again one day, because it was the best feeling ever. The celebrations were amazing. We went wild.

There were ten minutes left, which was a bit nerve racking, but we felt comfortable. They were playing into our hands. We trusted each other to deal with it all.

And then the final whistle goes. It was so special. It's hard to put into words. I'm so proud of the lads. To do it in that way was just brilliant.

It was third time lucky for me at Wembley as well. I'd lost with Wrexham in the FA Trophy final and of course the year before. When we lost to Forest Green, I never want to feel like that again. I don't think I've ever felt like that in football before. It hit me very hard.

So it was brilliant to get the win. I'm so happy for the fans and my family as well. They had come twice and seen me lose, so all around it me was an amazing day. It was a feeling I'll never forget.

Epilogue

Being back in the Football League does not mean Tranmere's work is done. Far from it. They are a team who, certainly over the last three decades, have been used to playing much higher up the pyramid, and the aim of Mark and Nicola Palios and Micky Mellon is to bring the glory days back to Prenton Park.

For the chairman, the plan is to keep building on this success. Rovers can be a hub for the local community. They can be a source of pride and joy. Those emotions have been rejuvenated in recent years, and he wants to carry that forward.

"I'm massively proud of what has been achieved," he beams. "I don't use the term vindication, because that implies that you're sticking two fingers up to people, but it's immensely satisfying. Wembley is a place I was involved in building, and if I'd known all those years back that there'd be a day that would come when this would happen, I'd have said 'you're joking'.

"For me, it was a culmination of quite a lot of effort and energy and resources. The family have put a lot into it as well. Two of the girls are working for the club when they could be working elsewhere. Nicky is fantastic as well. She's stood shoulder to shoulder with me through the hard times and bought into the way the club in the way I knew she would. More than anyone, she deserved the day at Wembley. She's also helped a lot in terms of creating the atmosphere that we've got. We were just sitting there at Wembley and we had a team hug.

"We had the civic reception at the Town Hall a few days later. I was a schoolboy at St Anselms, so to stand there on the steps with people chanting your name is just bizarre! Having been the Chief Executive of the FA, they don't really like stuff like that, so it's all quite funny.

"There's much more to do though. People would come up to me and say 'thank you for what you've done for the club'. I'd feel a total fraud because we were still in Non League. I always said 'we haven't done anything yet'. Now I'll reply 'well we've got lots to do'.

"I know what I want as you come into The Campus. I want it to be 'Tranmere Rovers', and I want it to say 'Better Never Sleeps', because that's one of my things. The Wembley thing is exactly that. This morning, I was planning in my head the pictures that go around that statement, which will be Wembley.

"It'll be something like 'Wembley 12th May 2018: It doesn't matter what happens, it's how you respond that counts'. I'll put the pictures in there and underneath it'll say 'Every day, not just May 12th'.

"I love it when you can take a team and take people away and they can realise the whole is greater than the sum of the parts. That's always been a big thing for me, possibly because I've always played a team sport. It's the same in business. Now, when you walk around, there is such a joyous feeling about the place. I keep on saying it, you can't buy that or get it. That's why you're in the game.

"It really is fantastic and is what makes it worthwhile. I could have gone and spent the money we've spent on the club on a fantastic boat, which is what I want to do at some stage, on Lake Garda in the sun. It would be great, but you would get nothing like the highs that you got in the semi finals and certainly that day at Wembley. It was just incredible.

"I felt a bit churlish by saying we'll have a swear box and that you can't mention Wembley. If you're speaking to fans or people outside of the club, that's fine, but inside the club, we've got to get on with next season.

"It will be tough. League Two is a hard league; harder than when we first came into it four years ago. It's a more difficult division, but for all of that, I think we're better equipped to deal with it than we were when we were relegated from League One. We will deal with it. I'll be disappointed if we don't get promoted."

Going up is the aim for Micky Mellon too. He played for Tranmere when they were in the Championship. He knows the potential this club possesses and after becoming just the fourth manager to get them promoted, he is eying even greater glories in the future.

"I've moved on now, I really have," Mellon insists. "I don't know if you become greedy for success. I think you have to though. Already, that's gone for me. It's a place that when you're having a few beers and you're chatting, you'll go back to it. But I'm very much focused on improving the football club.

"Look at my training facilities, my playing staff, the environment that I've created with the help of the players, chairman and the rest of it. Look at where I want to take it to and how I want to improve it - I'm concentrating on that. I know why I'm here, In my head, I know what I want to do and how I want to leave it.

"One day I will leave, because nobody is here forever. I will have left it, I hope, in a sustainable place that, if managed properly by everybody and with the correct expectations, will be a solid football club for the next 100 years. I know that's my part in it now. That's what we'll try and get it to.

"I've still got an awful lot of work to do, but it's organised in my mind and achievable. I've got the opportunity to move it on a bit further because of Wembley and the promotion, but we have to move it on and leave it in a sustainable place that everybody goes to.

"I want people to come to this football club, our training ground, meet my players and me and say 'fucking hell, what a place that is. What a football club that is. That is a proper football club.'

"People are starting to say that now. Wait until you see what they're saying when I hopefully get it to what I want. I'm confident I'll get it to the place I want to get it to."

Statistics

2015/2016

Date	Opponent	Result	Line-Up
08/08/2015	Woking	W 1-0 (Harris)	Davies, Sutton, Hogan, Ihiekwe, Hill, Maynard, Jennings, Harris, Ridehalgh, Norwood (Mekki), Stockton
11/08/2015	Gateshead	W 4-1 (Ridehalgh, Sutton, Ihiekwe, Hill)	Davies, Sutton, Hogan, Ihiekwe, Hill, Maynard, Jennings, Harris, Ridehalgh (Mekki), Mangan, Stockton (Holness)
15/08/2015	Braintree	D 0-0	Davies, Sutton, Hogan (Riley), Ihiekwe, Hill, Maynard, Jennings, Harris, Ridehalgh, Mangan (Mekki), Stockton (Norwood)
18/08/2015	Halifax	W 1-0 (Mangan)	Davies, Sutton, Ihiekwe, Riley, Hill, Maynard, Jennings, Harris, Ridehalgh Mangan, Margetts
22/08/2015	Boreham Wood	L 0-2	Davies, Sutton, Ihiekwe, Riley, Hill, Maynard (Blissett), Jennings, Harris, Ridehalgh, Mangan, Margetts (Mekki)
29/08/2015	Altrincham	L 2-1 (Maynard)	Davies, Sutton, Holness, Riley, Ridehalgh (Jackson), Maynard, Jennings, Harris, Mekki, Stockton (Mangan), Margetts (Blissett)
31/08/2015	Kidderminster	D 2-2 (Hogan, Mangan)	Davies, Sutton, Hogan, Riley, Ridehalgh, Maynard, Jennings, Harris, Mekki (Jackson), Blissett (Ihiekwe), Mangan
05/09/2015	Welling	D 1-1 (Maynard)	Davies, Sutton, Hogan, Ihiekwe, Hill, Maynard, Jennings, Harris, Ridehalgh, Norwood, Mangan (Holness)
12/09/2015	Chester	W 2-0 (Hogan, Norwood)	Davies, Sutton, Hogan, Ihiekwe, Hill, Dawson (Jackson) Jennings, Harris, Mekki, Norwood (Margetts), Mangan (Maynard)
15/09/2015	Southport	D 2-2 (Harris, Norwood)	Davies, Sutton, Hogan, Ihiekwe, Hill, Dawson, Jennings, Harris, Mekki, Norwood, Mangan (Jackson)
18/09/2015	Grimsby	D 1-1 (Blissett)	Davies, Sutton, Hogan (Holness), Ihiekwe, Hill, Dawson, Jennings, Harris, Mekki (Blissett), Norwood, Jackson (Maynard)
22/09/2015	Aldershot	W 3-1 (Norwood, Mekki, Mangan)	Davies, Maynard, Sutton, Ihiekwe, Hill, Dawson (Margetts), Jennings, Harris, Mekki, Norwood, Blissett (Mangan)
26/09/2015	Cheltenham	W 0-1 (Mangan)	Davies, Sutton, Hogan, Ihiekwe, Hill, Mekki, Jennings, Harris, Maynard, Dawson (Jackson), Mangan (Margetts)
03/10/2015	Bromley	W 4-0 (Mangan x2, Margetts x2)	Davies, Sutton, Hogan, Ihiekwe (Riley), Hill, Mekki, Maynard, Harris, Dawson (Jackson), Mangan, Margetts
06/10/2015	Wrexham	D 2-2 (Maynard, Mangan)	Davies, Sutton, Hogan, Riley, Hill, Mekki, Maynard, Harris, Dawson (Jennings), Mangan (Jackson), Margetts (Norwood)
10/10/2015	Eastleigh	L 1-2 (Jennings)	Davies, Sutton (Jennings), Hogan, Riley, Hill, Dawson (Ridehalgh), Maynard, Harris, Jackson (Mekki), Norwood, Mangan
13/10/2015	Barrow	L 0-1	Davies, Sutton, Hogan, Riley, Hill, Mekki, Jennings, Harris, Ridehalgh (Jackson), Norwood, Margetts
17/10/2015	Forest Green	W 0-2 (Taylor-Fletcher, Norwood)	Davies, Maynard, Hogan, Riley, Hill, Mekki, Jennings, Harris, Ridehalgh (Sutton), Taylor-Fletcher, Norwood (Jackson)

269

Date	Opponent	Result	Team
31/10/ 2015	Dover	L 0-1	Turner, Sutton, McNulty, Riley, Hill, Tomlinson, Jennings, Maynard, Ridehalgh (Mangan), Taylor-Fletcher, Norwood
14/11/ 2015	Lincoln	L 1-0	Davies, Sutton, McNulty, Riley, Hill, Tomlinson (Mekki), Jennings, Harris, Taylor-Fletcher, Mangan, Norwood
21/11/ 2015	Guiseley	W 2-1 (Norwood x2)	Davies, Hogan, McNulty, Riley (Maynard), Hill, Mekki (Tomlinson), Jennings, Harris, Taylor-Fletcher, Norwood, Mangan
24/11/ 2015	Woking	L 4-1 (Norwood)	Davies, Maynard, Hogan, McNulty, Hill, Mekki (Sutton), Jennings, Harris, Taylor-Fletcher, Mangan (Tomlinson), Norwood
28/11/ 2015	Boreham Wood	D 0-0	Davies, Vaughan, Hogan (Sutton), McNulty, Hill, Maynard, Jennings, Harris (Mekki), Taylor-Fletcher (Mangan), Tomlinson, Norwood
05/12/ 2015	Braintree	L 1-2 (Mekki)	Davies, Vaughan, McNulty, Sutton, Hill, Mekki, Jennings, Maynard, Ridehalgh (Dawson), Norwood, Mangan
19/12/ 2015	Halifax	D 1-1 (Norwood)	Davies, Vaughan, McNulty, Ihiekwe, Ridehalgh (Sutton), Mekki (Tomlinson), Jennings, Harris, Maynard, Taylor-Fletcher (Mangan), Norwood
26/12/ 2015	Macclesfield	W 1-2 (McNulty, Ihiekwe)	Davies, Vaughan, McNulty, Ihiekwe, Hill, Maynard, Jennings, Harris, Mekki, Taylor-Fletcher (Tomlinson), Norwood
28/12/ 2015	Altrincham	W 1-0 (Norwood)	Davies, Vaughan, McNulty, Ihiekwe, Hill, Maynard, Jennings, Harris, Mekki (Mangan), Tomlinson (Kirby), Norwood
01/01/ 2016	Macclesfield	L 0-1	Davies, Vaughan, McNulty, Ihiekwe, Hill, Maynard, Jennings, Harris, Hughes (Tomlinson), Mekki (Stockton), Norwood
09/01/ 2016	Barrow	W 3-4 (Mekki, Maynard, Hughes, Kirby)	Davies, Vaughan, McNulty, Ihiekwe, Hill, Maynard, Jennings, Harris, Hughes, Mekki (Kirby), Tomlinson (Stockton)
23/01/ 2016	Bromley	W 0-1 (Vaughan)	Davies, Vaughan, McNulty, Ihiekwe, Hill, Maynard, Jennings, Harris, Hughes, Mekki (Taylor-Fletcher), Norwood
30/01/ 2016	Torquay	W 2-1 (Taylor-Fletcher, Norwood)	Davies, Vaughan, McNulty (Sutton), Ihiekwe, Ridehalgh, Maynard, Jennings, Harris, Mekki (Mackreth), Taylor-Fletcher, Norwood
06/02/ 2016	Southport	W 1-0 (Norwood)	Davies, Vaughan, McNulty, Ihiekwe, Ridehalgh, Maynard, Jennings, Harris, Hughes, Taylor-Fletcher (Mackreth), Norwood
13/02/ 2016	Aldershot	D 0-0	Davies, Vaughan, McNulty, Ihiekwe, Ridehalgh, Maynard, Hughes, Harris, Mackreth (Taylor-Fletcher), Higdon, Norwood
20/02/ 2016	Cheltenham	L 0-1	Davies, Vaughan, McNulty, Ihiekwe, Ridehalgh, Maynard, Hughes (Kirby 70), Harris, Taylor-Fletcher (Mekki), Higdon, Norwood
28/02/ 2016	Chester	W 0-1 (Norwood)	Davies, Vaughan, McNulty, Ihiekwe, Ridehalgh, Mekki, Jennings, Hughes, Kirby (Mackreth), Norwood, Higdon (Taylor-Fletcher)
05/03/ 2016	Gateshead	W 3-1 (Norwood x2, Higdon)	Davies, Vaughan, McNulty, Ihiekwe, Ridehalgh, Kirby (Mackreth), Jennings, Hughes, Mekki (Taylor-Fletcher), Norwood, Higdon (Margetts)
08/03/ 2016	Guiseley	D 2-2 (Atkinson og, Kirby)	Davies, Vaughan, McNulty (Riley), Ihiekwe, Ridehalgh, Mekki, Jennings, Hughes, Kirby, Norwood, Higdon
12/03/ 2016	Dover	D 0-0	Davies, Vaughan, McNulty, Ihiekwe, Ridehalgh, Mekki (Maynard), Jennings, Hughes, Kirby, Norwood, Higdon (Harris)
19/03/ 2016	Forest Green	D 1-1 (Harris)	Davies, Vaughan, McNulty, Ihiekwe, Hill, Mekki, Hughes, Harris, Kirby (Mackreth), Taylor-Fletcher, Norwood

26/03/2016	Lincoln	W 3-2 (Norwood, Kirby, Mekki)	Davies, Vaughan, McNulty, Ihiekwe, Hill, Jennings, Harris, Hughes, Taylor-Fletcher (Fenwick), Kirby (Mekki), Norwood
28/03/2016	Kidderminster	W 0-2 (Norwood x2)	Davies, Vaughan, McNulty, Ihiekwe, Hill, Jennings, Harris, Hughes, Taylor-Fletcher (Fenwick), Kirby (Mackreth), Norwood
02/04/2016	Welling	L 1-2 (Vaughan)	Davies, Vaughan, McNulty, Ihiekwe, Hill, Jennings, Harris, Hughes (Mackreth), Taylor-Fletcher (Fenwick), Kirby (Higdon), Norwood
09/04/2016	Torquay	W 0-1 (Higdon)	Davies, Vaughan, McNulty, Ihiekwe, Ridehalgh, Maynard (Mekki), Jennings, Harris, Hughes, Norwood (Kirby), Higdon
16/04/2016	Wrexham	L 1-2 (Norwood)	Davies, Vaughan, McNulty, Ihiekwe, Ridehalgh, Jennings, Harris, Hughes (Taylor-Fletcher), Mekki, Norwood, Higdon (Kirby)
23/04/2016	Eastleigh	W 0-1 (Norwood)	Davies, Vaughan, McNulty (Riley), Ihiekwe, Ridehalgh, Maynard, Jennings, Harris (Taylor-Fletcher, Hughes, Kirby (Mekki), Norwood
30/04/2016	Grimsby	W 1-0 (Jennings)	Davies, Vaughan (Hogan), Riley, Ihiekwe, Ridehalgh, Maynard (Kirby), Jennings, Harris, Hughes, Mekki, Norwood

2016/17

Date	Opponent	Result	Line-Up
06/08/ 2016	Bromley	W 0-2 (Norwood x2)	Davies, Maynard, McNulty, Ihiekwe, Ridehalgh, S Jennings, Harris, Hughes, C Jennings, Norwood (Kirby), Cook (Mekki)
09/08/ 2016	Barrow	W 2-0 (Cook, Norwood)	Davies, Maynard, McNulty, Ihiekwe, Ridehalgh (Vaughan), S Jennings, Harris, Hughes, C Jennings, Norwood (Kirby), Cook
13/08/ 2016	Eastleigh	W 2-1 (S Jennings, Norwood)	Davies, Maynard, McNulty, Ihiekwe, Vaughan, S Jennings, Harris (Stephenson), Hughes, C Jennings, Norwood, Cook (Kirby)
16/08/ 2016	Boreham Wood	W 0-1 (C Jennings)	Davies, Maynard, McNulty, Ihiekwe, Vaughan, S Jennings, Harris, Hughes, C Jennings, Norwood, Cook
20/08/ 2016	Maidstone	W 2-1 (Cook, McNulty)	Davies, Maynard, McNulty, Ihiekwe, Vaughan, S Jennings, Harris, Hughes, C Jennings (Kirby), Norwood (Mekki), Cook
27/08/ 2016	Southport	D 1-1 (Cook)	Davies, Maynard, McNulty, Ihiekwe, Vaughan (Ridehalgh), S Jennings, Harris (Kirby), Hughes, C Jennings (Mekki), Norwood, Cook
29/08/ 2016	Guiseley	W 1-0 (Norwood)	Davies, Maynard, McNulty, Ihiekwe, Ridehalgh, S Jennings, Harris (Mekki), Hughes, C Jennings, Norwood, Cook
03/09/ 2016	Aldershot	L 3-1 (Cook)	Davies, Maynard, McNulty, Ihiekwe, Ridehalgh, S Jennings, Mekki (Stephenson), Hughes, C Jennings, Norwood, Cook (Kirby)
10/09/ 2016	Lincoln	L 0-1	Davies, Maynard, McNulty, Ihiekwe, Vaughan, S Jennings, Harris (Mekki), Hughes, C Jennings (Kirby), Norwood, Cook (Stephenson)
13/09/ 2016	York	D 0-0	Davies, Vaughan, McNulty, Ihiekwe, Ridehalgh, S Jennings, Maynard, Hughes, Stephenson, Norwood, Cook
17/09/ 2016	Sutton	L 1-0	Davies, Vaughan, McNulty, Ihiekwe, Ridehalgh, S Jennings, Maynard, Harris (Mekki), Kirby (Cook), Stephenson (Jones), Norwood
24/09/ 2016	Woking	W 3-1 (Cook x2, Norwood)	Davies, Sutton, McNulty, Ihiekwe, Ridehalgh, Tollitt (Duggan), S Jennings, Maynard, Almond (Stephenson), Norwood, Cook (Jones)
01/10/ 2016	Dagenham	D 0-0	Davies, Sutton, McNulty, Ihiekwe, Ridehalgh, Kirby (Jones), S Jennings, Maynard, Almond (Duggan), Norwood (Osborne), Cook
04/10/ 2016	Gateshead	L 0-1	Davies, Duggan, McNulty, Sutton, Ridehalgh, Kirby (Stephenson), Osborne, Harris, Almond (Tollitt), Jones, Cook
08/10/ 2016	Wrexham	W 2-0 (Jalal og, Cook)	Davies, Sutton, McNulty, Ihiekwe, Ridehalgh, Duggan, Harris, S Jennings, Tollitt (Osborne), Kirby (Stephenson), Cook
22/10/ 2016	Solihull	W 0-3 (Kirby x2, Norwood)	Davies, Vaughan, McNulty, Sutton, Ridehalgh, Maynard, S Jennings (Harris), Hughes, Kirby, Almond (Norwood), Cook (Stephenson)

Date	Opponent	Result	Team
25/10/2016	North Ferriby	W 1-0 (Cook)	Davies, Vaughan, McNulty, Sutton, Ridehalgh, Maynard, Harris (Tollitt), Hughes, Almond (Norwood), Kirby (Tollitt), Cook
29/10/2016	Dover	W 1-4 (Cook x2, Walker og, Tollitt)	Davies, Vaughan (Ihiekwe), McNulty, Sutton, Ridehalgh, Maynard, Harris, Hughes, Tollitt, Stephenson (Mekki), Cook (Jones)
12/11/2016	Chester	D 2-2 (Cook, Tollitt)	Davies, Vaughan, McNulty, Sutton, Ridehalgh, Kirby (Mekki), Harris, Hughes, Tollitt, Mangan (Ihiekwe), Cook
19/11/2016	Braintree	W 0-1 (Cook)	Davies, Vaughan, McNulty, Sutton, Ridehalgh, Dawson (Mekki), Harris (Maynard), Hughes, Kirby (Ihiekwe), Cook, Mangan
22/11/2016	Forest Green	D 2-2 (Maynard, Norwood)	Davies, Ihiekwe, McNulty, Sutton, Ridehalgh, Kirby, Maynard, Hughes, Tollitt, Cook (Norwood), Mangan
26/11/2016	Torquay	W 2-1 (Mangan x2)	Davies, Vaughan, McNulty, Sutton, Ridehalgh (Ihiekwe), Maynard, Harris (Kirby), Hughes, Tollitt, Mangan (Norwood), Cook
29/11/2016	Gateshead	W 0-1 (Tollitt)	Davies, Sutton, McNulty, Ihiekwe, Kirby, Maynard, Harris, Hughes, Tollitt (Dawson), Mangan (Norwood), Cook (Wallace)
03/12/2016	York	W 1-0 (Norwood)	Davies, Sutton, McNulty, Ihiekwe, Vaughan, Harris (Dawson), Maynard (Kirby), Hughes, Tollitt, Norwood, Mangan (Cook)
17/12/2016	Lincoln	L 2-1 (Hughes)	Davies, Vaughan, McNulty, Sutton, Tollitt, Hughes, Harris (Kirby), Maynard, Ridehalgh, Norwood, Mangan
26/12/2016	Macclesfield	W 1-0 (Hughes)	Davies, Vaughan, McNulty, Sutton, Ridehalgh, Tollitt, Wallace, Hughes, Kirby (C Jennings), Norwood, Mangan (Maynard)
01/01/2017	Macclesfield	L 4-2 (McNulty, Sutton)	Davies, Vaughan, McNulty, Sutton, Ridehalgh, Tollitt, Wallace (Maynard), Hughes, Kirby (Mekki), Norwood, Mangan (C Jennings)
28/01/2017	Dagenham	L 0-2	Davies, Vaughan, McNulty, Ihiekwe, Kirby (Tollitt), Hughes, Wallace, S Jennings (Norwood), Ridehalgh, Cook, Mangan (Stockton)
31/01/2017	Woking	W 0-3 (Cook, Tollitt x2)	Davies, Vaughan, McNulty, Ihiekwe, Tollitt, Maynard, Wallace (Harris), Hughes, Ridehalgh, Cook (Stockton), Norwood (Kirby)
11/02/2017	Bromley	D 2-2 (Cook x2)	Davies, Buxton, McNulty (Maynard), Ihiekwe, Ridehalgh, Tollitt, Hughes, Wallace (Kirby), Dunn (Mangan), Norwood, Cook
18/02/2017	Eastleigh	W 0-2 (Tollitt, Norwood)	Davies, Vaughan, McNulty, Ihiekwe, Ridehalgh, Tollitt, Hughes, Maynard, Dunn (Kirby), Cook, Norwood
21/02/2017	Boreham Wood	W 2-1 (Cook x2)	Davies, Vaughan, McNulty, Ihiekwe, Ridehalgh, Tollitt (Mangan), Hughes, Maynard, Dunn (Kirby), Norwood, Cook (Stockton)
03/03/2017	Chester	W 2-3 (Harris, Norwood, Cook)	Davies, Sutton, McNulty, Ihiekwe, Vaughan, Maynard (Harris), Hughes, Mekki, Ridehalgh, Mangan (Norwood), Stockton (Cook)
07/03/2017	Barrow	L 2-1 (Cook)	Davies, Sutton (Mangan), McNulty, Ihiekwe, Vaughan, Harris (Stockton), Hughes, Mekki (C Jennings), Ridehalgh, Cook, Norwood

14/03/ 2017	Torquay	D 0-0	Davies, Sutton, McNulty, Ihiekwe, Vaughan, Harris, Hughes, C Jennings, Ridehalgh, Mangan (Norwood), Stockton (Cook)
21/03/ 2017	North Ferriby	W 1-4 (Harris x3, Cook)	Davies, Sutton, McNulty, Ihiekwe, Vaughan, Harris, Hughes, C Jennings (Mekki), Ridehalgh, Cook (Mangan), Norwood (Stockton)
25/03/ 2017	Braintree	W 1-0 (Cook)	Davies, Sutton, McNulty, Ihiekwe, Vaughan, Harris, Hughes, C Jennings (Mekki), Ridehalgh, Cook (Stockton), Norwood
28/03/ 2017	Dover	W 1-0 (Stockton)	Davies, Buxton, McNulty, Ihiekwe, Vaughan, Harris, Hughes, C Jennings (Mekki), Ridehalgh, Norwood (Mangan), Cook (Stockton)
01/04/ 2017	Wrexham	W 0-1 (Vaughan)	Davies, Buxton, McNulty, Ihiekwe, Vaughan, Harris, Hughes, C Jennings (Mekki), Ridehalgh, Norwood (Mangan), Stockton (Cook)
04/04/ 2017	Sutton	W 3-2 (Ihiekwe x2, Eastmond og)	Davies, Buxton, McNulty, Ihiekwe, Vaughan, Harris, Hughes, C Jennings (Mekki), Ridehalgh, Norwood, Stockton (Cook)
08/04/ 2017	Solihull	W 9-0 (Stockton x3, C Jennings x3, Cook, Ridehalgh, Collins)	Davies, Buxton, McNulty, Ihiekwe, Vaughan, Harris (Sousa), Hughes, C Jennings, Ridehalgh, Norwood (Collins), Stockton (Cook)
11/04/ 2017	Forest Green	L 0-1	Davies, Buxton, McNulty, Ihiekwe, Vaughan (Sousa), Harris (Wallace), Hughes, C Jennings, Ridehalgh, Stockton (Cook), Norwood
14/04/ 2017	Aldershot	D 2-2 (Stockton, C Jennings)	Davies, Buxton (Sousa), McNulty, Ihiekwe, Vaughan, Maynard, Hughes, C Jennings, Ridehalgh, Norwood, Stockton (Cook)
17/04/ 2017	Guiseley	W 1-2 (Norwood, Cook)	Davies, Buxton, McNulty, Ihiekwe, Vaughan, Wallace, Hughes, C Jennings (Dunn), Ridehalgh, Cook (Stockton), Norwood (Mangan)
22/04/ 2017	Southport	W 4-1 (Norwood x2, C Jennings x2)	Davies, Buxton, McNulty, Ihiekwe, Vaughan (Dunn), Hughes, Wallace, C Jennings, Ridehalgh, Norwood (Mangan), Stockton (Cook)
29/04/ 2017	Maidstone	W 0-1 (Ilesanmi)	Pilling, Solomon-Davies, Gumbs, Drysdale, Clarke (Flemming), Dawson, Mekki (Devine), Lucy, Sousa, Collins, Ilesanmi (Coughan)
03/05/ 2017	Aldershot	W 0-3 (Stockton x2, Norwood)	Davies, Maynard (Mangan), McNulty, Ihiekwe, Buxton, Hughes, Wallace, C Jennings, Ridehalgh, Norwood (Dunn), Stockton (Cook)
06/05/ 2017	Aldershot	D 2-2 (Stockton, Norwood)	Davies, Maynard, McNulty, Ihiekwe, Buxton, Hughes, Wallace (Mangan), C Jennings, Ridehalgh, Norwood, Stockton
14/05/ 2017	Forest Green	L 1-3 (C Jennings)	Davies, Buxton, McNulty, Ihiekwe, Mangan (Dunn), Hughes, Maynard, C Jennings (Cook), Ridehalgh, Stockton, Norwood

2017/18

Date	Opponent	Result	Line-Up
05/08/2017	Torquay	D 0-0	Davies, Buxton, McNulty, McEveley, Jennings, Norburn (Sutton), Hughes, Harris, Ridehalgh, Alabi (Cook), Norwood
08/08/2017	Woking	W 3-1 (Cook, Norburn, McEveley)	Davies, Buxton, Sutton, McEveley, Dunn (Alabi), Norburn, Hughes, Harris, Ridehalgh, Jennings, Cook (Mangan)
12/08/2017	Sutton	L 0-1	Davies, Buxton, Sutton, McEveley, Dunn (Alabi), Norburn, Hughes, Harris (Mangan), Ridehalgh, Jennings, Cook
15/08/2017	Guiseley	D 0-0	Davies, Buxton, McNulty, McEveley, Dunn, Norburn, Hughes, Harris (Alabi), Ridehalgh, Jennings, Cook
19/08/2017	Eastleigh	L 2-0	Davies, Buxton, McNulty, Sutton, Jennings (Alabi), Norburn, Hughes, Harris (Dunn), Ridehalgh, Cook, Norwood
26/08/2017	Boreham Wood	D 2-2 (Cook, Mangan)	Davies, Sutton, McNulty, McEveley, Duggan, Norburn, Hughes (Harris), Jennings (Mangan), Ridehalgh, Alabi (Cook), Norwood
28/08/2017	Solihull	W 0-2 (Norburn, Cook)	Davies, Sutton, McNulty, McEveley, Duggan (Buxton), Norburn (Jennings), Hughes, Harris, Ridehalgh, Cook, Mangan (Norwood)
02/09/2017	Dover	L 0-1	Davies, Sutton, McNulty, McEveley, Duggan (Buxton), Norburn (Jennings), Hughes, Harris, Ridehalgh, Cook, Mangan (Norwood)
09/09/2017	Barrow	W 1-0 (Norwood)	Davies, Sutton, McNulty, McEveley (Jennings), Buxton, Norburn, Harris (Dunn), Hughes, Ridehalgh, Cook (Waring), Norwood
12/09/2017	Maidenhead	L 1-0	Davies, Sutton, McNulty, Gumbs (Dunn), Buxton, Norburn, Hughes, Jennings (Alabi), Ridehalgh, Cook (Harris), Norwood
16/09/2017	Ebbsfleet	D 0-0	Davies, Sutton, McNulty, McEveley, Buxton, Norburn (Waring), Hughes, Harris, Ridehalgh, Jennings, Norwood
23/09/2017	Wrexham	L 0-1	Davies, Buxton, McNulty, Sutton, Ridehalgh, Dunn (Cook), Norburn, Harris, Jennings, Norwood, Alabi (Waring)
30/09/2017	Bromley	W 0-1 (Norwood)	Davies, Buxton, McNulty, Sutton, Duggan, Norburn, Hughes, Jennings, Ridehalgh, Alabi, Norwood
04/10/2017	Leyton Orient	W 2-1 (Cook, Norwood)	Davies, Buxton, McNulty, Sutton, Ridehalgh, Tollitt (Mottley-Henry), Norburn (Harris), Hughes, Jennings, Cook, Norwood
07/10/2017	Chester	D 0-0	Davies, Buxton, McNulty, Sutton, Ridehalgh, Mottley-Henry, Norburn (Harris), Hughes, Jennings, Cook (McDonagh), Norwood
21/10/2017	Aldershot	L 2-1 (McNulty)	Davies, Duggan, McNulty, Sutton, Clarke, Mottley-Henry (McEveley), Norburn, Hughes, Harris, Jennings, Norwood (McDonagh)
24/10/2017	Hartlepool	D 1-1 (McEveley)	Davies, Duggan, McNulty (McEveley), Sutton, Ridehalgh, Mottley-Henry, Norburn, Harris, Jennings, Cook, Norwood

Date	Opponent	Result	Players
28/10/2017	Halifax	W 4-2 (Norwood x2, Cole, Mottley-Henry)	Davies, Duggan, McNulty, Sutton, Ridehalgh, Mottley-Henry, Hughes, Harris, Jennings, Norwood (Cole (Cook)), McDonagh
11/11/2017	Dagenham	W 2-0 (Norwood, Norburn)	Davies, Duggan (Harris), McNulty, Sutton, Ridehalgh, Mottley-Henry, Hughes (Cole), Norburn, Jennings, Norwood, Cook (McDonagh)
18/11/2017	Gateshead	L 1-0	Davies, Buxton, McNulty, Sutton, Ridehalgh (Gumbs), Mottley-Henry (Green), Banks, Norburn, Cole, Norwood, Cook
21/11/2017	Macclesfield	D 2-2 (Cole, Cook)	Davies, Buxton, McNulty, Sutton, Clarke, Mottley-Henry, Banks, Norburn, Cole (Jennings), Norwood (McDonagh), Cook (Kay)
25/11/2017	Maidstone	W 4-0 (Norwood x2, Cook, Norburn)	Davies, Buxton, Gumbs, Sutton, Clarke, Mottley-Henry (Green), Banks, Norburn (Kay), Jennings, Norwood, Cook
09/12/2017	Torquay	W 3-0 (Jennings, Cook x2)	Davies, Buxton, McNulty, Sutton, Clarke, Mottley-Henry, Banks (Harris), Norburn, Jennings, Norwood (McDonagh), Cook
23/12/2017	Sutton	W 1-3 (Buxton, Jennings, Cook)	Davies, Buxton, McNulty, Sutton, Clarke, Mottley-Henry, Banks, Norburn, Jennings, Norwood, Cook (McDonagh)
26/12/2017	Fylde	W 4-1 (Sutton x2, Cook x2)	Davies, Buxton, McNulty, Sutton, Clarke, Mottley-Henry (Gumbs), Banks (Hughes), Jennings, Norwood, Cook (McDonagh)
30/12/2017	Guiseley	W 4-0 (Norwood, Jennings x2, Cook)	Davies, Buxton, McNulty, Sutton, Clarke, Cole (Harris), Banks, Norburn (Hughes), Jennings, Norwood (Kirby), Cook
01/01/2018	Fylde	L 5-2 (Banks, Jennings)	Davies (Pilling), Buxton, McNulty, Sutton, Ridehalgh, Cole (Clarke), Banks, Norburn (Harris), Jennings, Norwood, Cook
06/01/2018	Barrow	D 1-1 (Norwood)	Taylor, Buxton (Ridehalgh), McNulty, Sutton, Clarke, Cole (Kirby), Harris (Hughes), Norburn, Jennings, Norwood, Cook
13/01/2018	Woking	W 0-1 (Cook)	Taylor, Buxton, McNulty (Ridehalgh), Sutton, Clarke, Cole (Hughes), Norburn, Harris, Jennings, Norwood, Cook
20/01/2018	Maidenhead	W 3-2 (Norwood, Ginnelly, Hughes)	Taylor, Buxton, McNulty, Sutton, Ridehalgh, Ginnelly (Hughes), Norburn, Harris, Jennings, Kirby (Mangan), Norwood
27/01/2018	Wrexham	D 2-2 (Sutton, Cook)	Taylor, Buxton, McNulty, Sutton, Ridehalgh, Ginnelly (Clarke), Norburn, Harris, Jennings, Norwood, Cook
03/02/2018	Ebbsfleet	W 3-0 (Cook, Norwood x2)	Taylor, Ridehalgh, McNulty, Sutton, Clarke, Ginnelly (Tollitt), Norburn (Hughes), Harris, Jennings, Norwood (Mangan), Cook

Date	Opponent	Result	Team
10/02/ 2018	Leyton Orient	D 1-1 (Sutton)	Davies, Ridehalgh, McNulty, Sutton, Clarke, Ginnelly (Tollitt), Norburn, Harris, Jennings, Norwood, Cook
17/02/ 2018	Bromley	W 1-0 (Jennings)	Davies, Buxton, McNulty, Sutton, Ridehalgh, Ginnelly (Tollitt), Norburn (Hughes), Harris, Jennings, Norwood, Cook
20/02/ 2018	Macclesfield	L 1-4 (Cook)	Davies, Buxton, McNulty, Sutton, Ridehalgh, Tollitt, Norburn, Harris, Jennings, Norwood, Cook
24/02/ 2018	Maidstone	W 2-3 (Cook, Finney og, Hughes)	Davies, Buxton, Sutton, Monthe, Hughes (Duggan (Tollitt)), Dunn, Norburn, Harris, Jennings, Norwood (Mangan), Cook
10/03/ 2018	Dagenham	W 0-4 (Cook x2, Norwood x2)	Davies, Buxton, McNulty, Monthe (Sutton), Ridehalgh, Ginnelly (Tollitt), Traore, Harris (Wallace), Jennings, Norwood, Cook
17/03/ 2018	Boreham Wood	L 2-1 (Norwood)	Davies, Buxton, McNulty, Monthe, Ridehalgh, Ginnelly (Tollitt), Traore, Harris, Jennings, Norwood, Cook
24/03/ 2018	Eastleigh	W 3-1 (Sutton, Cook x2)	Davies, Buxton, McNulty, Sutton, Ridehalgh, Tollitt (Mangan), Norburn, Hughes, Jennings, Norwood, Cook
07/04/ 2018	Chester	W 0-2 (Cook, Norwood)	Davies, Buxton, McNulty, Sutton, Ridehalgh, Tollitt (Harris), Norburn (Wallace), Hughes, Jennings, Norwood (Mangan), Cook
10/04/ 2018	Gateshead	W 4-2 (Cook x4)	Davies, Buxton, McNulty, Sutton, Ridehalgh, Tollitt (Cole), Norburn, Harris, Jennings, Norwood (Mangan), Cook (Traore)
14/04/ 2018	Aldershot	W 2-0 (Norwood x2)	Davies, Buxton, McNulty, Sutton, Ridehalgh, Tollitt (Cole), Norburn, Hughes, Jennings, Norwood (Mangan), Cook (Harris)
17/04/ 2018	Dover	W 0-1 (Cook)	Davies, Buxton, McNulty, Sutton, Ridehalgh, Cole (Harris), Norburn, Hughes, Jennings, Norwood, Cook
21/04/ 2018	Halifax	W 0-2 (Cook, Norwood)	Davies, Buxton (Harris), McNulty, Sutton, Ridehalgh, Cole (Ginnelly), Norburn, Hughes, Jennings, Norwood, Cook (Mangan)
24/04/ 2018	Solihull	L 1-2 (Green)	Taylor, Solomon-Davies, Drysdale, Monthe, Clarke, Rokka (Spellman), Duggan, Dunn, Ginnelly, Green (Walker-Rice), Mangan
28/04/ 2018	Hartlepool	L 1-2 (Hughes)	Davies, Harris, McNulty, Sutton, Ridehalgh, Ginnelly, Norburn, Hughes, Cole (Duggan), Norwood, Cook
05/05/ 2018	Ebbsfleet	W 4-2 (Norwood x2, Ginnelly, Cole)	Davies, Buxton (Monthe), McNulty, Sutton, Ridehalgh, Ginnelly (Harris), Norburn, Hughes, Cole, Norwood, Cook
12/05/ 2018	Boreham Wood	W 2-1 (Cook, Norwood)	Davies, Monthe, McNulty, Sutton (Harris), Ridehalgh, Ginnelly (Jennings), Hughes, Norburn, Cole (Clarke), Norwood, Cook

Other Stats (league only)

Games Played: 143 (Won 78, Drew 31, Lost 34)

Goals Scored: 220

Goals Conceded: 137

Biggest Win: 9-0 (v Solihull)

Biggest Defeat: 5-2 (v Fylde)

Most Appearances: Scott Davies (135)

Top Scorer: James Norwood (59)

Players To Make A First Team Appearance: 76